JESUS FRAMED

Jesus Framed is a collection of essays on reading the gospel of Mark. It uses literary theory, most notably the writings of Roland Barthes, to examine some of the difficulties in the text of Mark. A series of close readings of the gospel of Mark is compared to similar texts, both biblical and otherwise. Drawing on Mark's famous phrase that "to those who are outside all comes through parables" (Mark 4:11–12), *Jesus Framed* explores the boundaries between insiders and outsiders, those who can, and those who cannot, find a meaning in the text.

George Aichele is Professor of Philosophy and Religion at Adrian College, Michigan. He is author of *The Limits of Story* (1985) and, as a member of the Bible and Culture Collective, co-author of *The Postmodern Bible* (1995).

BIBLICAL LIMITS

We have to move beyond the outside–inside alternative; we have to be at the frontiers. Criticism indeed consists of analyzing and reflecting upon limits.
– Michel Foucault ('What is Enlightenment?')

This series brings a variety of postmodern perspectives to the reading of the familiar biblical texts. Books in the series will bring the traditional field of biblical studies face to face with literary criticism, anthropology and gender-based approaches, thus reaching new ways of understanding biblical texts.

EDITORS

Danna Nolan Fewell
Southern Methodist University, Dallas, Texas

David M. Gunn
Texas Christian University, Fort Worth, Texas

Gary A. Phillips
College of the Holy Cross, Worcester, Massachusetts

JESUS FRAMED

George Aichele

London and New York

First published 1996
by Routledge
11 New Fetter Lane, London EC4P 4EE

Simultaneously published in the USA and Canada
by Routledge
29 West 35th Street, New York, NY 10001

Routledge is an International Thomson Publishing company

Typeset in Garamond by Solidus (Bristol) Limited
Printed and bound in Great Britain by
T.J. Press (Padstow) Ltd, Padstow, Cornwall

British Library Cataloguing in Publication Data
A catalogue record for this book is available from the British Library

Library of Congress Cataloguing in Publication Data
Aichele, George.
Jesus framed / George Aichele.
p.   cm. – (Biblical limits)
Includes bibliographical references and index.
1. Bible. N.T. Mark–Criticism, interpretation, etc. I. Title.
II. Series.
BS2585.2.A42   1996   95-39726
226.3'066–dc20   CIP

ISBN 0–415–13862–0 (hbk)
ISBN 0–415–13863–9 (pbk)

TO JANELLE AND TINA,
THIS BOOK IS DEDICATED.

CONTENTS

PREFACE

> The Word is no longer guided *in advance* by the general intention of a socialized discourse; the consumer ... receives [the Word] as an absolute quantity, accompanied by all its possible associations.
>
> (Barthes 1967b:48)

This book draws very heavily on the work of Roland Barthes, for whose writings such postmodern themes as the relation between the sign and history, the identity of the reading subject, and the role of ideology in culture are central. Of particular relevance to the explorations of the gospel of Mark in this book have been Barthes's use of the related concepts of connotation and denotation (which Barthes borrowed from Louis Hjelmslev, but which are widely in use throughout linguistics and the philosophy of language), and of intertextuality (which Barthes borrowed from Julia Kristeva). Although Barthes does not often refer explicitly to the materiality of the physical text, that concept also is closely related to his discussions of "the pleasure of the text," "the rustle of language," "the grain of the voice," and his numerous other references to text as a "body." Barthes lurks in the background of every page of this book, and the reader who wishes to pursue further the issues raised here would do well to read his writings. English translations of most of his books are listed in the bibliography at the end of this book.

I also acknowledge Frank Kermode's *The Genesis of Secrecy* (1979), which has served during the writing of this book both as model and frequent provocation. In addition, although I do not follow the reader-response methodology outlined in and rigorously exemplified by Robert Fowler's *Let the Reader Understand* (1991), nevertheless Fowler's stress upon and unflagging attention to "the role of the reader" in relation to the meaning of text has been of great value to me. Varieties of reader-response criticism remain popular and influential in literary studies of the Bible, but they will not be discussed here, although some criticisms of reader-response theory may be inferred from the following. However, like both Kermode and Fowler, I find the "play" between reader and text to be of great interest. Finally, Stephen Moore's book, *Mark and Luke in Poststructuralist Perspectives* (1992), must be mentioned, for it moves in very much the same waters as this book, and yet in an opposite "direction." Moore's book buries the text of Mark beneath manifold and playful (very playful, but in another way than my own) readings, and these in turn generate an infinite rippling of meaning across Mark's text. Instead of enjoying the text of Mark as a meaningful plenitude, as Moore does, what I seek here are those places where the physical aspect of the signifier, which I also call the materiality or *hulê* (stuff) of the text, *interrupts* the flow of meaning. The crucial difference of this book from the books of Kermode, Fowler, and Moore, as well as much other biblical criticism, lies in its attempt to close in on the "text itself" and to produce readings of a text which is itself, finally, unreadable. It is in this sense that this book is "postmodern."

Members of the Semiotics and Exegesis Section and the Ideological Criticism Group of the Society of Biblical Literature, as well as students and faculty at Adrian College, have listened to, read, and commented helpfully on various parts of this book. I am also indebted to my colleagues in the Bible and Culture Collective – Fred Burnett, Elizabeth Castelli, Bob Fowler, David Jobling, Stephen Moore, Gary Phillips, Tina Pippin, Gina Schwartz, and Wilhelm Wuellner – for their comradeship and friendly provocation. Our group writing of *The Postmodern Bible* (Yale University Press, 1995) has profoundly stimulated my own work. Fred Burnett and Bob Fowler have furthermore read versions of the manuscript of this book and have offered many thoughtful and very helpful suggestions. In addition, the editorial team of Danna Nolan Fewell, David Gunn, and Gary Phillips have provided numerous corrections and suggestions, as have the anonymous Routledge readers.

I owe special thanks to Janelle Lutzke and to Tina Pippin. In addition to asking me hard questions and not letting me off with easy answers, both Janelle and Tina have pushed me in directions that I needed to go and have helped me to see things that I needed to see. Their wisdom and their generosity with advice and moral support is deeply appreciated. Following Janelle's lead, in this book I use the feminine pronouns "she" and "her" whenever the antecedent could be a human being of either sex; often, it is "the reader." If this book is needlessly obscure or otherwise defective, it is no doubt because I have failed to heed the advice of such careful friends.

INTRODUCTION: REWRITING THE TEXT

READING FROM OUTSIDE

To you are given the secrets of the Kingdom of God; but to those who are outside all comes through parables, so that they may have sight but not see, and hear but not understand, lest they be converted and forgiven.

(Mark 4:11–12)

In the language of the gospel of Mark, there is a fundamental division between the disciples and followers of Jesus, to whom the mystery of the kingdom of God is given, and "those who are outside." This division is described in Mark 4:11–12, cited above. For the reader, merely to have the words of the text pass before you, to read them without understanding (to sense the signifiers as physical objects without knowing their significance), is not enough. Something else must occur; a secret must be given. As Mark 4:11–12 suggests, this division between insiders (those who were with Jesus "when they were alone") and outsiders (the multitude) is based upon a distinction between two kinds or degrees of meaning, connotation and denotation. On this distinction hangs conversion and forgiveness.

Denotation and connotation will be discussed in detail in chapters 5 and 6 of this book. Connotation is the understanding of those who are on the "inside," who are given "the secrets of the Kingdom of God." Denotation is the fate of those on the "outside," to whom "all comes through parables." Along similar lines, Mark 4:33–4 states:

With many such parables he spoke the word to them ["those

1

who are outside"], according to what they could comprehend;
but he did not talk with them except in parables; but privately
with his own disciples he expounded all.

Those who are on the inside, who claim to know the secret, *to
mustêrion*, of the kingdom, are the putative legal owners of the text;
they are true disciples. The disciples understand the text as that
which both makes, and is made by, a canon of "holy scripture." For
them the text is complete, sufficient, and full of meaning. The text
contains a meaning, and it gives that meaning to those readers who
are on the inside.

For traditional biblical exegesis it is this meaningful completeness
which "is" the real gospel of Mark. The physical stuff of the text is
merely an outer husk to be shattered and penetrated and eventually
left behind. The gospel is a parable which must be transformed into
an allegory. The physical text must become invisible, so that the
inner secret may be given. This theology of the insiders is therefore
non-material or "spiritual." The great majority of theological and
biblical scholars, despite their diversity in other ways, attempts to
create such disciples, that is, to provide readers with a way inside the
text, authoritative and reliable access to the true meaning of the text.

Over the years this theology of the insiders has taken many
forms, from ancient and medieval allegory to modern historical–
critical reconstructions of the "historical Jesus," sociological and
anthropological investigations of the text's editorial *Sitz im Leben*,
or narratological and rhetorical analyses of the canonical scriptures.
Most frequently these studies have attempted to reconstruct a
situation of origin, either an actual, historical referent (Jesus, first-
century Judaism or Christianity) or the performance (oral or scribal)
and understanding of an authorized community of readers. Despite
(and yet because of) their pretense to scientific objectivity, these
reconstructions are thoroughly and profoundly theological.

While my focus here is on academic, liberal, biblical, and
theological scholarship, it should be noted that popular religious
fundamentalism also seeks to penetrate to the "inside" of the text. It
does so primarily through proper understanding of the biblical
canon as self-explanatory to those who truly believe. For fundamentalism, the Bible is inspired by God and therefore infallible. I argue
that both fundamentalism and academic liberalism create illusions of
naturalness for their inevitably ideological interpretations of the
Bible.

2

The readers from the inside, whether liberals or fundamentalists, stand in opposition to the reader from the outside, who appears to them as a thief, a violent, barbaric, and illegitimate reader. To the reader from the inside, the reader from the outside seems like a Judas who betrays the true meaning of the text. This binarism of insider and outsider is of course ideological. In fact, the matter of "insiders" and "outsiders" in Mark is a complicated and paradoxical one. According to Mark 4:11–12, the parables prevent access to the inside of the text, "lest [the outsiders] be converted and forgiven." However, in Mark 2:17 Jesus says to the Pharisees who have questioned why he eats with "tax collectors and sinners" that "I did not come to summon the just, but the sinners." This would seem to invert the outside/inside opposition. Can anyone be the legitimate insider of a text which suggests that the *outsiders* are insiders? Or, following a similar logic, if "he who wishes to save his life shall lose it; and he who loses his life for the sake of me and the gospel shall save it" (Mark 8:35), then only those who have given up the very idea of saving their lives have a chance of saving their lives. Surely anyone who "loses" her life *in order to* save it will not succeed, for she is still trying to save her life and therefore will lose it.

This obscurity concerning the relative value of outside and inside suggests the possibility, and the desirability, of reading the gospel of Mark from the outside. This reading would necessarily be a self-referential stutter, a failure of the text and of reading, even a non-reading. This book, this text which is itself about texts, must speak also about itself. Otherwise it will succumb finally (and perhaps it will, anyway) to the illusions of connotative meaning which it seeks to overcome. The strategy of reading from the outside entails a discourse excluded from, or at any rate marginalized by, the Western theological tradition. This discourse involves a theology of the text as a material thing, and therefore a theology of concrete, physical, and ultimately meaningless things (such as sheets of paper or ink marks). This reading is a discourse about the *possibility* of meaning, rather than about meaning itself.[1]

By disconnecting the reader from its referent, written text perpetually puts every reader on the outside, confused by the parabolic text. Reading from the outside is violent and barbaric, and yet it is also naive. It is the reading of denotation, a "stupid" reading, a reading which must fail. The failure of reading from the outside occurs when it "forgets itself" and becomes a reading from the inside; the desire for meaning overpowers the incoherence of the material text, and the binary opposition between outside and inside is rebuilt as soon as it collapses. Reading is always the *rewriting* of text (as Fredric Jameson has said), a rewriting which inscribes text with meaning, with ideology, and thus, inevitably, with the logo-centric theology of the insiders. Reading from the outside does not avoid the logocentric violence of reading, the thrust toward meaning and truth. However, it recognizes this violence by treating the text as artifice, as production, and as fiction. These themes will be developed in the following chapters.

Both insider and outsider re-read and rewrite the gospel text, but in fundamentally different ways. If the reader reads from the inside, then her reading seeks the truth of the gospel, a truth in which effects of ideology will always be invisible. For reading from the inside, the text is transparent, and it speaks with a clear voice; there is no secret that is not revealed. The violent refusal to read which defines the non-reading of Italo Calvino's fictional character Irnerio (1981)[2] is the negative image of the violence with which the reader from the inside, who "owns" the text, lays claim to the text.

Reading from the inside denies the necessity of non-reading, the zero degree of naive reading. The reading from the inside offered by logocentric theology assumes the possibility of a complete, self-identical, and meaningful text, and of a satisfied or successful reading. This reading disguises the fact that *every* reader is always an outsider.

If, however, the reader reads from the outside, then the inevitability of non-reading becomes evident, and the effects of ideology stand forth from the text even as they obscure it. Reading from the outside exposes the fundamental incompleteness and insufficiency of the material text. It reveals that the text is empty of meaning, and thus it uncovers the arbitrariness of the insider's reconstructions. Instead of speaking clearly, the text merely "rustles" (Barthes 1986). For reading from the outside, clarity of meaning is a symptom of the reader's bad faith, for all reading is finally ideological. Hence reading from the outside is always troublesome, never satisfying; it is subversive. "The opposition is between the class and those who are outside the class (*les hors-classe*). Between the servants of the machine, and those who sabotage it or its cogs and wheels" (Deleuze and Guattari 1983:255). To read from the outside sets the reader in tension with fundamental beliefs of the modern world. Because the desire for meaning is refused, reading from the outside defamiliarizes reality itself.

Reading from the outside requires close attention to those points at which the text resists interpretation, at which reading becomes "difficult," for any reason – such as the self-referentiality of "let the scriptures be fulfilled" (Mark 14:49), in which the text refers to itself as a moment of completeness, the bringing to totality of "the scriptures," which are of course written texts. But if texts are always incomplete, as they are for the reading from outside, then the textual fulfillment of the scriptures will itself need to be fulfilled by another text, and so on, endlessly. The desire for fulfillment is denied satisfaction by the very text which announces it. An irreducible, opaque remainder of text is emphasized by this reading, not in order somehow finally to be consumed and absorbed along with the rest, but as an undigestible excess, a marker of the limits of meaning. This unexplainable residue marks the text as fantastic (Todorov 1973:24–40).

All texts resist reading, although some are more resistant than others. Many of the difficulties that the gospel of Mark presents to the reader lie in this resistance. The abrupt and paradoxical ending of Mark at 16:8 produces the effect of a reading *coda*, a demand for return to the story's beginning and re-reading of the book (Fowler 1991:91). But instead of clarifying the secret of the kingdom, as one might hope, each re-reading of Mark only further deepens the uncertainties of its meaning. What the present book offers is a series of readings of the text of Mark – readings from the outside – each one at best an approximation and ultimately a failure. Yet through these failures the invisible, incoherent text of Mark does somehow, indirectly and evanescently, come to light, as does the ideological lenses through which it is read. Even as reading from the outside is unable to uncover "the text itself," a text without meaning, without ideology, it reveals the violence done to the text by reading.

THE BODY OF THE TEXT

> ... the Text is above all (or after all) that long operation through which an author (a discoursing author) discovers (or makes the reader discover) the *irreparability* of his speech and manages to substitute *it speaks* for *I speak*.
>
> (Barthes 1986:75, his emphases)

This book is a collection of essays written during the last several years, but chiefly during a sabbatical in the spring of 1993. The looseness of the chapter arrangement reflects one of the central claims that I want to make, which is that reading never entirely masters a text, but can only approach it through a series of ideological maneuvers by which the text is "rewritten." Therefore, this arrangement itself is an ideological maneuver, and also a theological one. In the following, I understand "theology" to be one point at which ideology, as the human and cultural force which most profoundly defines and determines who we are as individuals and communities, is made explicit and attempts to become intelligent.

Reading produces a meaningful text; this meaning "consumes" the text. The reading strategy which I undertake here begins with the claim that every reading strategy, as an attempt to uncover a text, inevitably fails. Reading can uncover only a text which it has itself produced. This book is an attempt to explore some of the points at which the text of the gospel of Mark escapes the closure of meaningful reading, that is, reading from the inside.

Therefore, the theoretical question which lies at the center of this book concerns the identity of text. In a postmodern world where old metaphysical categories no longer seem pertinent, how can one say – or can one say at all? – that two people, or one person at two different times, ever read(s) "the same" text? What are the limits of text? What is the relation between text and meaning? Between text and reader? These questions of identity are also questions of ideology. The question of the "proper," self-identical text comes down, in part at least, to the question of textual properties, or of text as (someone's) property, which is a question of drawing boundaries. Is the text nothing more than the material stuff of which it is made, or does "text" also refer to the linguistic, literary, and conceptual (and perhaps other) properties which readers find encoded in the physical object? My argument is that the material stuff endlessly disrupts the identity of the text as a meaningful work. This allows the text to escape the claims of its owners.

My focus in this book is as much on the text of Mark as it is on these theoretical questions. And yet my interest in Mark and my interest in the theoretical questions are not two separate things. The traditional distinction between theory and practice – like the distinction between reading and writing – is foreign to my interests in writing this book. Mark's gospel is a text whose properties resist analysis; it is a text which arguably has no identity, or whose identity, such as it is, refuses all propriety. Mark is not the only text of this sort. Insofar as all postmodern literature is this way, Mark is merely an early (but not the earliest!) case of postmodern writing.

A systematic, totalizing overview either of the gospel of Mark or of postmodern thought would be antithetical to my argument. Instead, I want these essays to reverberate off one another, to suggest the possibility of multiple and inconclusive readings ("productions") of the gospel of Mark – readings which open up Mark (and other texts) in provocative ways. These readings will always be partial in the double sense suggested by Deleuze and Guattari (1983:309): they will be always incomplete, and they will be always biased.

The sequence of readings in chapters 1–5 does not follow the order of Mark but rather a logic of their own, or as Roland Barthes might say, a "deviation," a postmodern para-logic. There are numerous links between these chapters, which the linearity of print can only suggest. Although they focus primarily on the text of Mark, chapters 1–5 are also very much concerned with theoretical issues, such as connotation and denotation, translation and transliteration, commentary, narrative completeness, and narrative integrity. Despite their attention to theory, chapters 6 and 7 also do their share of reading from the outside. Chapters 6 and 7 further explore selected theoretical issues uncovered in chapters 1–5.

This book seeks to undertake a series of readings from the outside, readings which are stupefied by the opacity of the text of the gospel of Mark. If such readings have been tolerated in the Western theological tradition, they have been relegated to the periphery of theological discourse. Their object, the physical materiality of a text, has been restricted to a place where it could only be glimpsed indirectly, or out of the corner of one's eye. Yet it is this materiality – which is ultimately the *hulê* (sheer physical stuff) of ink, paper, etc.[3] – which constantly disrupts and confuses assertions about the text's identity. The borderline status of these readings is in part an inevitable consequence of the great project of Western theology itself, and of the canonical status of the textual object, but it is also in the interest of modernist "bourgeois ideology" (Barthes 1976:10) to exclude or at least marginalize such ways of reading. It is also a direct consequence of the devaluation of the material text of the Bible in Christianity.[4]

In a book concerned with material aspects of the text, as this one is, the question of translation cannot be ignored or treated lightly. Unless otherwise noted, the English translation of the gospels used in this book is the one by Richmond Lattimore (1979). Lattimore uses the Greek text of B.F. Westcott and J.A. Hort, in which the ancient codex Vaticanus (B) has primary place (Aland and Aland 1987:14). Neither codex Vaticanus nor the contemporary critical edition of the Greek text (Nestle *et al.* 1979) which I have used in the following is the "original" text of Mark.

What would be the characteristics of an original text of a biblical book? What features could determine its identity as "original?" In relation to biblical texts, the notion of textual identity is especially troublesome. The concept of an original text of any book of the Bible, as I use the word "text," is obscure. Furthermore, the concept of an original neither avoids nor resolves the paradoxes of textual identity. However, in a book which interrogates the metaphysics of textual identity, as this one does, the problem (or nonexistence) of the original cannot be swept aside. Can we even imagine a single manuscript of Mark (or any biblical book) which is complete, which is not itself the copy of a complete manuscript, and from which all other complete manuscripts are directly or indirectly copied? How would we define that completeness? At what point in the trajectories of the traditions involved in the composition of the gospels does the text become complete – at what point does the legitimate "Mark" appear? It would probably be better to say "texts of Mark," and yet even so we would still need to assume that these texts – Lattimore's translation or others, Nestle *et al.*'s twenty-sixth edition of the Greek, various ancient codices – are all in some way the same text, the text of Mark.

However, even apart from the high historical improbability that any original texts of biblical writings remain in existence or could be recognized as such if they were found, the concept of "the original text" of Mark is, at best, vague. The problem of the identity and the limits of the text is crucial to the analysis of the gospel of Mark, as the following chapters will show.

Furthermore, Lattimore's translation is not an accurate one. Translation always brings with it both compromise and ideology or, as an Italian saying goes, betrayal. No translation can be an exact reproduction of the meaning (much less the materiality) of its source text. In fact, it is impossible to describe what an "accurate" or "exact" translation would be without presuming a metaphysics of language which would resolve all-too-easily some of the questions of textual identity. This metaphysics – namely, that the signified concept (the meaning or sense) can be identified in some practical way as distinct from the signifier word (the thing or event which means) – is fundamentally antithetical to my argument in this book.

I use Lattimore's translation of the gospels because I find it to be both concrete and defamiliarizing. Lattimore's translation comes close to a word-by-word rendition[5] of the incoherences of the Greek text of Mark; it avoids the temptation of readable follow-ability to which many translations of the Bible readily yield, and it approaches instead what Walter Benjamin (1968) called "literal" translation. Instead of smoothing over irregularities in the text by seeking a readable "dynamic equivalence" of meaning between the source ("original") and target (translated) texts, literal translation tends to emphasize obstacles generated by the physical properties of the text.[6]

The theological, and therefore ideological, dimensions of translation are not given serious consideration by biblical scholars often enough, perhaps because for them translation of biblical texts is generally not necessary. The exercise of Bible translation is usually left to missionaries and Bible societies, whose express interest is to make the Bible available and understandable to the greatest number of people – people not familiar with the original languages of the Bible. These groups of translators are often strongly committed to particular readings of the Bible. While their desire to disseminate the biblical texts is admirable (although the means to its accomplishment may be debated), these groups are necessarily opposed ideologically to acknowledgement of factors which inevitably make text *un*-available and *un*-understandable. Yet these elements of textual incoherence are inherent and unresolvable in any text, and they are the central topic of this book.

Lattimore's translation is helpful to me because it makes *difficult* the meaning of Mark's text; it forces me to turn again and again to the Greek text, as well as to other translations into English or other languages. This highlights critical transformations of the signifier. Because the materiality of text is important to my argument, fairly frequent citation of Greek words and phrases from the gospel of Mark are necessary at numerous points along the way. These citations may well seem intrusive to some readers, and they will probably be insufficient to others.

POSTMODERN READING

The postmodern would be that which, in the modern, puts forward the unpresentable in presentation itself; that which denies itself the solace of good forms, the consensus of a taste which would make it possible to share collectively the nostalgia for the unattainable; that which searches for new presentations, not in order to enjoy them but in order to impart a stronger sense of the unpresentable.

(Lyotard 1984:81)

Reading from the outside is postmodern, and deconstructive. The readings presented in this book are postmodern, in the sense that Jean-François Lyotard has given to that word. These readings presented are also deconstructive insofar as they apply pressure to structures of Mark's text until these structures come apart and the incoherence of Mark's text appears. However, the current popularity of the words "deconstruction" and "postmodernism" does nothing to reduce the marginal position of these readings. As "deconstruction" and "postmodernism" move increasingly into the mainstreams of popular discourse, their once-considerable power to define and even to feature the exclusion of the material text diminishes accordingly. The words have become so common and widespread in use that they are in danger of losing any semantic particularity.

The goal of the readings of the gospel of Mark in this book is to make apparent the dynamics of authority, ideology, and meaning that function in every act of reading. Every reading is an exercise of power; every reader reads in relation to a position of authority (her own or, more commonly, someone else's, such as a community of readers). These readings attempt to expose the exercise of this power, but they do not themselves escape from the dynamics of power. No reading can escape from responsibility; there is no innocent reading. I seek to explore ways in which the reader's desire for meaning transforms the text of Mark. This can be achieved only through a reading which inevitably does the very thing that is under investigation. Hence my readings are always self-referential and always incomplete.

Paradoxically, it is precisely the ease with which a text may be read and understood – the transparency of its representations – that renders its materiality invisible. If the text were only less readable (or "readerly" – Roland Barthes's term is *lisible*), then its materiality would be more visible. Insofar as the readings in this book fail to defamiliarize the text of Mark, to make it strange and difficult to understand, and therefore visible, they will have succeeded in reading that text, and vice versa.

One possible strategy for a postmodern reading would be to shred a highly readable text into its smallest coherent component parts – indeed, to the verge of incoherence – and in so doing to display how the ideological illusion of an authoritative reading, a reading from the inside, becomes possible. This was the technique used by Barthes in *S/Z*. He called the textual units into which he dissolved Balzac's story "lexias": "all we require is that each lexia should have at most three or four meanings to be enumerated ..." (Barthes 1974:13–14). At the level of the lexias, that which was "unpresentable" in Balzac's story appeared.

The strategy adopted in this book is a different one. This book pursues the difficulties presented by an unreadable (or "writerly" – Barthes's word is *scriptible*) text, such as the gospel of Mark. This is done with the hope of playing out the difficulties of Mark in order to unravel the text, to unsettle forever its possibility as a coherent text and as a narrative. Or following Barthes in the epigraph to part 2 above, to discover the irreparability of the text of Mark – to substitute "it speaks" for "I speak." I do not seek to resolve or explain these difficulties either theologically or historically – that is, to elucidate the text and overcome obstacles which it presents to understanding – as much previous scholarship has done. Yet as was noted above, if the reading from outside succeeds in realizing this hope, it fails, for as a reading, it is always coming "in," becoming theological. Inside becomes outside, and vice versa; the boundary of textual identity disappears. The opposition, which is always metaphysical, between outside and inside disintegrates.

1

JESUS FRAMED

THE FRAME

> Abba, father, for you all things are possible. Remove this cup
> from me. But not what I wish, but what you wish.
>
> (Mark 14:36)

Jesus's intimate prayer for release from suffering to come marks the
beginning of the story of his arrest and trials in the gospel of Mark.
Jesus addresses God as "father," *ho patêr*, in the garden of Gethsemane. The appearance in Mark's text of the Aramaic word *abba*
stands out as a redundancy, but it also resonates peculiarly with the
name "Barabbas" which marks the end of this story. The name of the
condemned man for whom Jesus is exchanged is no more necessary
to the story of Mark than are the names of Simon's mother-in-law
in Mark 1, or of the woman with the hemorrhage in Mark 5, or of
the centurion later on in Mark 15. Indeed, the names of these
characters do not appear in Mark, nor in the other gospels. The
intratextual play or resonance between these superfluous words,
"Abba" and "Barabbas," reflects and emphasizes the artificiality, and
therefore the profound fictionality, of the entire sequence of the
arrest/trials scenes in Mark.

The brief story of the release of Barabbas, one of the "insurgents
who had done murder during the uprising" (Mark 15:7), appears in
Mark 15:6–15. Barabbas does not appear as an active character in
Mark's narrative, but his name is used by "high priests" as the one
to be released when they "stir up the crowd" in order to demand the
crucifixion of Jesus.

> So Pilate wishing to satisfy the crowd released Barabbas to them,
> and had Jesus scourged and gave him over to be crucified.
>
> (Mark 15:15)

13

The introduction of the name Barabbas into the story is peculiar, perhaps especially in Mark, which uses few proper names even for characters who are active in the narrative. It is as though this character's sole purpose in the story is to function only as a name. However, although it is used as a proper name, "barabbas" is no more a proper name than "abba" is. "Barabbas is, in fact, almost impossibly odd as a semitic name" (Nineham 1963:416). The word "barabbas" transliterates the Aramaic phrase "son (*bar*) of the father (*abba*)." Furthermore, the statement in some manuscripts of Matthew 27:16–17 that Barabbas was also named "Jesus" generates an element of irony or even slapstick in the story: Jesus the son of the father ("abba") is condemned while Jesus the son of the father ("barabbas") is released (see especially Matthew 27:17). The political insurgent becomes a mock double of the Galilean preacher who has been arrested "as if [he] were a highwayman" (Mark 14:48); the mockery of Jesus then becomes quite explicit as the story continues in Mark 15:17–20 (Nineham 1963:418–19).

This alphabetical and conceptual doubling works both ways: Barabbas the revolutionary is in effect a would-be king of the Jews, but it is Jesus who ends up crucified as "King of the Jews" (Mark 15:26; also 15:32). The carnivalesque mocking play of language in this doubling seems out of place in the otherwise serious scene of Jesus's condemnation by Pilate. A similar effect was identified by Erich Auerbach in his well-known discussion of the scene of Peter's denial (1957:40ff.); Auerbach described the denial scene as a mingling of comic/realistic and tragic styles. The scene of Peter's denial (Mark 14:66–72) immediately precedes the story of Jesus's interrogation by Pilate (15:1–5), which is then followed by the exchange of Jesus for Barabbas.

As in the case of "talitha cum" in Mark 5:41[1] and several other such cases (which appear among the gospels only in Mark), the Greek transliteration, *abba*, of an Aramaic word for "father" is juxtaposed in the text with the Greek translation of the word, *patêr*. The conjunction in Mark 14:36 of *abba* and *ho patêr* establishes the conceptual possibility of identifying Jesus as "the son of the father" in Mark.[2] Elsewhere in Mark, Jesus refers to God as "your father in heaven" (11:25), and as father of "the son of man" (8:38), and he even opposes "the father" to "the son" (13:32). However, since Jesus never explicitly identifies himself as "the son," Mark 14:36 remains the only point in the gospel of Mark where Jesus unambiguously adopts son/father language in reference to his relation to God.

Only in Mark 14:36 and 15:6–15 does the reader find the linguistic play of Abba/Barabbas. The other canonical gospels avoid this verbal play altogether by omitting "Abba." These verses perform a function in Mark; they serve as a pair of palindromic brackets to frame and set off a highly orchestrated chunk of narrative material within Mark's passion narrative. The Abba/Barabbas play appears to be one of Mark's famous textual doublets,[3] in this case defining what has become for many readers the climactic episode of the entire story of Mark. Within these frames appear other double- and triple-units which play off against one another in syncopated rhythms.

The prayer to Abba is one of three prayers of Jesus in Gethsemane (Mark 14:32–42). While the three disciples (Peter, James, John) sleep, Jesus begs Abba to relieve him of the profound anguish of his soul "to the point of death." Jesus uses "the same words" (14:39) in each prayer, although the wording of the prayer (quoted above) is stated in Mark only once. Jesus receives no reply. The silence of Abba in Gethsemane is matched by the confusion or indifference of the disciples in Mark 14:40; "they did not know how to answer him," *ouk êdeisan ti apokrithôsin*. Abba's silence at this point in the story stands in striking contrast to the voice from heaven, or from a cloud, which speaks at the very beginning of Mark's narrative ("You are my son whom I love, with you I am well pleased," 1:11) and again at the transfiguration of Jesus ("This is my son whom I love," 9:7). After Jesus has been transfigured and just before the voice from the cloud identifies Jesus as "my son," Peter (once again with James and John) does not know what to say, *ou gar êdei ti apokrithê* (9:6), much as in Mark 14:40. Abba's silence in Gethsemane accompanies a moment of non-transfiguration. Is Jesus no longer the son of the Father? Has he already been abandoned by God (15:34)?

Jesus's prayer for relief in the gospel of Mark stands in strong contrast to his confidence in the gospel of John 12:27 ("what shall I say? Father, save me from this hour? But this is why I came to this hour"). In Mark 14:34 and the parallel in Matthew 26:38, Jesus instructs the disciples to "sit down here"; instructions to pray "that you may not be brought to the test" appear later in their respective versions of this scene (Mark 14:38, Matthew 26:41). Only Mark 14:35 emphasizes Jesus's desire that "the hour might pass him by"; Jesus is fearful and in anguish. In contrast, in Luke's parallel scene, Jesus's anguish is transferred to the disciples, who are instructed by Jesus to pray for themselves (Luke 22:40). Only in Luke 22:45 are the disciples said to sleep because of their sorrow.

These framing episodes are themselves about the "framing" (betrayal, delivery = *paradidômi*) of Jesus. The opening bracket of the frame, the Gethsemane episode, ends with the arrival of the betrayer, *ho paradidous*, Judas, on behalf of the high priests (Mark 14:10–11). The closing bracket of the frame, the story of Barabbas, concludes with Jesus's appearance before Pilate (Mark 15:1–15). After Jesus is delivered, *paredôkan*, to the Roman, Pilate asks Jesus two questions. He receives an enigmatic answer ("It is you who say it.") to the first question ("Are you the King of the Jews?" 15:2), which introduces the theme of "King of the Jews" in Mark. Pilate receives no answer at all to his second question ("Have you no answer?"), which only emphasizes that Jesus has in effect given "no answer" to the first question. Jesus's evasive answer to Pilate's first question also raises doubts about the meaning of his reply to a similar question of the high priest in Mark 14:61 ("Are you the Christ, the son of the Blessed One?").

Following Pilate's interrogation of Jesus, the crowd approaches Pilate – Mark 15:6 separates the scene into two distinct parts – and requests the release of a prisoner. Pilate asks the crowd three questions, which further pursue the theme of the "King of the Jews": "Do you wish me to release your King of the Jews?" "What then shall I do with the man you call the King of the Jews?" and "Why? What harm has he done?" In response to Pilate's questions, and at the instigation of the high priests, the crowd chooses Barabbas (who is thereby further identified as "King of the Jews"), and the crowd replies to the following two questions regarding the disposal of "the man you call the King of the Jews" (Jesus) with cries of "Crucify him." The episode ends with Barabbas released and Jesus delivered up, *paredôken*, to be crucified. In Mark's narrative, Barabbas and Jesus have exchanged places under the heading, "King of the Jews."

The textual juxtaposition of the name "Barabbas" and the phrase "King of the Jews" does not appear in the versions of this story in Matthew and Luke. However, the gospel of John, in a quite different account (18:33–40) which identifies Jesus's kingdom as "not of this world" and Barabbas as a "robber," does juxtapose these terms. There are additional differences. Luke omits Pilate's second question and Jesus's non-answer and adds details of the charges against Jesus as well as Pilate's comment (stated twice) that "nothing has been done by him to deserve death" (23:15, 22). Luke also adds an interview with Herod in which Jesus does not answer Herod's questions either. Matthew adds the brief note about Pilate's wife's dream, as well as a more specific question, "Which of the two shall I give you?" (27:21) together with the washing of Pilate's hands.

> These developments reveal the growing importance which came to be attached to the story [of the trial before Pilate], and the desire to emphasize both the innocence of Jesus and the guilt of the Jews. In comparison, Mark's narrative has greater simplicity and realism.
>
> (Taylor 1953:577)

Both of these episodes in Mark are constructed around a triple structure of question and answer (or non-answer), and each concludes with the handing over, *paradidômi*, of Jesus. In the Gethsemane episode, Jesus speaks and no one answers; he is abandoned or ignored by Abba and the three disciples, and betrayed by Judas. In the Barabbas episode, Pilate speaks and the crowd answers. Jesus is selected (for crucifixion) by the crowd – which is in effect a single individual here and throughout the gospel of Mark – and substituted for Barabbas. Pilate and the high priests function as narrative mechanisms through which the non-answer of Abba is replaced by the crowd's answers, by means of which the "son of the father" becomes "the king of the Jews." Pilate introduces the phrase "King of the Jews," which resonates throughout Mark 15, and he arranges the exchange of Barabbas for Jesus. The high priests introduce the call for Barabbas, and they arrange the arrest of Jesus, that is, the exchange of Jesus for money.

Modern readers are often justifiably uncomfortable with Mark's historically doubtful depiction of aggressive envy (15:10) on the part of the high priests and what seems to be, by comparison, a benign indifference on the part of Pilate. These readers are painfully aware that Gentile readings of this text, along with many other texts, have played a significant and indeed, deadly, role in the bitter history of Christian anti-semitism. Augmenting this discomfort is the desire of believers to read the text as though it were historically true; the roots of this desire run deep in Christian theology. Therefore, both the anti-semitic reader and her opponent argue about the text's historical accuracy. Those readers who oppose anti-semitism note historically inconsistent, improbable, or even completely false details such as the trial at night (14:53) followed by a second council meeting in the morning (15:1), or the custom of releasing a prisoner (15:6), as though fictional episodes in a biblical gospel were at all unusual.[4]

Yet if these passion story episodes were read as fictions, how would that change things? The entire section of Mark 14:32–15:15, which is of great importance for Mark's narrative, is characterized from end to end by the sort of narrative artifice noted above. The framing of these stories betrays their profound fictionality. It is the desire, always ideological, on the part of believing readers to read these stories as *non*-fictional which ignores the artificiality of the text and creates the theological predicament.

THE FRAME WITHIN THE FRAME

You come out with swords and clubs to arrest me as if I were a highwayman? Day by day I was near you in the temple, teaching, and you did not seize me. But let the scriptures be fulfilled.

(Mark 14:48–9)

Within the first set of frames appears a second set that consists of the twin betrayals of Jesus, first by Judas (Mark 14:42–54) and then by Peter (Mark 14:66–72). Just as the linguistic play of "Abba" and "Barabbas" establishes the larger frame of the passion narrative in Mark, so the narrative parallels between the two betrayers, Judas and Peter, establishes this inner frame. As disciples, Peter and Judas are emblematic (along with the nameless young man mentioned in Mark 14:51–2) of all those disciples who "left him [Jesus] and fled away" (14:50). Although the Abba/Barabbas play does not appear in these episodes, the twin betrayals serve in their turn as an inner set of frames, frames within the frames, which bracket the enclosed text, both separating it from, and tying it into, the surrounding narrative.

The narrative tension between the midnight arrest of Jesus in Gethsemane and the fulfillment of scriptures in the opening bracket of this second pair of frames is expressed through the ambivalence in both Judas's kiss and his reference to Jesus as "Master," *rhabbi* (Mark 14:45). Luke 22:48 in effect forestalls this ambiguity. Judas's expressions of affection and respect serve to identify the one betrayed. In fact, they present a double ambiguity, which concerns both betrayer and betrayed. If God wills Jesus to be betrayed, as is implied in the prayer-scene in Gethsemane, then Judas also does the will of God and deserves no condemnation.[5] However, if Judas betrays Jesus on his own and is therefore worthy of condemnation, then in what sense are the scriptures "fulfilled?" In fact, Mark says

18

nothing further regarding Judas (in contrast to Matthew 27:3ff. and Acts 1:18), although the longer added ending of Mark does refer to "the eleven" (16:14), suggesting that Judas is no longer counted among the disciples.

It is not clear what specific scriptures, if any, have been fulfilled in this story. The best *inter*textual candidate is perhaps the "servant song" of Isaiah 52:13–53:12. Or is the reference in Mark 14:49 to "the scriptures" simply a euphemism for God's will? However, another possibility is that the only "scriptures" which have been fulfilled are Jesus's three *intra*textual betrayal prophecies in Mark 9:31 and 10:33 (see also Mark 8:31). Could Mark's gospel be referring to itself in this passage as "scripture"? Could any single text possibly fulfill itself?[6] Furthermore, if Mark refers to itself in 14:49, then Mark may also refer to itself as scripture in 9:12 and 14:21 ("it is written"), texts which also refer to the suffering of the son of man. The parallel to Mark 14:49 in Matthew 26:56 rules out self-referentiality in that version, and Luke provides no parallel at all to Mark 14:49.

However, Jesus does *not* prophesy at Mark 8:31, 9:31, or 10:33 that he, Jesus, will be betrayed but rather that the "son of man" will be betrayed. Although readers often identify Jesus with the son of man, in Mark this identification is always equivocal. Mark 14 comes closer than any other chapter in that gospel to identifying Jesus with the son of man. It is almost as though this critical moment in the story demands the resolution of his identity. Nevertheless, even in these verses the identification remains uncertain. In Mark 14:18, Jesus does prophesy his own betrayal by one of the disciples, but then he shifts quickly to speak of the betrayal of the son of man in 14:21. A similar shift in reference from Jesus to the son of man occurs in Mark 10:32–3:

> ... he began to tell them what was going to happen to him: Behold, we are going up to Jerusalem, and the son of man will be given over to the high priests and the scribes, and they will condemn him to death, ...

In Mark 14:41–2, an even more abrupt shift, this time from the son of man to himself, again centers on the theme of betrayal: "the son of man is betrayed into the hands of sinners. Rise up, let us go; see, my betrayer is near."

To the saying at Mark 14:21, Jesus adds words of woe for the betrayer:

the son of man goes his way as it has been written concerning him, but woe to that man through whom the son of man is betrayed. It were well for that man if he had never been born.

This verse is traditionally read as though it refers to Judas. However, there is another betrayer in Mark 14, namely Peter.[7] The story of Peter's denial of Jesus forms the closing bracket of the inner frame of Mark's passion narrative. When Jesus prophesies that the disciples will all fail him – as "it is written" (Mark 14:27, citing Zechariah 13:7) – Peter insists that he will not abandon him. Yet Peter (along with James and John) sleeps in Gethsemane, even though Jesus asks them to keep watch with him (14:34ff.). Peter apparently flees with the other disciples when the crowd comes to arrest Jesus (14:50), although he follows (as does the unnamed young man) "from a distance" (14:54). When the young man is seized, he flees naked. When Peter is identified as a companion of Jesus in the high priest's courtyard, he denies (three times, before the cock crows twice) that he is "one of them" (14:66ff.).

Mark presents both Judas and Peter, then, as fulfilling the scriptures. Both of these characters share, along with numerous others in Mark, the responsibility for the death of Jesus. Although Peter does not betray Jesus in the same sense that Judas does, his failure as a disciple is strongly emphasized here and elsewhere in Mark. Once more, the other gospels tone down Mark's vivid scene and eliminate the ambiguities. Luke 22:47ff. and John 18:1ff. omit any reference to the flight of the disciples, and they alter the sequence in which Peter's denial appears in the series of episodes. Luke alone has Jesus look at Peter (22:61) at the instant of the third denial/second crow of the cock.

As in the Abba/Barabbas frame, Jesus has a speaking part in the opening bracket of the second frame, and once again he asks a question, although it is a rhetorical one. Judas is the only other character to speak. As a result of a shift in point of view (from priests and council to guards and bystanders), Jesus is once again silent in the closing bracket of the frame, and the questions are asked by the high priest's maid and the bystanders and answered by Peter. Just as Jesus, at a distance, is being interrogated by the high priest, so Peter is grilled by the maid. Only in Mark does the same woman ask Peter the first two questions, and Peter gives a double reply to the first question.

Samuel Sandmel notes that the gospel of Mark gives as much

attention to Peter's denial as it does to the trial of Jesus (1978:44). The scripture is fulfilled by the flight from Jesus of his disciples, but Mark itself is also fulfilled, for Jesus's predictions of Judas's betrayal[8] and Peter's denial are part of Mark's story, and they also have been fulfilled. Once again, Mark seems to refer to itself as "scripture," indefinitely suspending the possibility of its own fulfillment.

Thus the two inner frames both extend out into the surrounding parts of Mark's narrative by way of prophecies by Jesus of betrayal and denial. In addition, the story of Peter's betrayal is divided (intercalated) by the story of Jesus's trial, even as it divides the stories of Jesus's trials. Mark 14:53–4 ("And Peter had followed him from a distance, into the courtyard of the high priest, and he was sitting there with the servingmen and warming himself at the fire.") is appended to the Judas scene, perhaps to associate Peter with the young man, who appears only in Mark (14:51–2). The young man (is it the same one?) who appears in the tomb (Mark 16:5) instructs the women to "tell his disciples, *and Peter*" (italics added) that Jesus has risen and precedes them into Galilee.[9] However, the overlap of episodes in Mark 14:53–4 also associates Peter with Judas. After these betrayal scenes, neither Judas nor Peter appears again in Mark, although Peter is mentioned in 16:7; nonetheless, both he and Judas have been already dismissed from the story.[10]

THE FRAMED

Are you the Christ, the son of the Blessed One? ... I am he, and you will see the son of man sitting on the right of the power and coming with the clouds of the sky.

(Mark 14:61–2)

The passion narrative in Mark is therefore framed within two sets of frames. The outer frame is generated by the Abba/Barabbas play. The inner frame is generated by the twin betrayals of Jesus, by Judas and Peter. At the center of Mark's frame-within-a-frame appears the revelation of Jesus's identity before the high priest; here too, as elsewhere in the arrest/trials scenes in Mark, the reader is given an answer that is "no answer" (14:60–1, 15:4–5). Priests and council seek damning evidence: they want to frame Jesus. Yet they are unable to frame him, even though (or perhaps because) they call upon false witnesses, for "their testimony did not agree" (14:56, 59). Luke omits the false witnesses, and Matthew omits the inconsistency in their testimony. These witnesses, who give testimony that features a temple "made with hands" torn down and another one "not made with hands" built in "three days" (14:58), bring to mind saying 71 of the gospel of Thomas ("I shall destroy [this] house, and no one will be able to rebuild it"), and more so the gospel of John 2:19 ("Destroy this temple, and in three days I will raise it up"). Both of these texts refer to sayings of Jesus, and the temple that is "not made with hands" (Mark 14:58) sounds like it could be "the temple of [Jesus's] body" (John 2:21). Perhaps for this reason, many scholars (and maybe the authors of Matthew and Luke) regard the false claim in Mark 14:58 as in fact a true one – as a statement made by Jesus, despite Mark's own claims (13:2, 14:57) to the contrary (Taylor 1953:566–7). Like the witnesses at the trial in Mark, the testimony of the various gospels also does not agree. Only Mark by itself (without this intertextual rescue) can frame Jesus.

Yet within this central episode (Mark 14:55–65) there appears still another pair of frames! The unsuccessful attempt to frame Jesus by witnesses (14:55–9) and the act of condemnation (14:63b–5) serve as a further set of narrative brackets framing the central confrontation between Jesus and the high priest. The false witnesses that appear initially are replaced by council members and guards at the close of the episode. Once again, as in the outer, Abba/Barabbas frame, the episode ends with Jesus being "received" by others. In the course of Mark's passion narrative, Jesus is handed over three (or four) times, by various characters: by Judas, by the high priests or council (apparently twice, both before and after the scene of Peter's betrayal), and by Pilate.[11]

Thus at the core of Mark's passion narrative is that which is framed within these three-fold frames. It is the encounter between the high priest and Jesus in Mark 14:60–3a:

> Then the high priest stood up among them and questioned Jesus, saying: Have you no answer? What is this testimony that they bring against you? But he was silent and did not answer. Again the high priest questioned him and said: Are you the Christ, the son of the Blessed One? Jesus said: I am he, and you will see the son of man sitting on the right of the power and coming with the clouds of the sky. The high priest tore his clothing ...

Jesus answers only one of the high priest's two questions, just as he also answers, a few verses later, just one of Pilate's two questions.

The high priest's second question explicitly associates the king of the Jews ("the Christ") with the son of the Father ("the son of the Blessed One"). The answer which Jesus gives to this second question conjoins two scriptures, Psalm 110 and Daniel 7:13, but while it is more extensive than the answer that Jesus will give to Pilate, it is no less ambiguous.

This ambiguity is not usually recognized by readers; indeed, Jesus's bold answer in Mark's version of the story seems much less equivocal than the parallels in Matthew and Luke. "I am," *egô eimi*, is often read as an unambiguous affirmation that Jesus is in fact the son of the Blessed One and the messiah, or even as an assertion of identity with God ("I am" resonates with Exodus 3:14–15, God's answer to Moses from the burning bush). The latter reading would also support the priest's claim that Jesus has blasphemed (see Leviticus 24:16). As in the scene in the garden of Gethsemane, the high priest represents the silent Abba when he tears his robes (here in judgment, but originally a gesture of grief) in response to Jesus's answer. Jesus becomes the third and most spectacular betrayer within Mark's story; Jesus betrays himself.

However, reading Jesus's words in either of these ways is undermined by the remainder of his answer to the priest. If "son of God" is taken as equivalent to "messiah" (as the priest's question suggests), then Jesus's words about the son of man (*not* the messiah) do not provide unequivocal affirmation at all, but rather set up the paradoxical, and perhaps impossible, equation:

$$\text{messiah/son of god} = \text{son of man.}$$

This paradox undermines the apparent clarity of Jesus's statement of identity, "I am." Jesus's answer does not identify who he is; instead it identifies a lack of coherent identity. The apparently apocalyptic son of man of Mark 14:62 is hardly a political messiah ("King of the Jews"). The paradox is reduced in the parallels in Matthew 26:64 and Luke 22:67b–70 by an equivocation on Jesus's self-identification and further by the separation of this self-identification from the son of man saying; the paradoxical conjunction of sayings in Mark (*kai*, "and") becomes non-paradoxical opposition in both Matthew (*plên*, "but") and Luke (*de*, "but").

But is Jesus even saying, "I am ... the son of man"? How much does the reader of the gospel of Mark know about who Jesus is? The question of Jesus's identity is a theme which runs throughout Mark. The unclean spirits call him "the son of God." However, Mark's claim that the demons "knew him," *êdeisan auton* (Mark 1:34) is not enough to demonstrate who Jesus is, as one conclusion that may be drawn from this identifies Jesus with Satan; this is indeed the inference of the scribes and perhaps others in Mark 3:22ff. (see also 1:27). The words of the centurion ("In truth this man was the Son of God," 15:39) and even of the nameless voice from heaven or the cloud ("You are my son whom I love," 1:11, 9:7) are just as ambiguous. The opening verse of Mark describes Jesus as "messiah," but in the exchange of harsh words between Jesus and the disciples (especially Peter) at Caesarea Philippi, the messiah and the son of man are set in opposition to one another, as the thoughts of men versus the thoughts of God (Mark 8:33). The effect is to subvert the reader's attempt to establish an equation between messiah and son of man in Mark 14:61–2, and to raise doubts about the reliability of the narrator's language in 1:1.[12]

Perhaps most telling of all, in Mark 13:6, Jesus warns the disciples against those who come in "my name" and say *egô eimi*, for "they will lead many astray." Is the "name" of Jesus that of "the Christ, the son of the Blessed One" (see also Mark 1:1, 8:29)? Or is Jesus's name "bar abbas?" What is the name of Jesus in Mark?[13] Can his name be known if his identity remains uncertain? This name (or names) is referred to in Mark 6:14ff., 9:37–9, 41, 11:9, 13:6, 13; however, by the end of Mark, all possible names or titles have dropped away from Jesus except for "Jesus the Nazarene, who was crucified." Furthermore, in Mark 13:21–2, Jesus also says, "if someone says to you: See, here is the Christ; see, he is there, do not believe him. For false Christs and false prophets will rise up, and they will present signs and portents to mislead the chosen, if that may be done." Is Jesus masquerading as the Christ in Mark 14:62? Does his citation of Daniel 7:13 (also in Mark 8:38 and 13:26) present a sign? Jesus's own condemnation and eventual death (and associated events) result directly from his answer. Do these narrative events function in Mark as portents?

Frank Kermode (1979:156, n. 25) notes that Jesus's *egô eimi* in Mark 14:62 is unexpected and stands in counterpoint to Peter's denials in Mark 14:68ff. The apparent self-identification disturbs the reader's identification of Jesus (either as messiah or as son of man) with its paradoxical and fantastic oscillation between the supernatural and the natural (Todorov 1973:31–2). An alternative reading found in some manuscripts of Mark, "You say that I am," is much weaker, and it is closer to Matthew's and Luke's non-paradoxical versions of the episode. Besides Mark 13:6 and 14:62, the only other place where *egô eimi* appears in Mark is in the miracle story at 6:50, where Jesus speaks this phrase to the disciples as he walks on the sea toward their boat. It is not clear whether in this instance the significance of the phrase is analogous to that in Mark 13:6 or 14:62, or if Jesus is merely saying to the disciples, "it's me" (as both Lattimore and the Revised Standard Version [RSV] suggest). The response of the disciples is that "they were still all too much disturbed, for they had not understood about the loaves, but their hearts had become impenetrable" (Mark 6:51-2). The pre-death context of the walking on the sea turns what otherwise might be theophany into "mere" miracle and thereby effectively destroys the episode's plausibility as divine self-identification.

Has Jesus framed himself in his dialogue with the high priest? Shouldn't the warnings from Mark 13 be relevant to the events in Mark 14? Or are these two chapters to be read in reverse order, so that Jesus can announce his messiahship to the priest and thereby to the reader before warning against pretenders? To do that would require an inversion of the frames, turning the passion narrative inside-out, which is precisely what most readings of these episodes do to the story. Kermode (1979:128) speaks of chapter 13 as the largest of Mark's intercalations, "an incursion of the future, properly terrible, properly ambiguous, into a narrative which proleptically shapes and sanctifies it." The reader desires something like Mark 13 to be the true end of Mark's story, announcing a glorious sequel to follow the disappointing and confusing ending at 16:8.

However, no text (including that of the gospel of Mark) can successfully direct its own reading. While Mark's intercalations (such as the Temple "cleansing" in 11:15-18) do resonate in provocative ways with the stories into which they are inserted (the cursing and withering of the fig tree in 11:12-14, 19-21), they can hardly be said to explain them. The so-called "messianic secret" – the claim of many scholars that in Mark Jesus wants his true identity as the Christ to remain unknown until he begins his climactic journey to Jerusalem – may be the most spectacular consequence of this reading failure. The messianic secret is indeed "a literary device ... designed to emphasize the importance of a correct understanding of christological confession and christological testimony" (Perrin in Kelber 1976:89). However, the messianic secret is not a device that produces understanding, christological or otherwise, for this reading too must fail. If Jesus were secretly the Christ in Mark, there would be no son of man/messiah paradox in Mark 14:62.

> [T]he value of Wrede's theory [of the messianic secret in Mark] is less that it explains how Mark's book came to be as it is (why he had to put in so much, and so oddly, about secrecy) than that it compels us to see what is actually there: the antithesis of silence and proclamation, and its relation to a whole network of disjunct but collocated qualities throughout the work.
>
> (Kermode 1979:140)

Phrases such as "tell no one" echo throughout the text of Mark (1:44, 5:43, 7:36, 8:30, 9:9, 16:7–8; see also 11:33), and they contrast sharply with Jesus's messianic entrance into Jerusalem (11:1–11), as well as with passages such as Mark 5:19 ("Go home to your people and tell them what your lord did for you and how he took pity on you") and (perhaps) 10:46–52. Mark 9:9–10 ("As they came down from the mountain he charged them that they should tell no one what they had seen, except when the son of man should rise up from the dead. And they kept his commandment, while questioning among themselves what it might mean to rise from the dead.") is particularly puzzling. The inert, dead text of the written gospel is revealed most fully at Mark 16:8 ("And they said nothing to anyone, for they were afraid"), through the absence of the ambiguous messiah. Although the gospel will be "preached through all the world" (Mark 14:9), its message remains enigmatic and undecidable. In Roland Barthes's terms, Mark is a writerly text, an incoherent text, a text of bliss. As Barthes would say (1975:49–52), the sentence which forms this story is incomplete.

The framed contents of the elaborate series of frames-within-frames-within-frames at the core of the Markan passion narrative is itself a riddle in the guise of a revelation. Jesus's spectacular answer to the high priest turns out to be "no answer," paradoxical and finally incomprehensible without supplementation, either inter-textual (such as other biblical gospels might provide) or extratextual (the inversion of Mark in order to make it speak correctly, that is, according to Christian orthodoxy). For the Christian reader, this supplementation will be grounded in the ideology of the passion.

THE IDEOLOGY OF THE PASSION

Why do we still need witnesses? Did you hear the blasphemy?
What is your view?

(Mark 14:63–4)

Much scholarship on the gospel of Mark still takes as fact Martin Kähler's summation of that gospel as a passion narrative with a lengthy preface (1964:80).[14] According to this view, the first half of Mark introduces Jesus and presents collections of parables and miracle stories. The crucial dialogue at Caesarea Philippi (Mark 8:27–33), in which Jesus's identity is declared by Peter ("you are the Christ"), is a turning point in the story. Jesus then heads toward Jerusalem and proceeds decisively to the showdown with the Temple authorities, the outcome of which is central to a largely Pauline theology, which proclaims the centrality of Jesus's salvific death to Christian faith and which undergirds Mark's narrative. Important indicators of the centrality of the passion earlier in the story are the three predictions, at Mark 8:31, 9:31, and 10:33–4, of the suffering and death of the son of man.

However, the foregoing analysis of most of Mark's passion narrative suggests that Kähler's description applies more correctly to the way Christians *actually read* the gospel of Mark than it does to the arrangement of the text itself. This is indeed the diagnosis which Robert Fowler (1991) applies to most biblical scholarship, namely that the reader's attempt to make sense of the story says more about the process of reading than it does about the background, origins, or structure of the text itself. Jacques Derrida (1981:1–59) makes a similar point when he claims that every preface is written in the future perfect; it concerns that which will have already been written – that is, that which has already been read. Just as the reader reads the preface to any book in the light of her own (pre-)understanding of what the rest of the book will be about, so Christians read Mark backward from the passion account – they turn the first twelve chapters into a preface. Thereby they invert the framing of Jesus. The framed becomes the frame.

Mark's passion story does not terminate at 15:20, but it continues with the story of the crucifixion of Jesus itself. This succeeding story includes the fantastic events that take place at the moment of Jesus's death,[15] followed by the burial of Jesus (15:42–7) and then, after the Sabbath, by the visit of women followers to the tomb (16:1–8) with which Mark terminates. While these remaining episodes are perhaps the "bottom line" of Mark's story, it is the framed/framing sections discussed above that form the center of the passion narrative. How the reader understands Mark's ambiguous conclusion will be largely governed by how she understands the previous parts of the narrative, including the arrest/trials sequence. The episodes in Mark 15:21–16:8 shed no further light on the indeterminacies of 14:60–3a, but they continue a pattern of ambiguity that has already been well-established in Mark – a pattern that begins not at the beginning of the passion narrative but at the strange beginning of the gospel itself.[16]

Kähler is wrong; Mark is *not* merely a passion narrative with an elaborate preface – only the devout reading of Christian readers can transform it into that – but rather Mark is a continuously and conspicuously self-disruptive narrative which resists every attempt to define its identity or even to render it coherent. This observation in turn should raise doubts about the oft-stated view that Mark's "gospel" presents a Pauline theology. Just as Mark 13 presents an apocalypse the arrival of which "no one knows" (13:32, RSV), so the whole of the gospel of Mark presents a proclamation which is, like Jesus's responses to the high priest and to Pilate, "no answer."

Mark's passion story is itself one of the more convoluted and paradoxical segments in this pattern. One is reminded of *trompe l'œil* paintings in which a highly "realistic" picture frame is painted on the canvas itself, or contemporary art installations in which the contents of a painting spill out beyond the canvas on to the frame or even on to the wall on which the "picture" seems to be "hung." This postmodern characteristic also appears in the ancient gospel of Mark, where the framed scene of Jesus's trial splits the framing scene of Peter's denial. These aesthetic effects – indeed, all of Mark's intercalations as well as its references to itself – subvert the assumption that the frame determines a clear boundary between the content (that which is within the frame) and the context (that which is beyond the frame) of the reproduction. Mark's passion narrative frames reflect a much larger structure of the entire book.

> The practice is so often repeated as to become part of the habit of the book; and this repetition makes one wonder whether the intercalated stories do not exist to replicate, in particular episodes, some feature of the whole discourse. Should we think of the whole gospel as an intercalated story? ... All

Mark's minor intercalations reflect the image of a greater intervention represented by the whole book.

(Kermode 1979:133–4)

But an intervention in what? The fundamentally modernist ontology of the frame, which separates in order to join together content and context, representation and reality, fiction and history, is deconstructed by the self-referentiality of the text of Mark.

Mark's sequence of arrest/trials stories functions as a series of frames within frames, each frame containing a yet smaller frame. Constructions such as this raise the distressing possibility that there might be neither an ultimate framed content (an extratextual reality reproduced in the text) nor an absolute, outermost framing context (the extratextual reality which produces the text) – and that the sequence of frames might extend indefinitely into the opposed realms of the minuscule and the gigantic. This threat of infinite regression is averted only by the recognition that written text does indeed have a smallest atomic unit (the alphabetic letter) and that no narrative can successfully be boundless. Every narrative must have a beginning, a middle, and an end, as Aristotle said. The episodes of the story must be read in order, in a proper sequence. Matthew and Luke assist this reading, by consistently eliminating Mark's frames.

Has Mark "delivered" Jesus to the reader through this framing structure? Does the framing of Jesus by the text in fact produce its own inversion by the reader? Even though the text cannot direct its own reading, by establishing this pattern in the passion narrative, Mark appears to invite (or even seduce) the reader into reading *egô eimi*, the alphabetic bull's-eye at the narrative pattern's center, as the key to the entire story. Is this frame pattern truly "in" the text, or is it necessarily a construct (always intertextual) imposed upon the text by the reader? The fact that other readers make nothing of this pattern (for example, the play of Abba/Barabbas is rarely noted) indicates that it is at least in part a product of the reading. This fact may also indicate that this frame is very effective; it does not draw attention to itself. Yet the textual features themselves (*abba, Barabbas, paradidômi,* etc.) are physical, material objects, ink marks of specific color and shape on a page of specific texture and thickness, which are not subjective. These physical qualities are independent of every interpretation, but this does not mean that they remain uninterpreted. Without such features, there could be no pattern;

however, they alone are insufficient to the reading, because they alone are meaningless.

Something further is required in order to make sense of the text, and that is the ideology of the passion itself, which unfolds from intertextual networks of Christian belief and provides its own frame for the reading of these texts. Christianity as we know it is unthinkable without the passion of Jesus. This is not to deny the possibility of early groups within the "Jesus movements" for which Jesus's passion was not theologically important, and for which evidence is provided by Q (the common source of Matthew and Luke) and the gospel of Thomas. Not only is a passion story absent from both Q and Thomas, but the term "Christ" does not appear in either of them (see, however, Thomas 37, 44, and 61). However, whether or in what sense the groups which produced Q and Thomas were "Christian" is not clear.

The lack of a passion narrative may explain why these two writings were eventually eliminated by the Christian movement, either through association with heresy (Thomas) or absorption into more clearly orthodox writings (Q). As it has actually survived and developed, Christianity has taken the passion as a fundamental and indispensable christological concept. This concept has been central to Christian belief in Jesus as both human messiah *and* divine son of God, the unique incarnation of God, and also to Christian belief in the historical actuality of the event of Jesus's death and resurrection (rejection of Docetism). The proclamation of Jesus's death as the means of salvation which is essential to mainstream Christian self-definition requires a reading of the passion story as factual; for Christianity, Jesus must be both the son of the Father and the king of the Jews.

The story of Mark itself "betrays" Jesus as the son of man even as it fulfills itself, but it does so only as it is also betrayed by a community of interpretation which as a result of faith reads the gospel text as "scripture": "the son of man goes his way as it has been written concerning him" (Mark 14:21). By transforming the text into the Truth (the Word of God) the believing community transforms fiction into historical fact; narrative becomes theology. The text is consumed and digested, and the reading seeks to re-frame Jesus, to rewrite him, eliminating the ambiguities of his identity. That which was framed is opened up and itself becomes the frame through which the entire gospel is read.

The ideology of the passion arises from the desire of Christian readers to let go of the frames and keep the framed. But the desire of readers to mark elements of the passion story as historically inaccurate theological constructions (fictions) is merely the obverse of the desire of Christians to read the rest of the passion story as fundamentally truthful (factual), for the historical actuality and consequent theological truth of the passion story remain of central importance to Christianity. The elements identified as fictional remain of interest to those readers who want to reconstruct Mark's theology;[17] however, identification of narrative elements as fictional constructs disengages their relevance to contemporary exegesis and belief. This dividing of the gospel into history and fiction is performed in theological and narratological bad faith. Insofar as Christians continue to believe that only through the unique and historical passion of Jesus the Christ/son of God does salvation become possible, that through his passion Jesus has triumphed over death and powers of evil, and thus that Jesus's suffering and death are theologically indispensable, then anti-semitism also remains unavoidable in Christian belief.

In order for Jesus to answer the high priest's question, the question must first be asked. By explicitly raising the question of Jesus's identity, the question which has dominated the entire story of Mark, the high priest speaks for the reader. The enemies of Jesus procure answers for the reader. The transition from Pilate's inter- rogation of Jesus (Mark 15:1–5), where questions similar to the high priest's are asked, to Pilate's baiting of the Jerusalem crowd, which is agitated in turn by the high priests (15:6–15), is crucial. If Pilate is viewed as a sympathetic character (Nineham 1963:411–13), then a correlated understanding of the priests as lacking in sympathetic qualities will be required, and this places the reader in an interpretive bind. The reader collaborates with both Romans and priests in the framing of Jesus in the gospel of Mark.

One escape from this bind is to claim that it was clear who Jesus was all along, as many commentators do. The logic of the keryg- matic passion story requires the innocence of Jesus: only the sacrifice of the innocent one can bring salvation. However, if Jesus was innocent but was found guilty, then he must have been framed by someone, either the Jewish priests or the Romans. If his enigmatic answer to the high priest really means, "Yes, I am the Christ, the son of the Blessed One," then it is the priest who must be guilty of killing the messiah. On the other hand, if Jesus's answer to Pilate really means, "Yes, I am God's anointed King of the Jews," then

Pilate is the one who is responsible for Jesus's death, and Jesus must be a revolutionary like Barabbas. Christian belief requires the former answer.

The scapegoating of Jews (high priests, crowds, Pharisees) and relative exoneration of Romans (Pilate, the centurion) emerged from the political–existential situation of the early Jesus movements. The contemporary desire to clarify the socio–historical context of the gospels in the early Jesus movements, and especially to bring an end to Christian hatred of the Jewish people, is certainly praiseworthy, and long overdue. However, this is also where the desire to segregate seemingly anti-semitic elements in the gospel stories of Jesus as theological (or narrative) constructs arises for modern readers, who use the category of fiction to bracket and neutralize depictions of Jews (especially high priests and Pharisees) and Romans, while attempting to maintain the non-fictionality both of Jesus's answer to the high priest and of Jesus's necessary death. Contemporary scholarship uses historical analysis of the texts to provide a supplement to Mark (and the other gospels), both to "correct" Mark's inadequate account of the passion and to save important christological claims.[18]

Mark and other gospels undoubtedly have played historical roles in the production of Christian beliefs, including Christian anti-semitism. However, it does not follow from this history that those beliefs or any others are located somehow "in" the text of Mark or essential to its reading, any more than clear identification of who Jesus is can be found in Mark. Who dies in Mark 15? Whose tomb appears empty in Mark 16? Is it the son of the Father or the king of the Jews? Both? Neither? Anti-semitism belongs to the ideology of the reader (and the reader's community), not to the text itself. Perhaps the more difficult question is whether a non-anti-semitic ideology could ever "own" (or "steal") the gospel of Mark.[19] Such a reading of the gospel would depend upon the willingness (or ability) of readers to abandon theological claims regarding the importance and historical uniqueness of Jesus's passion and to read the *entire* passion narrative as self-referential fiction – that is, to contextualize and subvert the story as reference to historical truth. However, no reading could ever excuse or exonerate anti-semitism, and to read Mark as fiction does not entitle the reader to be comfortable with Mark's framing of Jesus.

By framing Jesus as it does, Mark both invites and resists the reader's readings. It raises vital questions: "From where does the man derive all this?" (6:2) "Who do people say that I am?" (8:27) "What might it mean to rise from the dead?" (9:10) "What must I do to inherit life everlasting?" (10:17) "By what authority do you do this? Or who gave you this authority, to do these things?" (11:28) But the gospel of Mark, like the character Jesus in its story, gives the reader "no answer." Its enigmatic style and paradoxical narrative provide no readerly satisfactions. Mark is a great tease, suggesting possibilities which it then fails to fulfill; as a story it is profoundly incomplete. It is not surprising, then, that readers, beginning with Matthew and Luke, go beyond Mark, re-framing Mark and rewriting it to satisfy their own desires.

2

DESIRE FOR AN END

THE LIMITS OF STORY

"Whole" is that which has beginning, middle, and end. "Beginning" is that which does not necessarily follow on something else, but after it something else naturally is or happens; "end," the other way round, is that which naturally follows on something else, either necessarily or for the most part, but nothing else after it ... [W]ell-constructed plots should neither begin nor end at any chance point but follow the guidelines just laid down.

(Aristotle 1967:30)

Aristotle's famous dictum (*Poetics* 1450b26–34) raises more questions than it answers. Can we conceive of any event which "does not necessarily follow on something else?" What does it mean to say of an event that "nothing else [follows] after it?" These definitions point toward an absolute beginning or end, a point in time when whatever happens before or after it, as the case may be, is entirely unconnected to a sequence of events, a plot. But Aristotle is talking about narrative events.[1] Could he mean that the narrator simply does not give the reader the sort of information from which the reader might infer a preceding event as necessary to the beginning, or a succeeding event as inevitable to the end? Is that even conceivable, as a narrative strategy, or can readers always assume that *something* must have happened before the story began, and after it ended?

The point of Aristotle's discussion of plot unity seems to be that stories cannot just start or end anywhere. Aristotle seeks both a metaphysics and a logic of narrative, as the words "naturally" and "necessarily" suggest: he is concerned with the identity of the story, what holds it together, what makes it this specific story and not another, or one story and not several. The practical reality that Aristotle seeks to explore within his theory of narrative is that stories must make sense. They must start somehow, and they must also end somehow. A story which begins in the middle of things or whose end is chopped off without apparent reason presses the reader to construct a proper, more complete beginning or end for the story – that is, a natural or necessary beginning or end of the sort that Aristotle requires. Otherwise the reader is not only frustrated in her desire for narrative completeness, but she is also in fact unable to understand the story at all.

As Aristotle's definitions suggest (the rest of the *Poetics* notwithstanding), the absolutely complete story is an impossibility, for there is always more that could be told, further questions that the story suggests but does not answer. The process of narrative production is infinite, although practical and ideological limits will inevitably be set for it. The "natural-ness" of the ending must always be illusory. As Frank Kermode says, more explicitly, "Endings, then, are faked, as are all other parts of a narrative structure that impose metaphor on the metonymic sequence" (1978:147). Along similar lines, Roland Barthes (1985:103) quotes an unnamed linguist as saying, "Each one of us speaks but a single sentence, which only death can bring to a close."[2]

The incompleteness of every story leaves open the possibility that additional information regarding events or characters in the story would throw into an entirely different light any story that the reader has been given. The reader's desire to complete the "poorly constructed plot" (as Aristotle might describe it) may be satisfied by additions to the story that extend the narrative past or future to encompass an acceptable beginning or end. Because they grope for that which is "necessary" and "natural," these extensions are profoundly ideological (Barthes 1988:173–8). The reader desires another story, a further story, sequel or prequel, which will supplement and therefore necessarily change the given story. However, the supplemental story, because it too is a story, will also inevitably be incomplete. The prospect of an endless progression (or regression) of stories is thereby opened up; each additional story promises to finish off the previous one(s) and always fails to do so. However – and this is Aristotle's main point – an endless story is by definition *not* a story. Its identity as a story is fundamentally deficient. In order for there to be a story, supplementation must eventually come to a stop.[3]

Readers and audiences are familiar today with the great demand for the sequel to popular movies, novels, comic books, and television shows. These authorized supplements to popular stories are widely accepted, and even intrinsic to certain genres, such as the comic strip and the TV serial.[4] The story recruits an audience which reacts with a kind of shock if an addition to the story is published that violates the values and expectations which they have inferred from preceding episodes – for example, if Sherlock Holmes or Superman dies. This shock is not just a response to narrative reversal; it is an index of the dominant ideology of the audience. Market research may dictate revision of a potentially unpopular story ending prior to the release of a new episode, or an additional sequel may explain that what appeared earlier to be the hero's death at the hands of a villain was only apparently so. (And it is also necessary for villainy to survive! There can be no story without contest.)

In the original, oral, situation of storytelling, the power of the communal audience to negotiate a narrative "contract" which among other things set limits to narrative proliferation was probably considerable. The "sense of an ending" was communal. In contrast, imaginary additions to a story's beginning or end satisfy the isolated reader of the written story without involving other readers, except insofar as other readers share in a community of readers that forms the reader's tastes and beliefs. Kermode notes that

> We depend upon well-formedness – less so, it must be confessed, in oral than in written language: in the written story there is no visible gesture or immediate social context to help out the unarticulated sentence, the aposiopesis.
>
> (Kermode 1979:64–5)

Yet if all narratives are inherently incomplete, then even the private responses of the reader of a written text will reflect negotiations not entirely unlike those of the preliterate community. Furthermore, it seems that with the development of popular literature and especially mass media such as cinema and television, the rewriting of incomplete written stories in the private imaginations of the readers of books has become once again a public matter. The demand for, general acceptance of, and popularity of public, authorized prequels and sequels to popular novels and movies (sometimes crossing the boundaries between media) extends phenomena such as the communal, oral, composition of folk tales and popular songs in folk tradition into the modern and postmodern realms of electronic media. The development of these extended narratives has always been reflective of ideology, regardless of the medium and the cultural milieu. In the contemporary world, dominated as it is by commercial interests, however, this development is governed by the copyright-protected control of the story's owner. This owner may or may not be the story's creator; the owner may even franchise the right to the story's extension to others.

Once the supplementation of the story begins – and this supplementation is probably as old as storytelling itself – the boundaries of the story as defined by Aristotle become unclear. Where then does the story begin or end? Can one draw a line, actual or hypothetical, between the story proper (in something like Aristotle's sense) and its accretions (imaginary or actual) at the hands of its readers? In most cases, the reader depends upon certain events in the history of the text's production to determine this distinction: the author's manuscript, the published text, the authorized translation, the critical edition. The problem is not simply (or primarily) historical, however, for the selection of one or another of these events as a criterion of narrative identity implies in turn a different understanding of what counts as "the story" – different metaphysics and a different logic. Much room remains for controversy over the identity of any story, and even if there were general agreement concerning what counted as critical events, serious difficulties would remain. It is impossible to define adequately the limits of story.

It is structurally impossible to define the precise point at which one story (or one version of a story) becomes different from another story (or version). When do the differences between two stories become significant? At what point are the two no longer "the same" story? For similar reasons, it is impossible to account fully for any story's beginning or end – that is, why a story begins or ends at one point and not another. To do so would require yet another story (to account for the first story), and so on, *ad infinitum*. As a result, Aristotle's third plot feature, the middle, the part that seems most sure in terms of identity, is also a site of incompleteness. Once the beginning and the end have been established, the middle also must follow "naturally" and "necessarily" – in other words, the middle of the story is also a product of ideology. In addition, the middle must somehow link together the beginning and the end, and it may indeed fail to do that as well. When this happens, then once again the completeness and the identity of the story becomes problematic.

The biblical text of the gospel of Mark fails Aristotle's identity test. Yet Aristotle's criteria for narrative identity can nonetheless tell us much about Mark – both what Mark is and what Mark isn't. Among other features which thwart narrative coherence, Mark offers the reader several distinct endings to its story. One or both of two additional endings usually appear in texts of Mark following verse 16:8, which is where the gospel ends in the oldest "complete" manuscripts known at present. Why were these supplementary endings added to Mark – or if 16:8 is itself a truncation of an original longer ending, as some scholars think, why was material removed from some manuscripts? My concern in the following is not with that historical question but with what the addition of these endings to Mark do to and imply about the "well-constructedness" of Mark's narrative. How do the various conclusions of Mark disguise and resolve the inadequacies of Mark's story – or do they? These multiple endings interrogate the identity of Mark as a text and as a narrative.

BEGINNING AND ENDING MARK

The beginning of the gospel of Jesus Christ. As it is written in Isaiah the prophet ...

(Mark 1:1–2a)[5]

And they went out and fled from the tomb, for trembling and panic had hold of them. And they said nothing to anyone, for they were afraid.

(Mark 16:8)

The gospel of Mark begins with the word *archê*, which means "the beginning." That the beginning of this gospel should actually start with the words "the beginning of the gospel," *archê tou euaggeliou*, suggests a degree of self-referentiality in this ancient narrative which would be more appropriate to a postmodern story.[6] However, that which is postmodern is not always a product of the twentieth century, as readers of *Don Quixote* or *Tristram Shandy* are aware. I have argued elsewhere[7] that postmodern characteristics appear at many points in the gospel of Mark. This self-referentiality creates a narrative loop that undermines Mark's beginning.

Furthermore, Mark 1:1 appears to be an incipit, an opening sentence which often functioned in ancient narratives as a sort of title or summary for the entire story. Whether the words of this verse simply refer to themselves only or whether they refer to the entire text of Mark as "the beginning of the gospel" is impossible to determine. The gospels of Matthew and Luke also begin with incipits, but their beginnings are not as glaringly self-referential as Mark's. In addition, the beginnings of Matthew and Luke are softened considerably by immediately succeeding genealogies and Christmas stories, which tend to remove the referential indeterminacy that is found in Mark 1:1. In Aristotle's terms, Matthew and Luke do a better job of starting at the beginning ("that which does not necessarily follow on something else"), with stories of Jesus's ancestry and birth. The gospel of John's opening prologue does not follow the strategy of Matthew and Luke, but instead it traces Jesus's beginning back to the creation of the universe, the beginning of everything. In Aristotelian terms, one could do no more than John does.

If Mark 1:1 is read as an incipit, then Mark begins with the story of the baptism of Jesus as though nothing in his life prior to that moment were of importance – that is, as though his baptism did not necessarily follow on from something else. The narrative of Mark would then begin at verse 2, not verse 1. This would also imply that the first word of the "proper" text of Mark, that is, the first word of verse 2, is *kathôs*, "as." Mark 1:2 begins with "as it is written," which is still curiously self-referential. Mark continues (after 1:1) to write (about) its own writing, even though the reference of the words in 1:2 is explicitly to the prophetic writing of Isaiah (it is in fact a mixture of quotations from Malachi and Isaiah). To begin a book with "as" is not entirely uncouth, or unknown, but in comparison to the smooth beginnings of the other biblical gospels, "as it is written" reads like a stutter, a searching around for some way to get the tale started. From here on, whenever Mark refers to that which "is written" (*gegraptai*) or to "the scriptures" (*hai graphai*), it will echo this reference to itself as a writing.

Other seemingly postmodern paradoxes and indeterminacies of reference appear in many places and in many ways throughout the gospel of Mark; "a good deal of the story seems concerned with failure to understand the story," as Kermode says (1979:69). Mark is "incomplete," not only at its beginning and end, but throughout. That deficiency of narrative identity begins at its beginning. Even though the beginning of Mark is not troubled with major variants like the end of Mark is, in fact the beginning is nonetheless quite "difficult" and requires supplementation. This difficulty extends beyond the lack of a Christmas story such as in Matthew or Luke. The self-referential and grammatically odd beginning of Mark is neither "necessary" nor "natural."

The multiple endings of Mark are even more disruptive of its narrative completeness or identity than Mark's beginning. The first and uncontested end of Mark[8] is at 16:8: *kai oudeni ouden eipan ephobounto gar*, "and they said nothing to anyone, for they were afraid." This is the last half of the final verse in Mark. "For they were afraid," *ephobounto gar*, is, to say the least, a strange ending (as many critics have noted) for "the gospel of Jesus Christ," or even for "the beginning of the gospel." As Kermode says,

> We have to explain why a book that begins so triumphantly and makes promises of a certain kind ends in silence and dismay, without fulfilling the promises.
>
> (1978:148)

Furthermore, to end a sentence, much less an entire book, with the preposition "for," *gar*, while not unknown in Greek, is highly unusual. Mark both begins and ends with grammatical oddities.[9] Robert Fowler (1991:262) suggests that the final *gar* marks a circularity in the text, like a musical *coda*, whose effect is to return the reader to the beginning, to start reading all over again. This circularity points once again in the direction of the postmodern: the text establishes an endless reading loop, like *Finnegan's Wake* or some of the stories of Jorge Luis Borges or Italo Calvino.

The strange grammar of Mark's ending at 16:8 highlights the ending's other unusual qualities. None of the other biblical gospels have endings at all like Mark, either in grammar or narrative content. If Mark ends at 16:8, then the narrative ends without an appearance of the risen Jesus. Jesus's miraculous triumph over death appears only indirectly, in the report of a mysterious young man who appears in Jesus's place in the tomb. Can this report be trusted? The women disciples respond to it by fleeing from the empty tomb. After the women flee, "they said nothing to anyone, for they were afraid." But, if they said nothing to anyone, then no one ever heard the message of the young man, or even that the tomb was empty. If the text of Mark ends here, then the very fact of its own writing remains a mystery if not a contradiction, unless Mark's story is merely a fiction, and questions of how its message came to be known are irrelevant. Mark narrates at 16:8 the impossibility of its own telling – again, a postmodern twist.

With its lack of post-resurrection appearances of Jesus, Mark's empty tomb ending is difficult enough. In addition, the strongly implied consequence of 16:8 is that the story never got out, which the written fact of Mark's text itself contradicts. Could we have here an instance of an unreliable narrator? Or is this anachronism excessive? Recent narrative studies of the gospel of Mark tend to treat the Markan narrator as both omniscient and reliable.[10] However, if Mark's narrator is considered to be unreliable, then this raises the possibility that the narrator has also misled the reader in yet other ways. If any valuable information has been disclosed in Mark's story, the uncertainty of its ending renders the truth-value of that information equally uncertain. Can the entire text of Mark be read as a disturbing attempt to say "nothing to anyone" (see also Mark 8:30)? Is Mark a text which, finally and forever, keeps a secret? Might even the so-called "messianic secret," which modern scholars regard as a central theme of Mark, itself be a ruse, deflecting Mark's reader from a secret about Mark's text so well-kept that it has never been discovered?

Or is it possible, as many Christians have long believed, that Mark did not originally end in this way? Two additional endings following Mark 16:8 have been preserved in many of the ancient manuscripts of the gospel of Mark. These endings indicate that even early Christians felt that some further conclusion to the narrative was necessary. Some commentators have suggested that the manuscripts which terminate at Mark 16:8 should be explained as products of a scribal tradition deriving from a mutilated text.[11] Others have conjectured a sequel to the canonical book, a Markan book of Acts, now lost. Contemporary translations of Mark in some cases note the problem of the end at 16:8 with an ellipsis (Today's English Version [TEV], Scholar's Version), or add notes suggesting that an original, longer ending has been lost (Jerusalem Bible 1966:89). All of these translations publish, in one form or another, the two added endings.

As was noted in the Introduction to this book, what would count as an original text of the gospel of Mark is in any case highly problematic. However, on text- and source-critical grounds, Mark 16:8 is generally held by contemporary biblical scholars to be the "original" ending of Mark.[12] Furthermore, the literary style and message of the added endings is different from, and arguably foreign to, the rest of the gospel of Mark, and the fact that there are two, incompatible additions also weakens the case for either. Finally, an ending of the book at Mark 16:8 ("for they were afraid") *is* consistent with the previous text of the gospel, the beginning and the middle of Mark, no matter how uncomfortable it may be for readers who want a story to strengthen their faith.

THE "SHORTER ENDING"

They reported briefly to Peter and to his companions all that they had been told. And after that Jesus himself sent forth through them, from east to west, the holy and imperishable proclamation (*kêrugma*) of everlasting salvation (*sôtêrias*).

The so-called "shorter ending" of the gospel of Mark immediately follows Mark 16:8 in several ancient manuscripts.[13] "They" (in the first sentence) apparently refers to the female disciples who fled from the tomb in fear and said nothing to anyone, according to Mark 16:8. The first sentence of the shorter added ending therefore requires the omission of "they said nothing to anyone" from 16:8 (this is indeed the case in Old Latin codex k), or else the supposition of something like "after a while" at the beginning of the additional statement – that is, a further supplement that believing readers would be willing to provide to the text. It is understandable that after the women's fear had subsided, they might tell others what had happened. In fact, the parallels to Mark 16:8 in Matthew 28:8 and Luke 24:9 attempt to resolve this problem, for they explicitly deny the silence of the women. However, the statement in the shorter added ending that they did tell Peter and the others "all that they had been told" flatly contradicts Mark 16:8. In the absence of temporal qualification, the statement in 16:8 that they said nothing to anyone implies that the women *never* said anything to anyone about their experience in the tomb.

Thus the shorter added ending requires either the elimination or the qualification of the claim that the women said nothing. In other words, it requires even further supplementation. It also shifts the focus of Mark's ending away from the women (at 16:8) to the young man's message ("all that they had been told"), which appears at Mark 16:6–7:

Do not be thus amazed. You are looking for Jesus the Nazarene, who was crucified. He has risen, he is not here. See the place where they laid him. But go and tell his disciples, and Peter: He goes before you into Galilee. There you will see him, as he told you.

If Mark ends at 16:8, the women do not obey the young man's instructions, but in the shorter added ending, they do obey. If Mark ends at 16:8, the final words describing fear and silence overshadow the message, which after all did not get delivered. In the shorter added ending, the fear and silence give way to the successful communication of the message. The young man's message also reinforces Jesus's earlier prophecy to his disciples (Mark 14:28) that he would precede them to Galilee after he was "raised up" (RSV), *egerthênai*. If Mark ends at 16:8, Jesus's prophecy itself remains unfulfilled, and unlikely to be fulfilled, since the women said nothing to anyone. This raises doubts about the truthfulness of the narrative. The reliability of the narrative and of its narrator are therefore increased by the shorter added ending.

However, the remainder of the shorter added ending makes nothing of this prophecy at Mark 14:28. One could suppose that after the women reported to the others, they all went to Galilee where they met Jesus, after which he "sent forth through them, from east to west," and so on, but the text gives the reader no reason to suppose this. Indeed, there seems to be a great deal missing between the first and second sentences of the shorter added ending; the phrase "after that" leaves much unanswered. As narrative, the shorter added ending is vague and general, unlike the specificity of the rest of Mark. The language of the shorter added ending is quite foreign to the rest of Mark.[14]

An alternative supposition might be that "all that they had been told" was indeed "the holy and imperishable proclamation of everlasting salvation," but there is no reference to this message of salvation being communicated in the encounter of the women with the young man in the tomb, or anywhere else in Mark for that matter. Some possible candidates for the proclamation of salvation are Mark 8:35–7 ("For he who wishes to save his life shall lose it; and he who loses his life for the sake of me and the gospel shall save it. For what does it advantage a man to gain the whole world and pay for it with his life? What can a man give that is worth as much as his life?"); 10:26–7 ("Who then can be saved? ... For men it is impossible, but not for God, since for God all things are possible"); 10:45 ("the son of man came not to be served but to serve, and to give his own life for the redemption of many"); 13:13 ("you will be hated by all because of my name. But he who endures to the end will be saved"); or 13:20 ("if the Lord had not cut short the days, no flesh would be saved; but for the sake of the chosen, whom he chose, he did cut short the days").

However, none of these passages suggests the language of the second sentence of the shorter added ending: the words *kêrugma*, "proclamation," and *sôtêrias*, "salvation," do not appear anywhere else in Mark. Forms of the verb *kêrussô* do appear in Mark in reference to the preaching of John the Baptist (1:4, 7: "He who is stronger than I is coming after me ...") and of the people of the Decapolis region (7:36–7: "He has done everything well ..."), and also in reference to the preaching of the twelve (3:14, 6:12) -- but not to any preaching by Jesus that is clearly a "holy and imperishable proclamation of everlasting salvation."[15]

In Mark, the most likely narrative model on which the shorter added ending is patterned is the earlier mission on which Jesus sent the twelve (Mark 6:7–13, 30). Although the disciples' inability to understand Jesus continues unabated throughout Mark, this mission is arguably the only point in that gospel (through 16:8) where the disciples are represented as models of faith and capability. The mission is apparently successful; the twelve drive out demons, heal the sick, and preach "the message of repentance." In Mark 6:7, Jesus "began to send," *êrxato ... apostellein*, the twelve, and in the shorter added ending, he "sent forth," *exapesteilen*, the proclamation of salvation through the disciples. The linguistic echo is weak. The connection between the two passages is tenuous, and much still must be supplied by the reader. Any connection between the preaching of the twelve or the message of repentance in Mark 6 and the sending of the proclamation of salvation in the shorter added ending remains unclear.

Nonetheless, if the shorter added ending is another sending of disciples modelled upon the earlier one in Mark 6, this at least brings to the end of Mark a note of faithfulness and strength on the part of Jesus's followers which is lacking at Mark 16:8. The reference to "the disciples and Peter" in 16:7, which is echoed in the first sentence of the shorter added ending, also serves as a point of connection between the shorter added ending and earlier portions of Mark. Both the women and men disciples are transformed, according to the shorter added ending. The women obey the instructions of the young man, for they report to Peter and others. The entire group of disciples then becomes the channel through whom Jesus sends forth the proclamation of salvation. They become ideal disciples, precisely what they (and especially Peter) had not been, except for the successful mission in chapter 6.

The shorter added ending, however, fails to provide that which would follow, to use Aristotle's terms, from the unsatisfactory ending of Mark at 16:8. The summary quality of the ending contrasts to the concrete language of the rest of Mark. In addition, the shorter added ending revises Mark's depiction of the disciples. The textual glue of "Peter and his companions" connecting the added ending to 16:7–8 is inadequate to the task; the phrase cannot carry the alteration of the role of the disciples in getting out the message of Jesus. What the message of salvation has to do with the words or deeds of Jesus in Mark, and whether the message bears any relation to the empty tomb or to Jesus going ahead into Galilee, also remains unclear.

Although the shorter added ending does nothing to alter or eliminate Mark's deficiencies as a well-constructed plot, it at least cancels the "bad taste" for Christian readers left by the possibility of an unreliable narrative in Mark 16:8. The shorter added ending also obscures the fearful, faithless, and stupid disciples depicted in Mark 1:1–16:8 with a closing image of female and male disciples who are able servants of their resurrected Lord. In this respect it reclaims Mark for Christian orthodoxy by sketching out a "happy ending" (appropriately by way of "Peter and his companions") that is even more fully-developed elsewhere, that is, in the longer added ending of Mark, in other gospels, and in the epistles of Paul, the creeds, and the writings of the church "fathers."

THE "LONGER ENDING"

Then after he had arisen early on the first day of the week, he appeared first to Mary the Magdalene, from whom he had cast out seven demons. She went and told the news to those who had been with him, who were mourning and weeping; and they, when they heard that he was alive and had been seen by her, did not believe her. After that he appeared to two of them as they were walking. It was in another form and they were on their way into the country. And they too went back and told the news to the others; but neither did they believe them. Later he appeared to the eleven themselves as they were at dinner, and he had blame for their lack of faith and the insensitivity of their hearts, because they had not believed those who had seen him risen from the dead. *And he said to them: Go out into the whole world and preach the gospel to all creation. He who believes and is baptized shall be saved, but he who does not believe will be condemned. And here are the signs that will go with the believers: In my name they will cast out demons, speak with tongues, hold snakes, and if they drink something lethal it cannot harm them, and they will lay their hands on the sick and these will be well.

After talking with them the Lord was taken up into heaven and sat down on the right of God. And they went forth and preached everywhere, the Lord working with them and confirming their message through the signs that accompanied them.

(Mark 16:9–20)

While several manuscripts of Mark present this longer added ending after the shorter added ending, nearly all other manuscripts of the gospel, from the fifth century and following, present only the longer added ending after Mark 16:8.[16] Contemporary translations of Mark usually print the longer added ending following 16:8, with the shorter added ending appended as a footnote.[17] The Jerusalem Bible states that the longer added ending is canonical, although "not necessarily" original, to Mark.

In effect, then, there are three possible combinations of endings that have been added to Mark 16:8: shorter added ending only, longer added ending only, and shorter plus longer. In addition, the fifth-century manuscript codex Freerianus (W) inserts the following text, the "Freer Logion," into the longer added ending after 16:14 (*above):

And they apologized and said, "This lawless and faithless age is under the control of Satan, who by using unclean spirits does not allow the real power of God to be understood. So let your justice become evident now." They said this to Christ. And Christ answered them, "The time when Satan is in power has run its course, but other terrible things are just around the corner. I was put to death for the sake of those who sinned, so they might return to the truth and stop sinning, and thus inherit the spiritual and indestructible righteous glory that is in heaven."

(Scholar's Version, modified)

This creates a fourth possibility. The "Freer Logion" is usually not printed in modern translations of Mark (but see the Jerusalem Bible).

Depending upon the ending option, the longer added ending fills in or replaces the general and summary quality of the shorter added ending with detail and narrative specificity, a good deal of which appears to be "borrowed" from resurrection stories from the gospels of Luke and John. This suggests that the early success of the other gospels' resurrection scenes led to pressure to create similar scenes for Mark. In its use of detail, the longer added ending produces a return to Mark's general literary style, although both vocabulary and narrative content are different; "the writer is a compiler whose methods and outlook are different from those of Mark" (Taylor 1953:611). When the shorter and the longer added endings appear together, the second sentence of the shorter added ending serves as a transition and introduction to the longer ending. However, the first sentence of the shorter added ending ("They reported briefly to Peter and his companions all that they had been told") remains in conflict with Mark 16:8 ("they said nothing to anyone"), and it also conflicts with Mark 16:9–14 in the longer added ending.

What can explain this multiplicity of alternative endings, which is unlike anything to be found elsewhere[18] in the gospels? The shorter added ending appears to have failed to solve the related problems of establishing the reliability of the narrative and its narrator and of bringing Mark to a satisfactory end. The longer added ending has apparently been added in order to "rescue" the shorter one. The longer added ending solves some of the problems of the shorter added ending, but otherwise it uses the same sort of strategies that the shorter added ending does to bring the gospel to an end.

If the longer added ending follows directly after Mark 16:8, then its opening sentence resolves the conflict over "they said nothing to anyone." First Mary reports her encounter "to those who had been with him" (compare Luke 8:2, John 20:18), then the two who had been on their way "into the country" (similar to Luke 24:13ff., but much condensed) also tell of meeting Jesus. As in Luke 24:11, the others do not believe them. Thus when Jesus finally appears to the eleven[19] in Mark 16:14 and criticizes them very harshly, their faithlessness and Jesus's anger at them "for their lack of faith and the insensitivity of their hearts" is consistent with the pattern established in Mark 1:1–16:8. Where this meeting occurs is not mentioned, but if the meeting is in Jerusalem, as seems likely (there is no intervening mention of a change of scene), that would seem to contradict Mark 14:28 and 16:7, where a meeting in Galilee is foretold. Once again, the prophecy is not fulfilled.

Mark 16:15–20 appears to refer to the sending through the disciples of the "proclamation of everlasting salvation" summarized in the shorter added ending. This is interrupted by Jesus's ascension to heaven at 16:19 (compare Luke 24:51, Acts 1:9), although Jesus ("the Lord") works with the disciples even after he is seated in heaven. Jesus's ascent to heaven and his seating "on the right of God" echoes Mark 14:62, and the going forth and preaching, *exelthontes ekêruxan* (16:20), reverberates linguistically with both Mark 6:7 and the shorter added ending. The sayings in Mark 16:15–18 – the parting words of Jesus to the eleven disciples before he is "taken up into heaven" – are reminiscent of post-resurrection sayings in other gospels and Acts, but there are no close parallels. Among these other texts, Matthew 28:19–20 ("Go out, therefore, and instruct all the nations, baptizing them in the name of the Father and the Son and the Holy Spirit, teaching them to observe all that I have taught you. And behold, I am with you, all the days until the end of the world") and John 20:21–3 ("Peace be with you. As the father sent me forth, so I also send you.... For any whose sins you forgive, their sins are forgiven. For any whose sins you keep fast, they are kept fast") emphasize a sending of the disciples, while Luke 24:50 describes Jesus's final blessing of the disciples.

The longer added ending also has noteworthy oddities. Not only the snake-handling and poison-drinking aspects of Jesus's statement are unusual, but the focus of the entire statement on signs which support and accompany faith is unlike other biblical post-resurrection messages. It is also inconsistent with the rest of Mark; Mark 11:22–3 is about the power of belief, but throwing mountains into the sea is not presented as a sign of faith. Do these sayings in the longer added ending produce a reversal of the general lack of faith that characterizes the disciples in the rest of Mark? Probably not, especially in light of Jesus's criticism of them in 16:14. The belief referred to in Mark 16:16–18 appears to be that of those who believe the preaching of the disciples ("Go out into the whole world and preach the gospel to all creation. He who believes and is baptized shall be saved ..."), not the belief of the disciples themselves. The attention to "signs," *sêmeia* (16:17, 20), that will accompany the believers is also reminiscent of the discourse in Mark 13. However, in Mark 13 the sign, *sêmeion* (13:4), portends the suffering of the disciples and perhaps the end of the world (13:8);[20] this seems quite unlike the signs which "go with" the believers and "confirm" the message in the longer added ending.

The claim that Jesus appeared to two disciples "in another form," *en hetera morphê* (Mark 16:12), is also noteworthy. Unlike the story in Luke 24:13–17, which claims only that the disciples "were prevented from recognizing" Jesus, in this case it seems as though Jesus's own appearance has been changed. In the transfiguration story in Mark 9:2, Jesus is described as "transformed" (Scholar's Version), *metemorphôthê*, before three disciples on the mountaintop. Mark 16:12 appears to be a second transfiguration story. Conversely, the transfiguration story may have originally concerned a post-resurrection manifestation of Jesus.[21]

In summary, both the shorter and the longer added endings provide the "happy ending" which Mark 16:8 does not. Perhaps more importantly, the endings explain how the story of Mark "got out," and thus they reinforce the reliability of the narrative and its narrator. The longer added ending presents in greater detail the transformation from weak disciples to strong apostles which is only summarized in the shorter added ending and entirely absent from the ending at 16:8. It is unclear what has caused this transformation of the disciples, unless it is their encounter with the risen Jesus; however, the "Freer Logion" appears in codex Freerianus at precisely this point of transformation, and that addition therefore may be an attempt to improve the construction of Mark's ending even further.[22] If so, it seems that the "Freer Logion" too has failed. The multiplicity of endings as well as the inconsistencies between the longer and shorter added endings, and between both the added endings and the rest of Mark, further sabotage the narrative reliability that they attempt to reinforce. In Aristotle's terms, the ending of Mark remains no more well-constructed after all of these supplemental endings than it was at 16:8.

WHAT MARK IS NOT

The *not saying* of something (or the pretending not to say it) is an ancient rhetorical device, and it has always had its reflection at the higher level of narrative rhetoric.

(Kermode 1978:155)

In order to hold that one of the various endings of Mark (including 16:8) is the proper or the original one, the reader must make certain assumptions about what defines the limits of the text – that is, about the identity of the gospel of Mark. Otherwise, "the gospel of Mark" ceases to have a determinable referent; what Mark is, and what Mark is about, changes as Mark's ending changes. The reader must assume among other things that the idea of an original or proper ending of Mark (or of any text) itself makes sense as a concept. In other words, to speak as Aristotle does of a well-constructed story may raise more problems than it settles, but there must be some point at which the narrative of Mark actually ends. An endless text cannot exist.

The ending point may be determined by the author's intention (as many literary scholars hold) or by the first published edition (whatever that might mean in the context of the Mediterranean world of the first few centuries CE) or perhaps by some other standard of textual production or identity. Any of these criteria will be ideological (and therefore theological)[23] and probably will be contested, for each criterion implies its own metaphysics and its own logic. Nevertheless, some criterion is necessary to establish the limits of the text; otherwise the narrative will evaporate into the limitless intertextuality of the supplements which it will in any case require. Mark then would become every story, and no story.

However, the criteria which establish narrative identity also themselves serve as supplements to the story. For example, in order to explain the intention of the author (assuming that she has some basis for knowing what that was), the reader must produce another story – a story of the writing of the text – which then necessarily will require further interpretation and thus the supplementation of yet other stories, and so forth. Most blatantly, this story of the text takes the form of the popular legends concerning the lives of the evangelists and why they wrote the gospels (John Mark the associate of Paul and Peter, and so forth) which have been popular since the early centuries of Christianity. More subtly, the same criterion takes the form of scholarly attempts to trace the editing of the text. In each case a second narrative is developed in order to explain and clarify the first one. In other words, the reader becomes a writer, a producer of text, whose intentions must also then be explained. The product of this reading–writing is always itself a story, which will then also need to be interpreted. Narrative identity is always incomplete; therefore supplementation is perpetual.

A similar proliferation of stories would be necessary to explain the original readers' understanding of the text, or any other standard by which the text's identity is determined. The chapters in this book also serve such a need. It is always the reader's intertextual supplementation, ultimately, which produces the meaningful text.

Both adoption and rejection of a standard of textual identity eventually dissolve text into intertext.

This paradox of textual identity is not entirely unlike Heisenberg's uncertainty principle, namely, that the observer's interests are crucial factors in the knowledge obtained as a result of those interests. In this case, the paradox is that whatever sufficiently identifies the limits of a text also creates the text's identity through the very process of identification. Whatever defines the text necessarily transforms the text; the reader is a rewriter. This paradox describes the dialectic of text and ideology. Readers must suppose that the text exists apart from themselves, otherwise reading becomes entirely solipsistic. Yet the text cannot be completely, objectively identified. To avoid the paradox is not possible, but it is possible to come up against the text as a negative power, that is, as something which resists understanding.

The alternative added endings to Mark provide a partial index of that negative power – of what the gospel of Mark, as of 16:8, is *not*. These endings mark by their own variation and multiplicity the *inadequacies* of the text of Mark. The added endings say what some readers have wanted Mark to say, and they show how those readers have tried (and failed) to rewrite Mark. Mark is not a story which ends happily or comfortably for readers who want the reinforcing of Christian faith. It does not end with a meeting between the disciples and the resurrected Jesus, nor with Jesus seated on the right of God. It does not end with an imperishable message of everlasting salvation spreading out from east to west, nor with the end of the reign of Satan, nor with a promise of heavenly glory, nor with Jesus transformed, nor with transformed disciples.

However, just as the additional endings are too much for Mark, so also the ending at Mark 16:8 is too little for the believing reader.

> If St. Mark did intentionally end his Gospel with this paragraph, he was certainly behaving with considerable literary sophistication and making great demands on the understanding of his readers.
>
> (Nineham 1963:442)

D.E. Nineham quotes the biblical critic W.L. Knox to the effect that such an ending would be extraordinary in the first century and is more characteristic of "modern literature." Indeed, because Mark stops at 16:8 it is appropriate to refer to this gospel as a postmodern text, for the uncertainties created by Mark's use of referential paradox and indeterminacy are not finally overcome by the triumph of the resurrected Christ but are left hanging at the end. The delivery of Jesus by both his betrayers and his opponents, and ultimately by the text of Mark itself, culminates in a non-delivery. The tomb is empty, simultaneously offering promise and disappointment. Jesus disappears into an oblivion from which there is no return, a message (that of the women) which never reaches its destination, concealed paradoxically in a non-message (that of Mark) which does nevertheless manage to get through. Mark is in fact unreliable.

The strong feeling of many biblical scholars, along with countless Christian readers perhaps since the time of its writing, that Mark just cannot have ended at 16:8, is another symptom of the desire for completeness described in part 1 of this chapter. This desire is amply demonstrated by the addition of the other endings to Mark, as well as by the endings provided in the other biblical gospels. It is the desire that Mark be a well-constructed story – that Mark be a "text of pleasure."[24]

As in the present-day proliferation of sequels, the desire to rewrite Mark's ending resulted historically in actual writings. However, more than one ending has been supplied for Mark, and the resulting multiplicity of endings requires that judgment be made about the ending at Mark 16:8 as well as the additional endings, as epilogues or as alternative final scenes. This multiplicity signals the incompleteness of Mark's gospel. The desire for completeness, which can be very strong even in relation to the most unimportant stories, becomes unbearable in relation to stories believed to contain fundamental truths or values. Mark is incomplete, and yet Mark is "scripture"; this is an intolerable state of affairs. It is, finally, the resurrection stories at the end of the gospels of Matthew, Luke, and John – stories which do succeed as narrative endings, while Mark 16:9–20 fails – that allow the reader to tolerate the narrative messiness of Mark's endings. If the glaring discrepancies between the much more elaborate post-resurrection stories in these other gospels can be overlooked by the believing reader, then Mark's own multiple endings can also be accepted.

The insufficiency of the ending at Mark 16:8 and the failure of the additional endings to provide adequate supplementation point to a deficiency of meaning, that is, a deficiency of connotation, in Mark's text. The connotation of a word is its secondary or associated meanings; the denotation is the word's primary meaning. Connotation and denotation will be discussed in more detail in chapter 5. "[T]he modern text, which aims at a certain destruction of meaning, does not possess associated meanings, connotations" (Barthes 1985:70). Roland Barthes's comment about meaning applies better to postmodern texts than it does to modern ones. In his distinction between the "modern" or "writerly" text and the "classic" or "readerly" text, Barthes consistently uses the word "modern" in much the same way that "postmodern" is used here. The postmodern text makes the reader work; because it lacks sufficient meaning, the postmodern text requires that the reader attach her own meanings to it. As one of these texts, Mark "aims at a certain destruction of meaning."

Read at the level of denotation, Mark 1:1–16:8 presents an incoherent, fragmentary narrative, requiring a second level of meaning, the level of connotation, to hold together and smooth over the many narrative gaps. Yet this connotative level is precisely what the postmodern narrative lacks. These gaps – and even more so, Mark's canonical status – provoke the reader to generate a well-constructed narrative, in Aristotle's sense. This requires that the reader produce a believable account (either popular or scholarly) of how the gospel of Mark came to be, which in turn requires a reliable alternative to "they said nothing to anyone." Otherwise, either the gospel could not have been written, or the narrative reference would be revealed to be unreal, a fiction. These accounts of how the gospel came to be are provided by the shorter and longer added endings.

The effect of the incompleteness of Mark's text is comparable to the incompleteness of Jesus's parables. Both Mark as a whole and the parables individually produce a division of interpretative responses, which is enacted for Mark in the alternative endings. Mark's "connotators" (such as titles for Jesus, metatextual commentary, disciples or other characters whose understanding and faith might mediate the reader's own understanding and faith) are themselves ambiguous and fantastic. They are unable to determine a proper reading of the text. Such interpretations as the connotators do provisionally suggest are eventually subverted by other features of the text of Mark. The "clues" which Mark provides for its own deciphering (such as 16:6–7, echoing 14:28) all fail the reader. Hence the desire for supplementary endings, whether they be explicitly added to the text of Mark or whether they be "read in" from other, neighboring gospels, the writings of Paul, or creeds.

Only the reader who refuses to choose an ending to Mark will not "get the message"; for this reader, the desire for belief is frustrated.

This reader then reads from the outside. The "poorly-constructed ending" of Mark must be rescued by the reader's belief, for the reader must choose one or another of the ending possibilities. Nonetheless, the text of Mark rejects each choice. It continually demands to be rewritten, and yet it refuses its own rewriting. The postmodern paradox of the gospel of Mark is that it fails to begin and it fails to end, and thus it could be said that the gospel of Mark has not yet been written.

THE RESURRECTION ACCORDING TO MARK

I myself cannot (as an enamored subject) construct my love story to the end: I am its poet (its bard) only for the beginning; the end, like my own death, belongs to others; it is up to them to write the fiction, the external, mythic narrative.

(Barthes 1978:101)

Even if Mark ends at 16:8, with no post-resurrection appearances of Jesus, it still has a few things to say about the resurrection. However, these things are once again characterized by rampant Markan ambiguity and uncertainty.[25] For example, three predictions (Mark 8:31, 9:31, 10:33) announce the death and resurrection "after three days" of the "son of man." After the transfiguration, Jesus instructs Peter, James, and John to "tell no one what they had seen, except when the son of man should rise from the dead" (9:9). Despite these announcements, these passages are troubled by the uncertainty running throughout Mark, of who the son of man is, and also by the ambiguity of Jesus's relation to the son of man. For example, the disciples' response to Jesus's instruction in Mark 9:9 is to "question ... among themselves what it might mean to rise from the dead" (9:10).

If Jesus is the son of man, then Mark 16:1–8 depicts the fulfillment of the resurrection predictions, just as Mark 14–15 has depicted the fulfillment of the passion predictions. However, the resurrection predictions are "fulfilled" in Mark 16:1–8 by nothing more than an empty tomb, a mysterious young man, and the problems of reliability raised by the women's response.[26] The "son of man" has disappeared from the narrative; the final occurrence of the phrase is at 14:62, Jesus's "confession" before the high priest. Jesus is now merely "the Nazarene, who was crucified." Perhaps some of the desire for added endings comes from the perceived insufficiency of this narrative self-fulfillment.

A less ambiguous foretelling of his resurrection by Jesus appears in Mark 14:28: "after my resurrection I will lead the way for you into Galilee." In the latter part of Mark, Jesus has become a fortune teller. He tells the disciples where to find the colt (Mark 11:1ff.) and where they will locate the "upper room" (14:13–15). It is to the prediction at 14:28, apparently, that the young man refers in Mark 16:7 ("But go and tell his disciples, and Peter: He goes before you into Galilee. There you will see him, as he told you"). Both of the added endings contradict the claim that the disciples will see Jesus in Galilee to the extent that they imply a post-resurrection meeting with Jesus in Jerusalem. In the statements at 14:28 and 16:7, Mark places the post-resurrection appearance of Jesus in Galilee in the future. To read Mark as though this future has already occurred is again to supplement its ending, either with one of the added endings discussed above, or with post-resurrection appearances from another gospel, or in some other way.

"You will see (*opsesthe*) him" in Mark 16:7 also resonates with "you will see (*opsesthe*) the son of man" in Jesus's apocalyptic words of Mark 14:62 (see also 13:26, *opsontai*). The young man first appears to the women on the right side, *en tois dexiois*, of the tomb (16:5), just as the son of man is to appear "on the right (*ek dexiôn*) of the power" (14:62; see also 12:36). Is Mark 16:7 then to be read in the same way as 14:62? Insofar as the young man here speaks for Jesus, is he telling the women (who may hear for the reader) that the resurrection has not yet occurred? Is he implying that the resurrection is even now, at the present moment of the reader's reading, a future event? Does his statement mean that the resurrection will be identical to the parousia (presence: the second coming of Christ) – that the parousia will be the resurrection of the son of man?

These questions remain nothing more than possibilities, uncertain loose ends of the text of Mark's gospel. The resurrection predictions in Mark point not only beyond the narrative of Mark but to something that Mark either could not or would not narrate. That these hints and clues were not enough for the early Christian movement is made evident by both the endings which were soon added to Mark, and even more by the elaborate and spectacular post-resurrection appearances of Jesus in the gospels of Matthew, Luke, and John. Other early gospels, Q and the gospel of Thomas, had no resurrection narrative and only at best vague hints concerning the death of Jesus. These books were either suppressed (Thomas) or rewritten into a more acceptable form (Q, by absorption into Matthew and Luke). With its cryptic and unreliable resurrection story, Mark suffered a different fate. Mark's fate was neither of these, but in some ways it was even worse: Mark was canonized, and placed between Matthew and Luke, so that its ambiguities and uncertainties could be resolved through the greater readability of its neighbor gospels.

3

TALITHA CUM

THE QUESTION OF TRANSLITERATION

... and going in he said to them: Why this tumult and weeping? The child has not died, she is asleep. They laughed at him. He drove out all the others, and took with him the father and mother of the child and those who were with him, and went in where the child was; and he took the child's hand, and said to her: Talitha cum; which is, translated: Little girl, I say to you: Awake. At once the girl got up and walked about, for she was twelve years old. They were seized with great amazement.

(Mark 5:39–42)

A Greek transliteration, *talitha koum*, of Jesus's Aramaic words appears in Mark 5:41. Since the transliterated words are immediately translated into Greek, *to korasion, soi legô, egeire*, they serve no informative function in the text. Either the reader knows Aramaic and the translation is unnecessary, or the reader does not know Aramaic and the transliteration plays no role in the story, except perhaps to add an exotic quality. A similar transliteration/translation combination appears in Mark 7:34 – "and [Jesus] looked up into the sky and groaned and said to him: Ephphatha, which means: Be opened." Here also there is no apparent reason for the transliterated word, "ephphatha." Other comparable transliteration/translation combinations appear at Mark 3:17, where the nickname "Boanerges" is translated as "sons of thunder," and Mark 7:11, where "Corban" is translated as "gift to God." Unlike Mark 5:41 and 7:34, these latter instances are not elements of healing stories.

Why these transliterated words are included in Mark's text along with translations of the words is not clear. All four of the transliteration/translation combinations appear in Mark in the direct discourse of Jesus.[1] Each is an oddity which disrupts the text: in each case, the translation which accompanies the transliterated words enables them to be understood, but the function of the transliterated phrase itself is not clear. In fact, the transliteration seems to serve no purpose at all. No deep narrative structure accounts for this surface effect, nor does the transliterated phrase appear to have any particular theological significance. It is significant that all of the respective parallels to these passages in Matthew (9:25, 15:30, 10:2, 15:5, 26:39), Luke (8:54, 6:14, 22:42), and John (12:27) omit the transliterations.

Other transliteration/translation combinations do appear in Mark and other gospels of the New Testament, but in these other cases there appears to be some reason for the transliteration. The actual Aramaic or Hebrew word is valuable in its own right, yet it also requires translation. In one case, Mark 15:34, the final cry of Jesus, the Aramaic phrase *"Elôi elôi lama sabachthanei?"* helps to explain misunderstanding on the part of bystanders in the next verse ("he calls to Elijah"). As Robert Fowler notes (1991:108–9), this transliteration/translation combination appears to divide those who do not understand (bystanders) from those who do (readers). In Matthew's parallel passage, the transliteration of the phrase (27:46–7) differs slightly from Mark's and apparently quotes the Hebrew text of Psalm 22:1, not the Aramaic. Nevertheless, the same narrative function is served.

Strictly speaking, proper names cannot be translated, as they have no sense, but only reference, the power to point out some object (Frege 1952). To say that someone is named "Sara" neither describes her nor implies anything about her. Different versions of a name may exist in different languages (Peter, *Petros*, Pierre, etc.), but they are not translations of one another. Therefore, in the gospels proper names are usually transliterated without translation, but there are exceptions. In Mark 10:46, "Bartimaeus" (as a name) stands in apposition to "the son of Timaeus" (as a description). The parallels (Matthew 20:30, Luke 18:35) omit the entire phrase. In Mark 15:22 (par. Matthew 27:33), the meaning of "Golgotha" is given as "Place of the Skull." Matthew 1:23 also translates "Emmanuel" as "God is with us," John 1:42 explains "Cephas" as "Peter," and John 9:7 translates "Siloam" as "one who has been sent." In each of these latter cases, the explanation of the name has theological significance for Christian readers.

John 1:38 and 20:16 translates "master," *didaskale*, for the transliterated words "rabbi," *rhabbi*, and "rabbuni," *rabbouni*, respectively, and John 1:41 translates "Christ" for "Messiah." The function of the Hebrew words as titles in the belief systems of early Christians may have required their inclusion in transliteration in the text. However, *rhabbouni* appears in Mark 10:51 without a Greek translation, as does *rhabbi* in Mark 9:5, 11:21, and 14:45. Both the RSV and Lattimore translate these words ("master") as though they were Greek words like the other words in the passage. Other Aramaic, Hebrew, and Latin words also appear in the gospels in transliteration but without any accompanying translation. It seems likely that words such as "hosanna" and "praetorium" had become sufficiently assimilated to the Greek language by the time the gospels were written that their foreign origin was almost invisible (much like "wigwam" or "spaghetti" in contemporary American English). Perhaps this is also the case for *rhabbi* and *rhabbouni* in Mark.

Why do both transliteration and translation of a word or phrase appear where there is no apparent reason for the transliteration? Although there are important differences among the four instances of this phenomenon which appear in Mark, the focus in the following is on *talitha koum* in Mark 5:41. That phrase and the story of which it is part are representative of the other texts of this sort – even those which seem to be explainable on theological or narratological grounds.

PRODUCING THE TEXT

The original is in the situation of demand, that is, of a lack or exile. The original is indebted *a priori* to the translation. Its survival is a demand and a desire for translation, somewhat like the Babelian demand: Translate me.

(Derrida 1985:152)

The apparatus to the Nestle *et al.* (1979) edition of the Greek New Testament indicates that *talitha koum* is the best attested spelling of the transliterated phrase in Mark 5:41, but there is also evidence among the ancient manuscripts of Mark for *talitha koumi* and *tabitha koum(i)*. The fifth-century manuscript codex D, famous for its Aramaic transliterations into Greek, has *rabbi thabita (= rhabitha) koumi*.[2] The RSV re-transliterates the Aramaic phrase as "talitha cumi," apparently in an attempt to reconstruct the original words of Jesus (*cumi* = feminine of *cum*).

A remarkably similar saying appears in the book of Acts 9:40, where Peter heals the disciple Tabitha ("which means Dorcas") with the command, "Tabitha, rise," *Tabitha, anastêthi*. The Aramaic phrase, if there were one, would be something like "*tabitha cumi*," a formulation which is supported by the Old Latin version of Mark 5:41 and close to the texts of the fifth-century Greek manuscripts D and W. Otherwise different stories bring together the transliteration of the words *talitha/tabitha* and the Greek verb *anistêmi*, the apparent death of a girl/woman, and the successful command to rise ("And he gave her his hand and lifted her up," Acts 9:41, RSV). This correlation between the two passages suggests a correspondence between the stories. The story in Acts strangely echoes Mark's story.[3] Nevertheless, both the story of Peter's raising of Tabitha in Acts and the parallels to Mark's story of Jesus's raising of Jairus's daughter in Matthew 9:18–26 and Luke 8:40–56 avoid the difficulties of transliteration combined with translation that appear in Mark's story.

One explanation for "talitha cum" in Mark 5:41 (and also for "ephphatha" in 7:34) is that the Aramaic phrase was valued among early Christians as a formula to be used by magicians or faith-healers in the early churches.[4] This explanation would not account for the instances where *korban* or *boanêrges* (or *abba*) occur along with their translations, for no healing occurs in the latter stories. Neither does Mark otherwise appear to be a collection of incantations; rather, the gospel continually presents Jesus's magical powers as fantastic and thus of uncertain nature (Aichele 1991a). In at least two episodes (Mark 5:25–34, 7:24–30), what if anything that Jesus has said or done to make the miracle happen is not clear. Many miracles are represented in Mark, but Jesus's healing techniques are not always described. Only in these two miracle stories do non-Greek words appear.

Jesus's language of healing is not ritualistic in Mark, although his healings are described in language suggestive of magical practice (Jesus "looked up into the sky and groaned," Jesus uses spittle [Mark 8:22–6]). Jesus's healings are thus distinct from the healing miracles of Elijah in I Kings 17:17–24 or Elisha in II Kings 4:32–7, where a set pattern of prayers and gestures seems to be followed. The transliterated phrase in Mark 5:41, "little girl, stand up," seems an altogether ordinary thing to say under the circumstances (assuming that the girl is not dead); it is not obviously a magical formula. The girl does indeed stand up. Likewise, if "ephphatha" in Mark 7:34, "be opened," is magical, it is not so because of the use of esoteric language, but because the word is addressed primarily to the man's ears, which are then opened. The man after all is deaf, and the phrase appears to address his ears as though they were conscious agents – as though they could hear (as though his ears had ears). It is this that makes the episode fantastic and "magical." The translations that accompany the transliterated terms remove any quality of esoteric strangeness from them, and thus the translations neutralize any magical power that the foreign words might have. Unless Mark was kept for private, esoteric use only, the translations would serve to thwart use of the words by would-be magicians.[5]

Some interpreters have suggested that these transliterations provide historical evidence that Jesus did not ordinarily speak Aramaic, and that it was therefore remarkable when he did use Aramaic words. If this were the case, then such rare sayings might have been preserved in their original form, as well as translated. Keeping the Aramaic terms might also make it seem that these are the very words (both Aramaic and Greek) of Jesus. According to this possibility, the foreign-ness of the Aramaic words serves as evidence for their historical authenticity, and therefore their retention in the narrative suggests that the larger Greek context of Jesus's statement was also authentic.

On the other hand, if Jesus actually spoke Aramaic in most circumstances, as many scholars believe, then transliteration of these particular Aramaic words, and none of the others, needs to be explained. If an Aramaic tradition of words or deeds of Jesus does lie "behind" the gospels, as many scholars have claimed, then retention of these transliterated words rather than others makes them stand out and emphasizes their difference. These words do not reflect unique teachings of Jesus requiring his "very words." There is nothing special or remarkable about "talitha cum." The common observation that these words add an exotic quality to the story does not adequately address the question, which remains: why transliterate *these* words?

While it is not clear which language Jesus and his followers would have been most likely to speak in various situations, it is unlikely that Aramaic was so rare in first-century Galilee that its utterance would have been especially noteworthy. Even if it were, the question would still remain, why would Jesus have said these specific words? Matthew Black (1967) presents substantial evidence that Mark is "closer" to an Aramaic tradition than the other biblical gospels. However, even if these transliterations are nothing more than vestiges of that tradition, the question is still unanswered: why these particular vestiges? For example, Mark 8:22–6, the healing of a blind man at Bethsaida, is otherwise similar to 7:31–7, the story in which "ephphatha" appears, except for the fact that it contains no transliterated phrase. The same is true for Mark 9:16–27, the healing of a boy with a "speechless spirit," which is similar to the story of Jairus's daughter. These instances serve to underscore the difficulty: neither the magical power of *talitha koum* nor its rarity as an Aramaic utterance of Jesus can account for the inclusion of the transliterated phrase in the story of the raising of Jairus's daughter.

WAKING THE GIRL

> [T]he saying, "The child is not dead but is sleeping," [Mark 5:39] is ambiguous and, together with the command "Damsel, arise," does not require the hypothesis of resurrection, although it is not inconsistent with it. In these circumstances I do not think that a modern reader need feel disquieted if he finds himself inclined now to this opinion and now to that.
>
> (Taylor 1953:286)

The episode of the "waking" of Jairus's daughter is part of a cluster of four miracle stories in Mark 4:35–5:43.[6] In these stories, Jesus is at the height of his miraculous powers in Mark's gospel. This section in Mark begins with Jesus and the disciples crossing the sea; Jesus calms the storm which threatens them. When they arrive on the other side, Jesus exorcises the Gerasene demoniac. After their return once again to Galilee, Jesus provides the "power" to cure the woman with the hemorrhage and then "wakes" Jairus's daughter. Each of these stories recounts a miracle, but of a different sort. Although the stories present Jesus's power as operating in a wide variety of ways, each is characterized by typical Markan ambiguity and paradox.[7]

Frank Kermode notes the symmetry between the two halves of Mark 5 – the story of the Gerasene demoniac in 5:1–20 and the double story of the woman with the hemorrhage and Jairus's daughter in 5:21–43 – divided by the return passage across the sea from Gentile to Jewish lands. Kermode treats this symmetry as an example of the subtle and complex literary structuring of Mark.

The Gerasene displayed a demonic excess of male strength, but his violence leaves him with the unclean spirit.... In the case of the woman with the hemorrhage the going-out of power into the unclean was effected through a garment; here [in the story of the demoniac] the going out of strength with spirit (this time unclean) is signaled by the adoption of clothes.... One cure is of an excess of maleness, the other of related effects of femaleness.

(Kermode 1979:135)

Jesus heals the Gerasene by casting the (Roman?) legion of demons into (unclean) pigs which then destroy themselves. In order to do this, Jesus agrees to Legion's request to send the demons into the pigs rather than "out of the country" (Mark 5:10). Why does he consent to Legion's request? The Gentile Gerasenes then ask Jesus "to leave their territory" (5:17). Do they ask this because he has destroyed their pigs, or because he does what the demons ask? This is also unclear. In any case, Jesus accedes to this request also. The cured demoniac then begs Jesus that he be allowed to "go along with him" (5:18), but Jesus refuses this request; apparently the cured man, like the demons, is not to leave the country. Jesus instructs the man to tell his people "what your lord did for you," but instead the man tells them "what Jesus had done for him" (5:19–20). Does the man obey Jesus, or disobey him? This subtle linguistic shift as well as Jesus's acceptance of the requests of the demons and of the Gerasenes reflect the ambiguity of Jesus's identity in Mark.

Both the woman with the hemorrhage and the sick girl are characterized by the number twelve; both are described as "daughter," *thugatrion/thugatêr*. Each has a serious disease: the woman has been treated unsuccessfully by many doctors, and the girl is (at the beginning of her story) near death. Both cures are instantaneous. Because the stories are interwoven, the dimension of the fantastic in each of them maintains and heightens that of the other. The woman is healed by touching Jesus's clothes, but without his consent or intention. Jesus's power exceeds his control. This is one of the stories noted earlier in which no magical gestures appear, nor are there any incantations; a similar story appears in Mark 7:24–30, where Jesus tells the Syrophoenician woman that her (Greek?) words have made her daughter well. In Mark 5:25–34 – the healing of the woman with the hemorrhage – magical power flows out of Jesus, but it is the woman's faith which leads her to touch him. It is her action, not his, that makes her well; both Jesus and the woman sense in their bodies that the exchange has occurred after the fact (5:29–30). As in the encounter with the Syrophoenician woman, Jesus's words merely confirm that the miracle has occurred (see also Mark 6:56 and 10:52).

The brief story of the woman with the hemorrhage interrupts Jesus's movement toward Jairus's house and establishes a lapse of time during which the girl either dies or goes to sleep. Jairus's greeting of Jesus and evident confidence in him, as well as the thronging of the crowd, contrast sharply with the Gerasenes who have just expelled Jesus from their territory. Jesus takes with him the disciples Peter, James, and John. These three men often appear in Mark as a sort of inner circle of disciples; elsewhere in Mark they are alone with Jesus at the transfiguration (9:2ff.) and in the garden of Gethsemane (14:32ff.). Along with Andrew, they also constitute the audience for Jesus's apocalyptic discourse in Mark 13. These four are the first disciples that Jesus recruits (Mark 1:16–20), which may suggest that they hold a privileged status within the larger group of disciples.

It is not clear where Jesus is when he claims that the girl is sleeping. This ambiguity contributes to the fantastic quality of the story, a quality which appears whenever a story generates an uncertainty or "hesitation" over whether the narrative refers to a natural event or to a supernatural one, as Tzvetan Todorov argues (1973:31ff.). Jesus has already "entered (*erchontai*) the house" (Mark 5:38), but then "going in," *eiselthôn* (5:39), Jesus speaks to the mourners. If he is already in the house, then to what does he "go in?" It cannot be the girl's room, for there is yet a third entrance into her room. After the mourners laughed at him and he "drove out all the others," Jesus "went in (*eisporeuetai*) where the child was" (5:40).

It is between these last two entrances that Jesus makes his statement that the girl is not dead and the people who are there laugh at him. These are the two most perplexing elements of the episode. Is a single act of arrival at or entry into the house depicted twice in 5:38–9, followed by a separate entrance into the girl's room in 5:40, or do 5:39–40 refer twice to Jesus's entrance into her room? Or are there three distinct entrances, or only one entrance, described three times? The timing and location of Jesus's statement that the girl is sleeping and of the consequent laughter of the mourners are both uncertain. If he has not yet entered her room when he announces that she is sleeping, then only a very small miracle has occurred, namely, Jesus's precognition that Jairus's daughter is not dead but in fact sleeping. This miracle then displaces the much greater miracle of her resurrection.

The contrast between the claim by people from Jairus's house that the girl is dead, *apethanen*, and Jesus's claim that she is not dead but merely asleep, *ouk apethanen alla katheudei* (Mark 5:39–40), is particularly odd. That the others interrupt their mourning to laugh at him is also strange. The mourners' laughter contrasts sharply with the great respect shown to Jesus by Jairus.[8] Even those who bring the news of his daughter's death say to Jairus, "Why do you continue to trouble the master?" Is Jesus then speaking ironically or even jokingly when he says that the girl is sleeping? Mark says that Jesus "disregarded"[9] the report of her death, and the people apparently think that he is a fool. Both Jesus's statement and the mourners' laughter seem quite inappropriate given the seriousness of the moment, the politeness and earnestness of Jairus's request in the first place, and the promptness with which Jesus accompanies Jairus in response to his request. Jesus does not reply verbally to Jairus's request, but he goes with him, apparently without delay, until the encounter with the woman with the hemorrhage interrupts the story of Jairus.[10]

In Matthew 9:18 and Luke 8:53, the girl is described as dead. Commentators on Mark often assume that the girl is indeed dead,[11] although Mark does not say this – in fact, Jesus asserts the contrary (Mark 5:39, par. Matthew 9:24, Luke 8:52). When Jesus says that the girl is asleep, his statement is interpreted by the commentators as a euphemism, or as an attempt to protect the secret of his messianic identity. If Jairus's daughter is not dead but has instead recovered from her illness while she slept, then Jesus's request that she "be given something to eat" (5:43) is not evidence that she is not a ghost, as the commentators argue, but is, under the circumstances, quite an ordinary thing to say. Yet it seems rather improbable that the family should mistake sleep for death. If the girl is dead, then this miracle of her resurrection is comparable to Jesus's raising of the Widow of Nain's son in Luke 7:11–15 and his raising of Lazarus in John 11:1–44. "He took the child's hand" apparently refers to a magical practice which is found in various miracle stories (for example, Mark 1:31, 9:27). The close connection in 5:41–2 between *egeire*, "wake up" (in Jesus's words), and *anestê*, "rose up" (in the narrative of the girl's action), is also suggestive of a resurrection scene.[12] The bystanders' response of great amazement, as in the "ephphatha" story (Mark 7:37) and eventually the story of Jesus's own resurrection (16:8), indicates that something quite remarkable has occurred – something fantastic, in Todorov's sense of the word.

IMPLICATIONS

> My little daughter is at the point of death; so come and lay your hands upon her, so that she may recover and live.
>
> (Mark 5:23)

How seriously should the reader take Jesus's claim that the girl is not dead? Is Jesus making a joke of it all? Is this why the others laugh? Jesus seems quite serious in his claim that Jairus's daughter is sleeping, and after the mourners laugh at him, he drives them out of the house. Or is Jesus's driving out of the mourners also part of the gag? Either Jesus sincerely thinks that the girl is asleep, or else his attempt to downplay what he has done (and by implication who he is) has failed miserably.

Regardless of the reason why Jesus might have claimed that the girl was only sleeping, this passage presents serious difficulties for the reader. Two contradictory readings of the story are equally plausible. In the first reading, the family of the girl have made a gruesome (but finally harmless) mistake, while in the second reading, Jesus is unable to keep from saying ridiculous things even while performing a tremendous miracle. In either case, as Charles Hedrick (1993) notes, the identity of Jesus is at stake. If the girl really is asleep, then Jesus has performed no great miracle. However, if she is dead, then Jesus has performed a very great miracle indeed. If the latter is true, then in all of Mark's gospel only Jesus's calming of the sea in Mark 4:39 would approach the greatness of this achievement.

This episode thus simultaneously sustains two opposed readings: a reading in terms of interpretive codes of the supernatural (the "marvelous"), and a reading in terms of codes of the unusual but nevertheless quite natural (the "uncanny"). The reader's hesitation between these two readings marks this text as fantastic (Todorov 1973:33). These readings rely upon connotation, and therefore they are sensitive to ideological nuances and cultural implications of the story. Read according to the reference codes[13] of ancient wonder-working, such as Elijah's raising of his landlady's son in I Kings 17, the story depicts a miracle of the highest order, even though the miracle worker denies in effect that a miracle has occurred (perhaps according to the hermeneutic codes of the "messianic secret"). The alternative reading focuses more on the empirical level of action (the proairetic codes) and finds nothing at all supernatural in Mark's story. For this reading, all the cues and hints are false fronts, distractions which are wisely ignored by Jesus. The girl's sickness has departed; Jesus merely wakens her and tells the parents to feed her. The bystanders, however, seriously misunderstand what has happened.

Each of these two readings requires the "reading out" of a different ideology from the text. Each ideology will determine what the story of the raising of Jairus's daughter implies about who Jesus is and what he has achieved. The ideology will in each of these cases take the form of an understanding of the order of the natural world, and whether or how supernatural miracles occur in the natural world. Therefore, either of these readings of the raising of Jairus's daughter will reflect an intertextual rewriting of the text of Mark 5:41. The reader brings to bear on the text connotative codes acquired from other narratives (such as synoptic parallels, or other healing stories). These codes in turn reflect and maintain previously acquired beliefs about who Jesus is (for example, about the messianic secret, or Jesus's relation to God), beliefs about the nature of reality (derived from historical reconstructions of first-century Galilee, scientific studies of illness, or metaphysical theories of the irreversibility of death), and beliefs about the genre of the gospel narratives as well as a much more general and less conscious awareness of "how stories are supposed to go." In these beliefs all of the reader's previous readings come into play. These codes filter out narrative material which is inconsistent with the reading and either fill in or allow the reader to overlook gaps within the text itself.

Any reader, using any hermeneutical strategy, engages the play between connotation and denotation as she determines the meaning of the story. Reading according to connotation determines whether Jesus's power belongs to the human world or to some other world. Connotation is often described as "built upon" and therefore secondary to denotation, which is usually considered the more fundamental, "dictionary" level of linguistic meaning. Accordingly the connotative reading, regardless of the direction it takes in relation to the story of Jairus's daughter, will be derived from a reading according to denotation. However, purely denotative (non-connotative) reading is conceivable only as an extreme or utopian case, a "zero degree" of connotation. Denotative reading is culturally stupid and non-rhetorical; it is superficial and naive. It presupposes a general familiarity with the language but draws upon neither the beliefs nor the experiential context of the reader. This is the situation encountered by Barthes's hypothetical Martian reader (1988:173–8), which will be discussed further in chapter 5. A purely denotative reading is, in short, impossible; all actual readings of any story are more or less connotative.

Nevertheless, the theoretical concept of a purely denotative reading serves as a useful standard against which readings of connotation can be compared. Denotation marks out the space of parabolic exclusion which is the space of "reading from outside" (Mark 4:11–12). For the denotative reading, the story of the resuscitation of Jairus's daughter is a point of obscurity that divides insider from outsider. Reading according to denotation cannot determine where Jesus is when he says that the girl is sleeping, or what he means by this statement. Read according to the codes of denotation, the story of Jairus's daughter in the gospel of Mark approaches incoherence. How can any connotative reading out of what has "really" happened according to the story be based upon this denotative obscurity? If the reader cannot identify, at the level of denotation, what the story is about, then its ideological dimensions cannot be explored. The reader must determine these matters among others, because the narrative alone does not; at these points the reader imports ideology into the story under the cover of denotative clarification.

There are of course a great many ways to read the story of Jairus's daughter, as there are many ways to read any story. In most stories, the plurality of possible readings poses no serious difficulty for the reader's understanding. Because linguistic connotation is impossible without denotation, the two levels of reading will ordinarily be more or less compatible with each other; in fact, they will reinforce each other. However, the story of Jairus's daughter makes explicit a fantastic conflict between two incompatible connotations. The denotative incoherence of the story functions to sustain this conflict and thus to subvert textual production by causing an oscillation of meaning that increases to a level of self-destruction. The failure of language to refer unequivocally comes itself to language at this point, and as a result, determination of a consistent reading for the story becomes impossible. The stage for this failure of reading is set in the mutual rejection of Jesus and the mourners. Either the girl is dead or she isn't, and the reader must choose. But if the reader chooses to believe Jesus, then no miracle has occurred.

"Talitha cum" and its translation are the textual site where the conflict between connotations in this story explodes. The conflict is presented as a multiple text, a confrontation between an original and its translation. The transliteration/translation combination is a curious example of what Walter Benjamin calls "literal translation" (1968:69ff.).[14] Benjamin's ideal of literal translation is the interlinear text, the "crib" in which corresponding lines and words of the source and target texts are placed one above the other. The transliteration/translation combination in Mark 5:41 is *intra*linear, not *inter*linear, but the result is the same.

This juxtaposition of texts, Benjamin claimed, reveals a "pure language" lying behind or within all actual languages – a Kabbalist image of a mystical unity to which all translation aspires but which is itself unspeakable. In literal translation, the pure language imprisoned within the original text is "liberated" (Benjamin 1968:80) and it speaks. However, the language speaks only itself; it gives no meaning. For literal translation there is no extratextual world – at least, none which can be spoken about, except in a negative, quasi-mystical sort of way – no referents to complete the proper meaning of the text.

As Benjamin describes it, literal translation does not present the prospect of accurate transfer of meaning. On the contrary, it suggests language beyond meaning, language without meaning. Literal translation is for "those who are outside" (Mark 4:11), that is, those readers who understand only denotation and from whom "the secrets of the Kingdom of God" have been withheld. Literal translation does not bring these outsiders inside, but rather it acknowledges the ineradicable opacity of language. In the gospel of Mark, connotation fails, not just once, but again and again. These cases of unexplained transliteration plus translation are cases of Benjaminian literal translation. They are among the numerous points in the gospel where connotation fails.

It is significant that all of the instances of unexplained transliteration and translation in the gospels are found in Mark. It may also be significant that in each instance it is Jesus's words that are transliterated. There are no similar cases in the other biblical gospels. The reading of the other biblical gospels is rescued by the patterns of connotation which they develop and reinforce. The failure of reading is made explicit in Mark, where denotation subverts the reading of connotation. Is there a connection between this feature of Mark and the fact that Mark has always been the least popular of the biblical gospels?

Literal translation highlights the role played in any translation by the aspect of meaning which Gottlob Frege called "sense." For the signifier, the physical stuff of the sign, there can be no translation, only transliteration. For the signified, which is the sense or intellectual content of the sign, translation is possible, provided that the sense points to an unambiguous extralinguistic referent.

> Somebody observes the Moon through a telescope. I compare the Moon itself to the meaning [referent]; it is the object of the observation, mediated by the real image projected by the object glass in the interior of the telescope, and by the retinal image of the observer. The former I compare to the sense, the latter is like the idea or experience.
>
> (Frege 1952:60)

It follows from this that if the referent of a sentence (or a story) is ambiguous or does not exist, then the sentence can refer only to its own sense. This creates a referential loop which short-circuits meaning. Frege speaks of such self-referentiality as the "indirect reference" of the sign to itself. The equation in this case of sense and reference results in an undecidable meaning – a perpetually incomplete sentence. If Mark ends at 16:8, then it is in effect an incomplete sentence (see chapter 2). As a sign, the signifier must refer to some signified; but if the signifier is its own signified, then the process of signification can never be completed or brought to closure. Self-referentiality creates non-identity within identity.[15]

What does this have to do with the story of Jairus's daughter? In Mark 5:41, a transliterated signifier, "talitha cum," confronts its translated signified in the form of a linguistic phrase, "little girl, I say to you: Awake." The referent of this double phrase is ambiguous: is the girl sleeping or dead? In effect, the text quotes itself, indirectly and paradoxically, like M.C. Escher's cartoon of a hand drawing itself. At 5:41, 7:34, and the other transliteration/translation combinations noted in part 1, the gospel of Mark acknowledges that its own Greek text, and especially its reproduction of the language of Jesus, is a translation. Yet this admission is itself a literary device; this transliteration/translation combination both denotes and connotes.

The intralinear confrontation of source text ("talitha cum") and target text ("little girl, I say to you: Awake") in Mark 5:41 denotes the confrontation between connotations: either the girl is dead or she is asleep. The Aramaic phrase denotes an ordinary thing to say to a sleeping girl, but in the Greek text the exotic words connote "a magical formula," a recipe for resurrection. Yet as translation the Greek words in all their denotative ordinariness are also connoted by the Aramaic source phrase. This confrontation between connotations reproduces in miniature the fundamental indeterminacy of the larger story of Mark. It leads to yet another question: if the entire verse denotes the linguistic equivalence – "which is, translated," *ho estin methermêneuomenon* – of the Aramaic and Greek phrases, then what might the verse itself connote? In order to answer this question, the reader must understand what has "really" happened to Jairus's daughter (is she asleep?). It is that understanding which the story of Jairus's daughter itself obstructs.

THE TEXT RUSTLES

Rustling, entrusted to the signifier by an unprecedented movement unknown to our rational discourses, language would not thereby abandon a horizon of meaning: meaning, undivided, impenetrable, unnamable, would however be posited in the distance like a mirage.

(Barthes 1986:77–8)

That which is represented within and through a story – especially a written story – is necessarily not present; if it were present, the narrative would be superfluous. Regardless of its medium of presentation, narrative appears as a dialogue between two poles, an implied author and an implied reader, with whom the actual readers or authors identify to a greater or lesser extent. This implied dialogue "presents" the story's absent referent, that is, it creates an illusion of reality. This is true of even the most fabulous "unreal" stories. This illusion is in part made possible by the non-presence of the story's referent. As a result, the reader must work to connect the story to its absent referent. The meaning of the story is at least in part the product of the reader's ability to locate the implied dialogue within a possibly vast intertextual network, which in turn provides codes in terms of which the narrative structure can be interpreted.

As implied dialogue, the narrative is always "being told" – it involves an exchange, a "contract" between two or more parties, in which the gratification of an expectation, or the answer to a question, is both deferred and sublimated – and eventually given. "In an [economic] exchange, the debt must be cancelled, and quickly. In a narrative, it must be recognized, honored, and deferred" (Lyotard 1988:178). Narrative, and especially fictional narrative, presents a particularly interesting case of what Frege called indirect reference. In indirect reference, the reference of the story is to the sense of the words through which it is narrated. Hence every story is at least somewhat self-referential. Even in narratives that readers consider to be more or less transparently referential, or "realistic" (such as historical or biographical narratives), sense dominates over reference. In extreme cases, self-referentiality is emphasized and made paradoxical, with fantastic logical and conceptual results. In those extreme cases, the materiality of the text threatens to overwhelm the meaning of the work and to deprive the reader of the pleasure of its possession. The episode in the gospel of Mark in which *talitha koum* appears is of this self-referential variety.

How does this paradoxical self-referentiality affect the reading of Mark, and especially the reading of the story of the raising of Jairus's daughter? Christians tend to focus on the sacred content (the signifieds) of the biblical words and not on the actual words themselves (the signifiers).[16] Their attention is given to possible theological connotations of the story. The primary attitude of Christians toward the text is "Greek" and not "oriental," to use the distinction made by Kurt and Barbara Aland.

> Greeks and orientals view the written word differently. For orientals the very letter had a sanctity of its own. The Hebrew text of the Old Testament, like the text of the Quran, is alike in all manuscripts (except for unintentional errors). For Greeks it was the message contained that was sacred.
>
> (Aland and Aland 1987:286)

For the "Greek" view, it is the message of the story that is important. If the message does not get through, then all is lost. In fact, the message is an already meaningful one; the connotations have largely absorbed and obscured the denotations.

Many Christian Bible translators, in contrast to Benjamin, consider language to be transparent to meaning. The New Testament is always already translated into Greek. If translation of the message from the "original" texts is impossible, then Christianity itself is also impossible. Christian Bible translators therefore regard reading in translation as the successful reception of a (connotative) message passed from within the source text through the target text to the reader. These translators have downplayed or ignored the material aspect of the signifier in order to convey what they considered to be the proper signification (the signified connotation) of the words. This view of translation is often referred to as "dynamic equivalence."

In a similar fashion, most readings of Mark's story of the healing of Jairus's daughter have seen no slippage or friction between the two signifiers, the Aramaic phrase and its Greek translation. Coincidentally, the confrontation of the two incompatible connotations has also been invisible. The reader assumes the dynamic equivalence of "talitha cum" and "little girl, I say to you: Awake." The reader ignores the duplicity of the text, just as she overlooks the ambiguity of Jesus's words, and the ambiguity of what has happened in the story. But it is this ignored materiality of the text, represented in this story in the doubled phrases of the transliteration/translation combination, that is crucial in the gospel of Mark.

In Mark 5:41, denotation and connotation are at war with each other. As in all works of fiction, but more so than in many, Mark's text loops back upon itself self-referentially. What the phrase "talitha cum" (and "ephphatha," and the others) is about, finally, is its own redundancy. Through this phrase the text confesses that it is a translation; it is not the "original." How then can it be "holy scripture" (Faur 1986:192)? This translation confession is itself a product of the text, one of Mark's many stories about its own production.[17] Transliteration and translation in combination set up a referential loop within the narrative, a lack of significance at a critical point in this seemingly significant story. The loop is generated by an interlinear (or in this case, intralinear) text, that is, a place where language speaks itself and nothing more. Through this loop of self-referentiality, the text speaks Benjamin's "pure language."

As a writing this text is both holy and non-holy – it is scripture, ineffable and utopian. The speaker who conjoins translation and transliteration is neither an author nor a reader (actual or implied), neither the narrator nor the character Jesus, but merely the text itself. The text is the flesh of language. Through this textual flesh language – pure language – speaks, just as when I speak, my vocal cords, tongue, and lips of flesh must also speak. The text does not say anything; it merely "rustles," to use Roland Barthes's term. It speaks itself speaking. No referential, extratextual truth emerges from this speech; instead it manifests itself merely as a disruption of every attempt to understand the text.[18]

4

THE TEXT READS
ITSELF

THE DESIRE FOR COMMENTARY

[By] passing from text to the Text, we must change numera-
tion: on the one side, the Text is not a computable object, it is
a methodological field in which are pursued ... the matter
commented on [the *commenté*] and the matter commenting
[the *commentant*]; on the other side, there is no necessity that
the Text be exclusively modern: there can be Text in ancient
works.

(Barthes 1986:73)

From its beginning, writing has required commentary. This demand
is recorded initially as the belief that only the spoken word is
genuine and dependable and the concomitant fear that writing is
inherently out of control. Instances of this fear and this belief appear
in Socrates's story of Theuth and Thamus in Plato's *Phaedrus*, in the
desire in Judaism for an oral Torah to clarify and complement the
written Torah, and in the confidence of Christianity that the Holy
Spirit guides the reading of the scriptures. The spoken word is active
and "alive," the written word inert and "dead." Spoken words can
only be uttered within a context of spatial and temporal immediacy
which "guarantees" that both speaker and hearer understand the
message; if either speaker or hearer doesn't understand, she has no
one to blame but herself. However, once a word has been written,
it is detached from its original context and continually in need of
being "rescued," as Socrates says, from misunderstanding. Written
texts by their very nature are inert and passive; they are helpless.

[O]nce a thing is committed to writing it circulates equally
among those who understand the subject and those who have

75

no business with it … if [the written word] is ill-treated or unfairly abused it always needs its parent [the spoken word] to come to its rescue; it is quite incapable of defending or helping itself.

(Plato 1973:96–7)[1]

The mere act of writing down spoken words transforms them. No matter how "close" the transcription is to the original utterance, the hermeneutical difference is immense. Writing is inherently incomplete and fragmentary; it demands a supplement, a commentary which will rescue it from invalid interpretation and provide it with proper meaning. Commentary is necessary to fill in the hermeneutical gap. The commentary provides in effect a second reading, an explicit rereading, which invests the text with authority. Commentary identifies the text as worthy of attention.

However, every written commentary is also a text and thus subject to further commentary. It is in principle unable to determine and clarify completely the meaning of the text. The commentary identifies the text commented on as authoritative, but what establishes the commentary itself as authoritative? Written text cannot be conclusively explained by or resolved through any supplement; writing resists hermeneutical closure. All commentary is itself incomplete and therefore fails to complete the text. Thus writing both provokes and refuses the hermeneutic strategy of commentary. Far more than speech – or at least more obviously than speech – writing at once provokes, endures, and resists multiple and potentially endless interpretations generated through an indefinite network of intertextuality. As Socrates said, writing is a drug, *pharmakon*, to which the reader becomes addicted (Derrida 1981:63ff.); once she has started reading, the reader can't stop.

The commentary is an instance of what Roland Barthes (following Louis Hjelmslev) called "metalanguage." The signifiers of a metalanguage take as their signifieds another language, another signifying system (SIGNIFIER $\Rightarrow$ SIGNIFIED).[2]

Metalanguage (commentary):   SIGNIFIER $\Rightarrow$ SIGNIFIED

Language (text):   SIGNIFIER $\Rightarrow$ SIGNIFIED

The commentary consists of a sequence of words (signifiers) which refer to a text (the signified) as a "matter commented upon" (Barthes 1986). However, the text itself also consists of a sequence of words (signifiers) referring to some topic (signified). The commentary is a "second language" which depends upon its object, the "first language" which is the text itself (Barthes 1987a:80). Commentary is a parasite which steals from its host text, but like any parasite the commentary also plays a crucial role in the economy of the host (Serres 1982). The commentary both mutilates and obscures the text, but it also adds currency and relevance to the text; it helps the text to "live." Commentary dis-incarnates and consumes the (obscure) text, reincarnating the text as the (meaningful) "work." The goal of commentary is to secure the meaning of the text, and ultimately, the Transcendental Signified (Derrida 1981); these gains are therefore inevitably theological. Commentary is a risky business, but the potential gains from it are great. But this business always fails: the commentary is a (re)reading, but a reading which is always also a "writing," in Barthes's sense of that word. Commentary rewrites the text.

As long as commentary remains physically distinct from the host text, that is, as a separate text, its parasitical role in relation to the host text can be clearly delineated. Commentary and text are in this case two distinct physical things. However, what if commentary were to appear within, and be indistinguishable from, the host text itself? At its greatest extreme, this would take the form of a book teaching the reader how to read. Not how to read fast, or efficiently, but simply how to read, starting with identifying the letters of the alphabet, etc.. If the text provided instructions to the reader about how it should be read, or in effect read itself, then parasite and host, second and first language, commentary and text commented on would become inseparable; in fact, they would be the same thing, one single thing.

Unlike biological parasites, which are of different species than their hosts, the commentary metalanguage in this case would be the same language as the primary language of the text. In fact, the metalanguage would *be* the primary language of the host. Given Barthes's understanding diagrammed above, this would create a loop of meaning: the two levels of signification would be identical, or rather, there would be only one SIGNIFIER $\Rightarrow$ SIGNIFIED, but it would produce a double effect, at once referential and self-referential. The self-commenting text would result in a text that is perpetually trying, and inevitably failing, to signify itself.

Insofar as it examines the functioning of commentaries, and especially of texts which comment upon themselves, this chapter is also an example of metalanguage. My desire, however, is not to comment further upon the commentaries considered below as such (although that cannot be entirely avoided), but rather to explore denotative and connotative implications of commentary, and especially of self-commentary. My thesis is that written text simultaneously and continually demands commentary and condemns every commentary in advance to failure, and that this demand and failure has profound consequences for Mark's gospel's attempt to comment upon itself.

METATEXT

> Commentary is undoubtedly a timid form of dialogue since it allows two authors to perform different parts, instead of mingling their texts genuinely together. When applied by the author himself to his own text, it can nevertheless give some standing to the idea that a text is at one and the same time definitive ... and infinitely open.
>
> (Barthes 1987b:39)

Metatextual self-commentary takes several forms. One familiar type is found in Lewis Carroll's well-known story, *Through the Looking Glass*. In chapter one, Alice reads the poem, "Jabberwocky," in a book which she finds on the White King's table. Her response to the poem is one of perplexity:

> "It seems very pretty," she said when she had finished it, "but it's *rather* hard to understand!" (You see she didn't like to confess, even to herself, that she couldn't make it out at all.) "Somehow it seems to fill my head with ideas – only I don't exactly know what they are! However, *somebody* killed *something*: that's clear, at any rate –"
>
> (Carroll n.d.:166, his emphases)

As the parenthetical (and itself metatextual) aside to the reader suggests, Alice's reaction to the poem is perhaps fairly close to that of the reader, here addressed parenthetically as "You." Indeed, in the two famous books in which she is the central character, Alice is frequently placed in a position similar to that of a reader of those very books – a reader confronted with an obscure and confusing text. As a result, Alice's adventures are amusing and instructive exercises in reading and/as misunderstanding. One suspects that Alice would not be at all surprised by the poststructuralist notion that understanding is always *mis*understanding (that there is no correct reading of any text), although whether she would approve of that view is another matter.

Whether Alice ever succeeds in reading the text which produces her as a character is doubtful. However, she is eventually offered an interpretation of the poem. Later on in Carroll's novel, in chapter six, Humpty Dumpty explains to Alice the meaning of the first verse of "Jabberwocky."

> 'Twas brillig, and the slithy toves
> Did gyre and gimble in the wabe;
> All mimsy were the borogoves,
> And the mome raths outgrabe.

"That's enough to begin with," Humpty Dumpty interrupted: "there are plenty of hard words there. '*brillig*' means four o'clock in the afternoon – the time when you begin *broiling* things for dinner."

"That'll do very well," said Alice: "and '*slithy*'?"

"Well, '*slithy*' means 'lithe and slimy.' 'Lithe' is the same as 'active.' You see it's like a portmanteau – there are two meanings packed up into one word."

"I see it now," Alice remarked thoughtfully: "and what are '*toves*'?"

"Well, '*toves*' are something like badgers – they're something like lizards – and they're something like corkscrews."

"They must be very curious looking creatures."

"They are that," said Humpty Dumpty: "also they make their nests under sun-dials – also they live on cheese."

"And what's to '*gyre*' and to '*gimble*'?"

"To '*gyre*' is to go round and round like a gyroscope. To '*gimble*' is to make holes like a gimlet."

"And '*the wabe*' is the grass-plot round a sun-dial, I suppose?" said Alice, surprised at her own ingenuity.

"Of course it is. It's called '*wabe*,' you know, because it goes a long way before it, and a long way behind it –"

"And a long way beyond it on each side," Alice added.

"Exactly so. Well, then, '*mimsy*' is 'flimsy and miserable' (there's another portmanteau for you). And a '*borogove*' is a thin shabby-looking bird with its feathers sticking out all round – something like a live mop."

"And then 'mome raths'?" said Alice. "I'm afraid I'm giving you a great deal of trouble."

"Well, a 'rath' is a sort of green pig: but 'mome' I'm not certain about. I think it's short for 'from home' – meaning that they'd lost their way, you know."

"And what does 'outgrabe' mean?"

"Well, 'outgribing' is something between bellowing and whistling, with a kind of sneeze in the middle: however, you'll hear it done, maybe – down in the wood yonder – and when you've once heard it you'll be *quite* content."

(Carroll n.d.:240–1, his emphases)

Humpty Dumpty explains the meaning of the poem by providing definitions for each of the nonsense words in it. The ordinary grammatical function of each word is maintained; words which would appear from their placement in the poem to be nouns are defined as nouns, what seem to be adjectives are indeed adjectives, and so on. The words are all quite pronounceable and seem like they could be English words. The comical and fantastical quality of Humpty Dumpty's definitions is heightened by the fact that Alice so willingly accepts them; as was noted above, she serves as a trusting master–reader of her own story; in effect a reliant narratee.

Humpty Dumpty's commentary provides Alice (and the reader) with access to an amusing and improbable dictionary. The words and their definitions belong to several categories. At least one of the words, "gyre," is an English word, although perhaps not one that a young girl would know. Humpty Dumpty's equation of the two English words, "lithe" and "active," is questionable at least. Several other words are, as Humpty Dumpty says, portmanteau words, and he defines them by listing their component words, which are also common English words. (The idea of a word that contains other words would especially appeal to Humpty Dumpty; see his discussion of meaning just prior to this episode [238–9].) "Brillig," "wabe," and "gimble" are also loosely derived from other English words whose ordinary meaning somehow relates to the meaning given for these words. However, other words in the poem, such as "toves," "raths," and "outgribing," bear no apparent relation in any way to the English words used to define them.

This authoritative word by word commentary is provided by one character in Carroll's story for another character in the same story. The commentary is an etymological one, not in the historical, philological sense usually given to "etymology," but in Barthes's sense of denotation as the proper meaning, the *etymon*:

> Denotation would be here a scientific myth: that of a "true" state of language, as if every sentence had inside it an *etymon* (origin and truth).... Each time I believe in the truth, I have need of denotation.
>
> (Barthes 1977b:67)

Poststructural interpretation (which Barthes calls "textual analysis") favors close reading and plays with etymology; it deconstructs the "scientific myth" of denotation. Denotation, often thought of as the foundation of linguistic meaning, is carried away in the endless whirl of intertextual reading, for which there is no final "origin and truth" of meaning.

In contrast to this poststructuralist view, Humpty Dumpty anchors the meaning of the poem in the meanings (*etyma*) assigned to its component words. He offers denotation as the explanation of the poem and thereby tries to raise Alice (and the reader of *Through the Looking Glass*) from the level of a non-reader, for whom "Jabberwocky" is utter nonsense, to that of a naive reader, who reads at the word by word level of denotation only. Humpty Dumpty's answers create an interlinear confrontation between two texts, that is, a "literal" translation which is also an interplay between words.[3] His lexicon depends upon the fantastic denotation of these words, that is, their reference is neither symbolic nor realistic (Todorov 1973:58ff.). Whether the definitions provided clarify the overall meaning of the poem is not important. The autocommentary does not clarify the meaning of the text but rather creates it, almost *ex nihilo*.

For modern scholars, the value of etymology is controversial at best. The connection between words and their meanings is often understood to be determined primarily by the actual usage of the words, the social, historical, or cultural contexts in which the words are spoken or read, not by some alleged original sense. Words are tools to be used, not pointers to eternal Platonic ideas. However, Humpty Dumpty appears at another point in Carroll's story to be just such a modern reader. In fact, at that point in the story he carries the modernist idea of usage to a ridiculous extreme: "When *I* use a word ... it means just what I choose it to mean" (Carroll n.d.:238). Alice is reluctant to accept Humpty Dumpty's view that the meaning of a word is its usage, for in the extreme form that he presents it this view would destroy meaning altogether.

Indeed, Humpty Dumpty's literal, word by word translation of the "Jabberwocky" stanza contradicts his own belief regarding the nature of meaning; he is one person who can never satisfy Alice's desire to understand this poem. Do the poem's words actually mean what Humpty Dumpty says they do (are his definitions the true *etyma*)? Or, are the definitions that he provides to Alice merely whatever he chooses these words to mean? This indeterminacy underscores the desire for further commentary already explicit in *Through the Looking Glass*.

What does the textual self-commentary represented in Humpty Dumpty's analysis of "Jabberwocky" suggest? One never reads a text that is totally without sense nor comprehends as such a disembodied, non-linguistic sense. Even nonsense words and sentences, in order to be recognizable as such, must be provided with a sort of minimal sense; the reader does not know what "brillig" might mean as an English word, but she can recognize from its alphabetic structure that it could be a word and from its syntactic position that it is probably an adjective. The paradox and self-referentiality inherent in Humpty Dumpty's commentary appear primarily in the droll and absurd quality of his explanations. "Green pigs which have lost their way" may translate "mome raths," but the net effect on Alice's (or Carroll's reader's) reading of the poem is minimal. In either case the words refer to a reality which is alien to the reader's everyday world. As a result, the reader can just as easily reject Humpty Dumpty's interpretations as accept them, with little effect on the reading of "Jabberwocky."

THE LAW OF THE BOOK

The meaning constituted by the allegorical sign can then consist only in the *repetition* (in the Kierkegaardian sense of the term) of a previous sign with which it can never coincide, since it is of the essence of this previous sign to be pure anteriority.

(de Man 1983:207)

A different type of self-commentary appears in Franz Kafka's novel, *The Trial*. Towards the end of that novel, the principal character, K., enters into an extended discussion with a priest. At the center of their dialogue is a story which the priest tells "in the very words of the scriptures" (1964:269), concerning "a man from the country who begs for admittance to the Law" (1964:267).[4] The doorkeeper who stands before the Law insists that the man cannot enter "at this moment." The man waits for many years and tries on numerous occasions to get past the intimidating doorkeeper by either begging or bribing him. Finally as he lies dying, the man asks the doorkeeper why, even though "[e]veryone strives to attain the Law," no others have come forward to enter the door. The doorkeeper replies that "this door was intended [only] for you. I am now going to shut it" (1964:269).[5]

In the dialogue which follows the priest's telling of the story, K. and the priest seek to paraphrase the story as a meaningful whole, or as Barthes might put it, to transform the story into a coherent sentence. K. argues that the story is about deception of the man, even though the word "deception" occurs nowhere in the text of the story. The priest counters that the story is about duty and the faithfulness of the doorkeeper. Citing "commentators" on these scriptures, the priest defends the character of the doorkeeper at all cost, turning every incident and aspect of the story to his defense. The priest then reverses himself and presents a different interpretation, one in which the doorkeeper is entirely at fault. In the priest's first reading of the story, the doorkeeper is the intimate of the Law, its perfect servant; the doorkeeper is, in effect, already inside the Law. In the second reading of the story, the doorkeeper is at an infinite distance from the Law, an outsider to the Law, not unlike readers who struggle to understand Kafka's story itself. Speaking of the conflict between these two interpretations and of the difficulty in understanding the story, the priest says, "The scriptures are unalterable and the comments often enough merely express the commentators' despair" (1964:272–3).

The two interpretations put forward by the priest seem equally legitimate. Each serves as an allegory, in which every action by and every statement of the doorkeeper contributes to the revelation of hidden truth. In each interpretation, the Law is eternal, perfect, and divine, and the doorkeeper is its human medium, the ambiguous "text" on which the priest's comments actually focus. However, as K. notes, the two interpretations do not contradict one another. Nor do either of the priest's interpretations contradict K.'s view that the man from the country has been deceived. To this the priest replies that in any case the doorkeeper "belongs to the Law and as such is beyond human judgment.... [T]o doubt his dignity is to doubt the

Law itself" (1964:276). It does not matter which interpretation of the doorkeeper is accepted. The priest goes on to argue that it is not necessary to believe that the doorkeeper speaks the truth, but only to accept what the doorkeeper says as necessary. K. concludes that this "turns lying into a universal principle." The Law is the universal principle, the categorical imperative or Transcendental Signified (Derrida 1981) to which the man (and K., and the reader of Kafka's story) seeks admittance, and which the doorkeeper (and the priest) defends. But this Law states that every statement should always be a lie. In other words, the commentary subverts its own desire for revelation, and deception wins out after all.

Kafka's story and its metatextual commentary depict the struggle between the reader and the "law" of the book. Like the man from the country, the reading of the book is outside of its law, but it makes the law both possible and necessary. The commentary that K. and the priest provide for the reader is a dialogue, not entirely unlike the one described above between Alice and Humpty Dumpty. However, Kafka's dialogue lacks the denotational and etymological finality of Humpty Dumpty's unquestioned definitions. The priest's readings, and K.'s desire to understand, attend instead to the story's connotation, that is, to inferences derived from the story's surface level but not stated in the story itself (for example, the theme of deception). In other words, the priest uses a set of interpretive codes which operate in quite different ways than those of Humpty Dumpty. These codes turn the doorkeeper and the Law (and implicitly, the man from the country) into allegorical symbols.

The priest does provide a close reading of the story, but by no means is his reading a word-by-word interpretation. However, none of the words in the story of the man before the Law is nonsense, in contrast to all the crucial words in "Jabberwocky." The priest does not contradict himself as Humpty Dumpty does, but by skipping from one well-justified reading to a very different one he implies that no one interpretation best fits the story. As in *Through the Looking Glass*, the priest's two interpretations point to an indeterminacy that requires still more commentary.

Finally, K.'s concluding remark ("A melancholy conclusion. It turns lying into a universal principle.") challenges and undermines the value not only of the entire commentary – and perhaps of any commentary – but also of the story of the man from the country itself. The revelation that the true Law that all people desire to have revealed is in reality the universality of deceit, is tantamount to the final disappointment for the man from the country. Here the commentary not only fails finally to elucidate the text, but it threatens to destroy any prospect of meaning whatsoever.

THE SOWER OF THE WORD

... the work of commentary, once it is separated from any ideology of totality, consists precisely in *manhandling* the text, *interrupting* it.

(Barthes 1974:15, his emphases)

And he said to them: You did not read this parable? Then how shall you understand all the parables?

(Mark 4:13)

In Mark 4:11–12, Jesus cites Isaiah 6:9–10 in order to distinguish between those who have received "the secret (*to mustêrion*) of the kingdom of God"[6] and "those who are outside," to whom "all comes through parables." Some commentators argue that the word *parabolais*, "parables," in Mark 4:11 would be better translated as "riddles." The parables are riddles or puzzles that divide insiders who are given supplementary instruction from outsiders who are not, "lest they [the outsiders] be converted and forgiven." In Mark, the insider group consists primarily of Jesus's disciples ("his followers along with the twelve"), and these insiders get the secret instruction. For the outsiders – the crowd – there is only the denotation of the parables; the connotation or secret that carries the possibility of repentance is missing. Connotative meaning has been withheld, "so that they [the outsiders] may have sight but not see, and hear but not understand" (Mark 4:12). Frank Kermode (1979) argues that this text makes outsiders of everyone who does not understand the parables, and it legitimizes an institutionalized hermeneutic – the training of insiders.

Mark 4:33–4 also separates "them" from "his own disciples," although the referent of the word "they" in these verses is ambiguous: is it the crowd?[7]

With many such parables he spoke the word to them, according to what they could comprehend; but he did not talk with them except in parables; but privately with his own disciples he expounded all.

The division between "them" and the disciples here seems less harsh than in 4:11–12, for Jesus speaks the word in parables "according to what they could comprehend." Furthermore, in Mark 7:14, where Jesus calls upon "the multitude" to "listen ... and understand," Mark's story seems to suggest yet a different tactic (or even a different understanding of the crowd) on Jesus's part. Is the narrative of Mark inconsistent at these points, or does Jesus's attitude toward the outsiders change during Mark's story?

Throughout Mark the implied reader of the story, like the disciples, is privy to secret instruction, including the commentary on the sower parable. However, in Mark 4:11–13, as in 4:24–5 and elsewhere, the implied author steps forward in the form of the character Jesus and addresses the reader, inviting careful reading of the text.[8] D.E. Nineham (1963:139) notes that Mark 4:13 implies that Jesus had expected that the disciples would understand the sower parable (4:3–8), and that Jesus had been disappointed. Robert Fowler (1991:102) argues that Mark 4:11–12 is ironic, and Werner Kelber (1983:126) suggests that this saying is itself parabolic. Like both Carroll's Alice books and Kafka's stories, the gospel of Mark is both an exercise in (re)reading and in the futility of its own reading. Thus it is quite appropriate that Richmond Lattimore translates the phrase *ouk oidate* in 4:13 as "You did *not read* ...?" even though nowhere else in Mark does he translate any of the many instances of the root verb *idein* in this way. *Idein* is usually translated "see," "know," or "understand."[9] Thus in Lattimore's English translation, Mark 4:13 resonates with the phrase, "let him who reads this take note of it" which appears in Mark 13:14, in the midst of Jesus's announcement of apocalyptic disasters to come. These verses explicitly identify the gospel of Mark as a *writing* addressed to a *reader*.

Neither the gospel of Matthew nor the gospel of Luke has a saying parallel to Mark 4:13 ("You did not read this parable? Then how shall you understand all the parables?"). In addition, both Matthew and Luke soften the quotation from Isaiah 6 in Mark 4:12, from "so that they may have sight but not see, and hear but not understand, lest they be converted and forgiven" to "because they have sight but do not see, and hearing but do not hear or understand ... so that they may never see ... and turn back, so that I can heal them" (Matthew 13:13, 15) and "so that though they have sight they may not see, and though they have hearing they may not understand" (Luke 8:10, with no mention of forgiveness). Nevertheless, both Matthew and Luke do include parallels to both the sower parable and its metatextual commentary, which together comprise the Markan context of 4:12–13.

The words in Mark 4:12–13 are apparently quite troublesome and invite rewriting. Jesus's parables are obscure and his commentary is withheld from the outsiders in Mark, *in order that, hina ... mêpote*, they may not "be converted and forgiven." Yet these troublesome verses set the stage for Jesus's commentary on his parable of the sower:

> The sower sows the word. And these are the ones beside the way where the word is sown, and as soon as they hear it Satan comes and snatches the word that has been sown among them. And there are some who are as if sown on stony ground, who when they hear the word accept it with joy; and they have no roots in themselves but are men of the moment, and when there comes affliction and persecution, because of the word, they do not stand fast. And others are those who were sown among thorns; these are the ones who hear the word, and concern for the world and the beguilement of riches and desire for other things come upon them and stifle the word, and it bears no fruit. And the others are those who were sown upon the good soil, who hear the word and accept it and bear fruit thirtyfold and sixtyfold and a hundredfold.
>
> (Mark 4:14–20)

At first glance Jesus's self-commentary looks somewhat like Humpty Dumpty's commentary on "Jabberwocky." The interpretation is not contested; in fact, no one responds to it at all. Although the disciples requested the commentary, there is no indication that they have heard it. However, unlike "Jabberwocky" the words of the sower parable are not nonsensical; the denotation of the parable is coherent and clear. Furthermore, unlike Humpty Dumpty's commentary on the poem, Jesus's commentary does not attempt to explain the parable word by word, but rather phrase by phrase. Beginning with an initial interpretive "key," in which the seed, *to speirein*, is equated with the word, *ho logos*, Jesus explains each of the different environments into which the seed falls as a different sort of person or reception of the word. However, Jesus's commentary vacillates here, for that which is sown is at first identified as "the word," but then the seed is described in terms of those who hear the word.[10]

The net effect of Jesus's commentary is thus not so much

etymological and denotative, as in *Through the Looking Glass*, but rather allegorical, as in *The Trial*. "Kafka, whose interpreter dies outside, is a doorkeeper only; so was Mark" (Kermode 1979:45). The sower parable lacks the evident paradox of the doorkeeper who forbids the man from entering the door which was intended for him alone, and which demands explanation. Nonetheless, the parable's reader, who like the disciple should be an insider, requires an explanation anyway.[11] Like Kafka's priest, Jesus presents a connotation of the sower parable in his commentary, completing the bare denotation of the words which would otherwise exclude the disciple/reader/man from the country. Yet the sower commentary is not entirely analogous to Kafka's. Does the reader question this explanation, like Kafka's K., or accept it, like Carroll's Alice? Does Jesus, like the priest, offer conflicting interpretations, or are the consequences for the various seeds consistent with one another?

This is not the only place in the gospel of Mark where "how-to-read-it" instructions are provided for the reader. The text offers numerous "asides" to the reader, of which the most famous is the phrase "let him who reads this take note of it" in Mark 13:14 (par. Matthew 24:15). References to "the gospel" throughout Mark's text[12] are also important ways in which the story of Mark refers openly to the fact that it is a writing and therefore that it needs to be rescued from the dangers of misinterpretation. Like every written text, Mark needs a supplement, but Mark makes this need explicit. One might even argue that the ambiguous "them" in Mark 4:33 refers best to the reader, with the crowd's hearing representing the reader's reading.

Mark's reference to itself as written text appears also in other ways. For example, Samuel Sandmel (1978:32) notes that in Mark 7:1–8, Jesus rejects the oral Torah ("the tradition of men": the tradition of rabbinic commentary) in favor of the written Torah ("the commandment of God"). Furthermore, in Mark 16:6–7, the implied author once again steps forward and becomes a character in the story who gives final directions to disciples and to readers ("go and tell his disciples, and Peter: He goes before you into Galilee. There you will see him, as he told you"). Appropriately enough, the mysterious young man is a fantastic double of Jesus (on the right of the tomb, just as the son of man would be seen on the right of God [14:62]). As we saw in chapter 2, the young man's words are in effect a commentary on a text that isn't there – the ending of Mark. The young man's words promise a conclusive encounter with Jesus beyond the text.

For decades, biblical scholars have typically resolved the incongruities between text and metalanguage in Mark 4 by regarding the commentary as "secondary."[13] Both intra- and intertextual evidence supports this position: for example, the language of the commentary is unusual for Mark, and the version of the sower parable in saying 9 of the gospel of Thomas, while otherwise close to Mark, has no commentary. To treat the self-commentary in Mark 4:14–20 as secondary, however, is to avoid reading the commentary as part of the larger narrative in Mark. The immediate context in Mark 4, which groups parables according to similarity of theme, and beyond that the larger narrative frame of the gospel, also serve as implicit metatextual commentaries which help the reader to resolve ambiguities in the sower parable. By being explicit about the difficulty of understanding, Mark 4 creates an illusion of successful understanding. The gospel disguises by writing it the deficiency that produces it: the hermeneutic insufficiency of text. In contrast, the gospel of Thomas's version of the sower parable lacks narrative context; like most of the other sayings in Thomas, saying 9 appears as a more or less random item in a list of sayings, preceded only by the introductory phrase, "Jesus said." This lack of context leaves the opaque and parabolically exclusionary quality of saying 9 more readily apparent. In Mark 4, the sower parable is followed first by Jesus's commentary and then by a series of additional sayings and parables, several of which also refer to seeds or to the hidden made manifest. The commentary serves not only as a guide for the sower parable but also as instructions on how to read the next several sayings and possibly the entire gospel of Mark itself.[14]

However, despite Jesus's commentary on his own parable, the disciples in Mark remain uncertain, or even stupid. Instruction does not produce faith or understanding, as the disciples' response to the storm and to Jesus's calming of it shows in the very next episode, Mark 4:35–41. The twelve have not paid attention to what they have heard. Does this failure on the part of the disciples imply that the reader has also failed? Is Mark's implied reader also stupid? According to the commentary's interpretative key, the parable is itself about the act of teaching in parables, the sowing of the word. Has this seed/word, not only the sower parable but its commentary as well, fallen then on inhospitable soil? Mark's story narrates the failure, not only of the parable, but also of the commentary. The secrets of the kingdom lie in a metaphoric abyss, an enigmatic text. The reader is apparently already one of the disciples, but a disciple who has not yet seen the resurrected Jesus in Galilee (Mark 16:7). Insiders remain outside, and non-disciple outsiders such as the Syrophoenician woman in Mark 7 or the scribe in Mark 12 are on the inside.

Despite the narrative depiction of Jesus's oral performance in Mark 4 and elsewhere, the parables of Jesus are *written* texts, requiring but necessarily eluding the rescue offered by the self-commentary.[15] In these textual parables especially, language comes close to tearing away from meaning, as Socrates noted; these parables require commentary, to secure their meanings.

> At one end of the scale there is a zero point, a strong saying, perhaps, with no narrative content to speak of; and at the other is the well-formed story which, as structuralist exegetes like to demonstrate, exhibits all the marks of narrativity. But there is another scale to consider. Parables are stories, insofar as they *are* stories, which are not to be taken at face value, and bear various indications to make this condition plain to the interpreter; so the other scale is a measure of their darkness....
>
> All require some interpretative action from the auditor; they call for completion; the parable-event isn't over until a satisfactory answer or explanation is given; the interpretation completes it.
>
> (Kermode 1979:24, his emphasis)

Ironically, the failure of the commentary in Mark delivers the sower parable from its narrative context. The goal of every commentary, if Socrates is right, is to provide what is lost when the spoken word (or the word in the mind) is written down, that is, to come to the "rescue" of the written text. The independence of the parable text from a "present," oral context continually regenerates the desire for interpretation, even as it frustrates the satisfaction of that desire; as was noted above, writing infinitely defers completion. Meta-textual inclusion of the commentary in Mark's text introduces the narrative effect of a writing that defers itself *into the text itself*. The commentary "completes" the text by generating an endless loop out of the separation of the text from itself. Because Mark's text comments upon itself, the commentary and the text are one, and therefore it (the commentary as text, the text as commentary) cannot be "rescued." The gospel of Mark remains unread. This non-identity and non-presence constitutes writing as what Jacques Derrida calls *différance* (1973:129ff.).

The parable "is quite incapable of defending or helping itself" and requires its "parent" (the commentary) to rescue and restore its proper meaning. Disputes about reading the parables arise from different hermeneutical choices being made, which in turn are the results of the readers' different theological or methodological commitments. Insofar as the biblical gospels attempt to resolve these disputes through metatextual commentary such as Mark 4:14–20, they merely raise the level of disagreement. If the gospel of Mark itself is structured as a kind of great parable, as a number of biblical scholars have argued, then the commentary on the sower parable, along with other metatextual comments in Mark, allegorizes the entire narrative. Furthermore, if Mark is a parable, then Jesus's comment at 4:13 ("You did not read this parable? Then how shall you understand all the parables?"), like his statement at 13:14 ("let him who reads this take note of it"), applies to the entire book, not just to its proximate textual context. Thus the narrative of the entire gospel of Mark enacts the failure of commentary in 4:14–20, which ironically is the failure of its own reading. The failure of the sower commentary is the failure of every written text. As a written document, Mark has been cut loose from any oral supplementation which it might have had originally, and all readers are by necessity "those who are outside," to whom "all comes through parables" (4:11).

> The secret of the Kingdom of God is *perhaps* given to characters in the story [of Mark] but is definitely *not* given to the narratee through the discourse. For the reader of the Gospel, the giving of this secret lies behind an opaque veil.
>
> (Fowler 1991:168–9, his emphases)

In parable, "language overflows the speaker who makes use of it, by a kind of excess of meaning. He has said more and another thing than what he wanted to say" (Marin 1980:242, n. 132). Because it is writing, parabolic saying is by its very nature independent of hermeneutic control and can no longer be rescued by its "parent" if it is "ill-treated or unfairly abused" (Plato 1973:97). The sower commentary does not answer questions provoked by the parable; instead, it creates further questions. For example, who are those persons from whom "as soon as they hear it Satan comes and snatches the word that has been sown among them?" What does it mean to "hear the word and accept it?" While Mark's metatextual commentary lacks the evident self-mockery of the commentaries in

Carroll's and Kafka's texts, it joins with them in referring to a failure of the narrative.

COMMENTARY AND CANON

> The critical aspect of the old system is *interpretation*, i.e., the operation by which one assigns to a set of confused or even contradictory appearances a unitary structure, a deep meaning, a "veritable" explanation. Hence, interpretation must gradually give way to a new discourse, whose goal is not the revelation of a unique and "true" structure but the establishment of an interplay of multiple structures: an establishment itself *written*.
>
> (Barthes 1986:154, his emphases)

The reader always desires to read the text from the position of an insider. However, written text betrays a loss or transformation of memory, a separation from the immediacy of speech, which places the reader on the outside (Derrida 1973). Sometimes a text seeks to restore the reader to the inside through a metatextual frame in which the text becomes its own commentary, as in Mark 4:14–20. This metatextual frame attempts to meet certain fundamental needs of the reader: to eliminate ambiguity and produce in its place decidable referentiality (extratextual truth); to replace the polysemy of the text with univocal, legitimate interpretation, authorized by the text itself, which then must either be accepted or rejected; and to establish a believable cosmos (an ideology), featuring an imaginable time and space. Yet because Mark's metatextual commentary is part of the same text (the gospel of Mark) as the parable that it explains, it parodies both that text and the operation of any possible commentary.

When a text comments upon itself, this self-reading is an attempt to circumvent any other reading; the autocommentary anticipates and forestalls other (external) interpretations of the text. However, as Barthes notes, this strategy necessarily fails as all commentary fails, for self-commentary also cannot satisfy the desire for meaning. There will still be a need for further commentary. The failure of the self-commentary disrupts both its own clarification of the text's meaning and the functioning of the text itself; the metatext is thus always writerly. Self-commentary is the ultimate form of reading from inside – reading from inside the text itself. However, as a result of this, the *failure* of metatextual commentary necessarily places the reader on the outside. Ironically, that which would bring the reader "in" and make her a disciple, excludes her.

As the physical, material aspect of the signifier, text itself has no meaning; only in context – any context – does text acquire meaning. No written text can ever guarantee its "proper" context. Every actual reading is a compromise, an approximation to understanding which is limited by its context. Self-commentary attempts to enable the text to incorporate metatextually its own context – in other words, to liberate the text from the extratextual context. This task is in principle unfinishable. No matter how many words or phrases are added, rearranged, or substituted, there still remains some aspect of the original text which has not been completely specified or explained, and which therefore requires some further commentary.

> It has been said that there is no meta-language: or rather, there are only meta-languages, *language upon language*, like a foliation without a kernel, or better yet, because no language has control over another, the game of topping hands.
>
> (Barthes 1976:166)

Therefore the perfectly complete self-commentary, like the perfectly literal translation, will never be written (or read).

The desire to achieve complete mastery of the text, to read from the inside by means of the perfect commentary, is profoundly theological. It is the desire to be one of the disciples, in the presence of the living words of Jesus. This desire motivates traditional understandings of the biblical texts, and indeed of all texts. These understandings seek to establish the authenticity of the text's meaning, the unity of the narrative, the possibility of a correct reading, or of an accurate translation. What Barthes called the writerly text resists this desire for coherence, which as a theological desire is also therefore ideological.[16] The writerly text appears – it reads itself – whenever reference is suspended or otherwise incomplete. *The Trial* is one such text, and *Through the Looking Glass* is another; the gospel of Mark is a third.

The word by word and line by line commentary on "Jabberwocky" which Humpty Dumpty offers to Alice both reproduces and parodies the tradition of Western textual commentary, not only biblical commentary but also secular literary commentary, epitomized in Barthes's *S/Z*. Kafka's commentary also reproduces and parodies. The dialogical and ambiguous commentary in which K.

and the priest engage in *The Trial* tends in the direction of midrash;[17] it is reminiscent of those features of rabbinic exegesis which revel in textual polysemy and are willing to play with the scriptures. These two types of commentary do not exhaust the range of possibilities, but they do represent distinct positions on a scale between which many commentaries can be found.

Writing always desires commentary, and the writerly text makes this desire explicit. The desire for commentary, however, becomes even greater when writing is identified, as some texts are identified in Judaism and Christianity, as "Holy Scripture." When the text is canonized, the form of the text is thereby frozen (Kermode 1978:151; 1979:x). Once the text becomes "holy," it becomes the vessel of God's Word, the Eternal Truth. Such a text cannot be changed. Prior to the actual moment of canonization (which cannot be defined precisely), the text is still in production, subject to modification. Neither its physical form nor its message is yet definitive. Openness to revision allows inclusion of additional text, or clarification or elimination of ambiguous or objectionable material. Prior to canonization, a physical rewriting of the text is possible. Kurt and Barbara Aland claim that copyists of writings which eventually became the New Testament varied widely in their production of the texts, from "strict" (word by word) to "free" duplication (featuring substitution of synonyms, "correction" of "errors," etc.), until the third or fourth century (1987:64). Prior to the moment of canonizing, the texts that became the New Testament were like any other texts; they could be wrong and they could be changed.

Development of an institutionalized hermeneutic begins with desire for a canonized text. Indeed, it is commentary that creates canon – that is, which establishes the canonicity of the text on which it comments. Something like this process is recorded in the Bible itself, in the story of the discovery of the scroll in the Temple during the time of Josiah (II Kings 22). No text, of course, can validly assert its own canonicity, just as no text can comment on itself in a satisfactory way. By canonizing the text, the institution lays ideological claim to it and takes possession of it. In its turn, canonization of a text demands commentary for the text. Yet even before any texts are canonized the demand for commentary is already evident; in the Bible itself, many of the writings function as commentaries on other biblical texts.[18]

The New Testament contains four distinct and not readily

reconcilable gospels, not just one. This multiplicity suggests that the gospels are analogous to rabbinic midrashim, "oral" commentaries on the "written" Jewish scriptures.[19] Much of what became the New Testament consists of commentaries on writings which Christians eventually called the Old Testament; references to "the scriptures" or that which "is written" are points at which the New Testament texts manifest themselves as midrashic rewritings. Kermode (1979) notes the intertextuality of "fulfillment" between the Old and New Testaments. Thus the New Testament as commentary ratifies the canonicity of the Old Testament even as it threatens through its own canonicity to sweep it away. The New Testament presents the dilemma of a second canon, or rather a meta-canon which rewrites the Jewish canon.[20] The Christian double canon, as much as anything else, lies at the root of Christian anti-semitism. This double canon has deeply influenced the development of Christian theology, and it is a problem which Christians have never adequately faced.

Canonization ends the fluidity of production of the written text, for the canon is by definition always closed and complete. One consequence of canonization is that the material text can no longer be modified, short of heresy. The supposition, which is widespread among many contemporary biblical scholars as well as among ordinary readers, of the historical necessity of "original" texts (perhaps autographs), now lost, to ground the identity of the biblical texts, attests to the ideological power of canon. These originals would be the "true," authoritative texts which are secured by the canon.

In the oral culture context of earliest Christianity, one result of canonizing was to insure the stability of the biblical texts. Given the limitations of chirographic technology, innumerable variations between manuscripts of the biblical texts inevitably appeared, of course, until widespread use of the printing press created the possibility of endlessly identical copies. In contemporary print culture, however, the limits, the form, and the message of a text are better guaranteed by the publishing house and the copyright notice than by ecclesiastical acceptance.

A second result of canonizing was to secure the beliefs of the religious community – to divide insiders from outsiders. Insofar as the biblical books are owned ideologically (that is, intertextually) by powerful religious institutions, the concept and authority of the canon are secure. In the contemporary world, however, religious institutions have lost the power to enforce their canonizing decisions upon readers.[21] No two readers of the Bible necessarily read the "same" canon. Each reader may have her own preferred books, passages, verses (the canon within, or beyond, the canon), and there are other books and so forth that she rarely, or never, reads. Readers in effect create their own canons; even traditional biblical scholarship acknowledges this. Yet the modern fluidity of the canon is also symptomatic of a desire for a canon. Contemporary discussions about how to guarantee the authenticity of electronic texts increasingly available on computer networks reveal how strong the desire for something like canon remains, even in relation to non-biblical texts. The reader may physically rewrite the electronic text as much as she wants (the fact that it is on a computer screen makes it no less physical), but there is a strong general sense that some means must be provided to preserve an unaltered archive copy.

Canon establishes an authoritative, exclusive context in which the commentary game can be played. It provides a constant basis for exegesis and dispute. After canonization, those parts of the text which remain (or become) unclear, or run counter to prevailing beliefs of readers, must be re-interpreted through commentary, either oral or written. These commentaries produce an external rewriting of the text, in contrast to the internal rewriting performed by the self-commentary. Irregularities, awkwardnesses, and incoherences remaining in the material text (after its canonical limits have been established) must still be smoothed over, but the option of an actual physical rewriting is no longer available (except at the risk of theological rejection by the community). Instead, the commentaries provide a *spiritual* rewriting; in this respect they serve a purely ideological function. The commentaries which arise in response to the need established by canonizing the text may contest one another, but they all agree in protecting the interests of the text's owners. Just as the canon excludes certain texts, so the institutional commentary traditions exclude certain interpretations; the commentaries guarantee the correctness of reading.

This spiritual rewriting by external commentaries is impeded from within the text by metatextual commentary. Texts such as the gospel of Mark (but also the texts of Kafka and Carroll) are saved from the oblivion of not being read through the promise of an elusive meaning to be uncovered by those insiders who know (whether Jesus, the priest, or Humpty Dumpty). In each of these three texts a narrative context, a metatext, comes to the rescue, attempting and yet failing to replace the lost oral "parent." This division of the text against itself, however, becomes a problem and an obstacle for the commentary tradition which arises in the wake of canonization; the autocommentary must be eliminated so that the external commentaries can go about their endless business. In the conventional reading of the churches from the very beginnings of Christianity, for example, Jesus's commentary on his own sower parable absorbs the parable itself, and the enduring secret of the kingdom of God, according to the gospel of Mark, goes unnoticed. Scholarly readers, on the other hand, generally retain the mysterious parable and dismiss the metatextual commentary as secondary. In either case the tension between the text (parable) and the metatext (commentary) has disappeared. Like disciples, the readers search the remains of the text in hopes of producing its absent "author," whether Jesus or the implied author of Mark, in order to short-circuit the metatextual paradox, and to rewrite the gospel of Mark, that is, to make it their own.

When canonizing freezes the text, the material space or *chôra* (what Julia Kristeva calls the semiotic) which makes signification possible becomes evident in the incoherences which remain in the text. The semiotic *chôra* appears in the failure of meaning, the slippage of the metatext. The text's resistance to meaning can never be entirely overcome, and in this respect each commentary necessarily fails; the text remains perpetually incomplete. Because the desire for canon is the desire for completeness, the supplement which desires to rescue the text eventually becomes an endless string of commentaries, as each commentary itself is also a text and requires further commentary (Kermode 1978:151–2).

The inevitable failure to rescue the text by rewriting it from within comes to expression in the reader's amusement or disillusionment or non-understanding. In *The Trial* and *Through the Looking Glass*, this failure can be, and is, tolerated and even enjoyed; it is part of what makes these stories exciting and provocative. The failure of these texts to read themselves is part of their larger success as writerly narratives. Other literary qualities also redeem the stories of Carroll and Kafka, and of course neither of them has biblical status. The gospel of Mark has both biblical and literary status. However, other, much more readerly, versions of "the same" story (the other biblical gospels) are available, bound up in the same canonical collection (the New Testament). The reader is pressed to take the story of Mark seriously, but this can be done more easily with one of the other versions. The failure of the metatextual rewriting of the sower parable is more evident in Mark, as one sees in the scramble of commentators to explain and discount the "difficult" saying at Mark 4:12 and especially the metatextual commentary of Mark 4:14–20, insofar as it fails to explain the parable of the sower. Mark has somehow made it into the biblical canon, and now its awkwardnesses must be explained away. The disciples' failure to read the parable ("You did not read this parable? Then how shall you understand all the parables?") is also Mark's failure to read itself, and therefore it is also the reader's failure to read Mark.

When a man has, he shall be given; when one has not, even what he has shall be taken away from him.

(Mark 4:25)

5

JESUS'S FRANKNESS

THE DISCOURSE OF JESUS

[He] began to explain to them that the son of man must suffer much and be rejected by the elders and the high priests and the scribes, and be killed, and rise up after three days. He was telling them frankly.

(Mark 8:31–2a)

The first of Jesus's three passion predictions in the gospel of Mark comes immediately after Peter identifies Jesus as "the Christ" and immediately before the exchange of rebukes that ends when Jesus identifies Peter as "Satan." The larger unit that contains this passage, the dialogue of Jesus and the disciples at Caesarea Philippi (Mark 8:27–9:1), has often been regarded as a narrative hinge joining together the two halves of Mark. In the first half of this gospel, Jesus apparently reveals himself to both demons and disciples as the miraculously powerful son of God, in Galilee and its vicinity. However, in the second half of Mark, Jesus's weakness and frustration grows as he moves toward apparent defeat and death in Jerusalem.

This brief passage is therefore a crucial one, a culmination and turning point in the identification of Jesus and therefore in the plot of Mark's story. Its significance is both theological and narratological. The passage's importance in this respect makes particularly troublesome two of the ambiguities which characterize the passage: first, that Jesus was speaking these words "frankly," *ton logon elalei parrêsia,* to the disciples, and second, that anyone could speak frankly of "the son of man" at all. Only in Mark could Jesus speak frankly of the son of man, because only in Mark is Jesus's frankness a signifier of the disruption and breakdown of denotative meaning.

"Frankness" here opens up not the connotative meaning of the text, but rather a textual abyss into which meaning vanishes.

It has long been observed that the gospel of Mark appears to be an incomplete, fragmentary text. However, the arguments have usually centered upon the alleged awkwardness of Mark's style and especially the abrupt ending of the gospel at 16:8. Soon after Mark was written, early readers attempted to rewrite and repair this ending with various supplements. The beginning of Mark is also less than satisfactory, especially when compared to the other biblical gospels. Mark's endings and its beginning are discussed further in chapter 2. However, the incompleteness of Mark is more far-reaching than what is apparent at its end or its beginning. Mark's incompleteness is also to be found in this saying of Jesus which Mark 8:32 underlines as "frank," as well as at numerous other points where the narrative in effect confesses its own failure.

Why is it strange and confusing that Jesus should speak frankly, *parrêsią*, to his disciples? The translation in which this word appears is that of Richmond Lattimore. Both the RSV and the New English Bible (NEB) translate *parrêsią* as "plainly"; other translations use "openly" (Jerusalem Bible, Scholars Version) or "very clear" (TEV). "Frankly" as used in Lattimore's text seems stiff and formal, out of place in this confrontation between Jesus and the disciples. For this reason I think that it is appropriate that Lattimore uses "frankly" in Mark 8:32, for only in Mark is "frankness" on the part of Jesus unusual, and therefore remarkable. In his translation of the gospel of John, which uses *parrêsią* nine times,[1] Lattimore never once translates the word as "frankly"; for that gospel he prefers instead what seem to me to be words that are more fitting in such contexts, such as "openly," "plainly," or "in public." Lattimore's use of "frankly" in Mark 8:32 points to something strange that is happening.

The word *parrêsią* seems out of place in the gospel of Mark. This verse is indeed the only time that *parrêsią* appears in Mark. In the Markan context this word stands in opposition to the parabolic speech which Jesus reserves for "those who are outside," in order to keep them from understanding (Mark 4:11–12).[2] Several times in Mark, Jesus draws the disciples away from the crowd in order to explain to them (frankly?) what he has been talking about. In similar fashion, at various points in the text the narrator interrupts the story to "explain" to the reader what Jesus's words mean. Yet if Mark is frank with the reader at these points, it is no more so than Jesus is with the disciples. Mark's frankness is no more successful than Jesus's frankness. Jesus's statements to the disciples as well as to the crowd are ambiguous and paradoxical throughout Mark.

The very notion that Jesus might say anything "frankly" runs up against one of the more important dimensions of Mark's narrative, which biblical scholars have long described as the "messianic secret." This is the reading of Mark which holds that Jesus initially desires to keep his messianic identity a secret and only in the latter half of the gospel does he openly reveal his true nature to others. Jesus's "identification" by Peter at Caesarea Philippi is usually regarded as the point in Mark's story where Jesus begins to reveal the secret. It's not entirely clear in what sense there is a secret in the story of Mark, or what the secret is, but Mark's Jesus is in any case an enigmatic character, the meaning of whose words and the nature of whose deeds are often indeterminable.

In Mark, the disciples are resistant to whatever Jesus says. Put more bluntly, they are stupid. Shortly before the Caesarea Philippi episode, Jesus complains to the disciples about their lack of understanding, despite the fact that they have been given the secrets of the kingdom of God ("Do you not yet see, do you not understand? Are your hearts impenetrable? Do you have eyes, but do not see, and ears, but do not hear?" [8:17–18; compare 4:11]). Like the disciples, the implied reader of Mark is apparently an insider, privy to explanation of Jesus's sayings, but also requiring and receiving explanation. Does the reader understand Jesus's sayings any better than the disciples do? Is the reader a true insider of Mark's text? Or is the reader finally just as stupid, confused, and fearful as the disciples? In Mark it is outsiders such as the Syrophoenician woman (7:24–30) and the scribe (12:28–34) who appear to understand Jesus best.

In Matthew and Luke the disciples are much more likely to understand and to approve of Jesus's words than in Mark. Yet neither the gospel of Matthew nor the gospel of Luke ever uses the word *parrêsiq*. Both Matthew 16:13–28 and Luke 9:18–27 offer parallels to the Caesarea Philippi episode, and yet both omit *parrêsiq* from their accounts. In each of these gospels, the relation between Jesus and his disciples is from the beginning depicted as a frank one. The disciples have little difficulty understanding what Jesus says and does, and who he is. Therefore the use of the word "frankly" in either Matthew or Luke would be redundant.

There may be in Mark's use of *parrêsiq* an echo of the speech of the resurrected, "living" Christ – a discourse which, however, never appears as such in Mark's story, assuming that Mark ends at 16:8. Such open or frank speech is more typical of gospels such as the gospel of John which are composed primarily of extended discourses of Jesus (Kelber 1990:75–6). In non-biblical writings such as the early post-resurrection discourse, *Pistis Sophia*, Jesus speaks to his disciples "openly" and "face to face without parables" (Hennecke and Schneemelcher 1963:255–6). Similarly, in the non-biblical *Apocryphon of James*, Jesus's pre-death parables are contrasted to his post-resurrection open speech with his disciples at 7:1–10 (Cameron 1982:59ff.).[3] The open speech of the resurrected Jesus in these writings stands in striking contrast to the ambiguous, parabolic language of the pre-Easter, earthly Jesus favored in the synoptic gospels.

The reader might expect then to find the word *parrêsia* in the transfiguration episode (Mark 9:2–13), which follows immediately after the encounter at Caesarea Philippi. The transfiguration story appears to be a post-resurrection story which Mark and other synoptic gospels have transplanted to a pre-crucifixion setting. John Dominic Crossan has argued that Mark, which contains no post-resurrection appearances of Jesus, has transposed elements of a resurrection tradition from the non-canonical gospel of Peter back to an earlier point in the narrative (1985:172; 1988:*passim*). Crossan's argument is supported by the explicit juxtaposition of transfiguration and resurrection in *Pistis Sophia*. Thus it is somewhat surprising that even in Mark's transfiguration story, *parrêsia* does not appear. The disciples are terrified and do not understand what Jesus says. What has happened is not clear to them, although Jesus once again speaks of the son of man (9:9, 12), as he did in the Caesarea Philippi episode.

The gospel of John often uses *parrêsia* in reference to Jesus's words. John's usage is not without its own ambiguity, however, for Jesus's withholding and giving of plain teaching plays an important part in John's gospel. John is quite ambiguous about Jesus's "openness," and John contrasts this openness explicitly to Jesus's speech in "figures," *paroimiai*, (John 16:25–9). This play between openness and secrecy may be found in several of the passages in John where *parrêsia* occurs. Although John's narrative has no direct parallel to the Caesarea Philippi encounter, a similar episode does appear at John 6:67–71. *Parrêsia* does not occur in this episode, but it does appear (for the very first time in John) three times in the next chapter, in relation to questions of openness and hiddenness.

In summary, in the gospel of John the word *parrêsią* is common, and in the gospels of Matthew and Luke the word is unknown; only in Mark is *parrêsią* unusual, both linguistically and theologically. It would seem that Mark's use of the word highlights a prevailing *lack* of frankness – that is, this narrative moment is a unique one for Mark, a moment which attracts the reader's attention. This is not the case for the other canonical gospels. For these reasons it is remarkable that the gospel of Mark would have Jesus speak frankly (or plainly or openly, for that matter). *Parrêsią* is symptomatic of something peculiar in Mark which does not figure in the other gospels.

Why is this peculiarity significant, and what does it signify about the gospel of Mark? *Parrêsią* is a term that was used in antiquity to characterize the candor and lack of reserve on the part of the Cynic philosophers. It referred to the harsh and shameless speech of those eccentric men, which was often accompanied by outrageous behavior (Vaage 1992). According to Heinrich Schlier (Kittel V 1967:871–4), the word refers to freedom from restraint in speech. *Parrêsią* is sometimes treated as synonymous with, or at least closely related to, *exousia*, a noun which, along with the verb *katexousiazousin*, appears eleven times in Mark. *Exousia* is often translated as "authority" (e.g. Mark 2:10), and in Mark *exousia* is usually understood as referring to the possession of a power or right to do or say something.

However, we must be careful not to exaggerate the relation between *parrêsią* and *exousia* in Mark. In Mark's narrative, Jesus's *exousia* is uncertain because of narrative ambiguity regarding his identity, as in Mark 1:22 (teaching with authority), 1:27 (healing with authority), and 2:10 (the son of man's authority), where those who are with Jesus are astonished or amazed at his words and deeds. In 11:28–33, the word appears four times as Jesus's *exousia* is contested by the chief priests, scribes, and elders in the temple ("fulfilling" the prediction of 8:31). In Mark 6:1–6, where the word does not appear, Jesus definitely lacks authority, and it is his turn to marvel. In 3:15 and 6:7, Jesus gives *exousia* to the disciples; in Mark 10:42, the "great men" of the Gentiles "exercise power (*katexousiazousin*) over them"; and in Mark 13:34, the master gives authority to his servants.

Although the gospel of Luke never uses the word *parrêsią*, this term does appear twelve times in Luke's sequel, the Acts of the Apostles.[4] Is it significant that the two volumes of Luke and Acts reserve this word for the second volume only? *Parrêsiạ* appears eighteen times in the New Testament epistles, most frequently in Hebrews and 1 John. In these texts, the term generally seems to refer to the ability of an apostle to speak freely because of power given to that apostle by Christ or God, and in these cases, the context suggests that the meaning of *parrêsiạ* is close to that of *exousia*. In Colossians 2:15, *exousias* and *parrêsiạ* are set over against one another ("[God] disarmed the principalities and powers and made a public example of them," RSV). In this case, *tas exousias* ("the powers") is conjoined with *tas archas* ("the principalities"). *Parrêsiạ* is relatively rare in the Septuagint (the Greek translation of the Jewish scriptures), where it sometimes is associated with God but just as often is not. In 3 Maccabees 7:12, *parrêsiạ* is apparently set over against the *exousia* of the king ("freely and without royal authority or supervision," RSV).

Thus *parrêsiạ* in Mark 8:32 does not necessarily carry overtones of *exousia*. In fact, the word *exousia* does not appear with *parrêsiạ* in Mark 8:31–2, or anywhere else in Mark's Caesarea Philippi story.

> Then Jesus and his disciples went forth to the villages of Caesarea Philippi; and on the way he questioned his disciples, asking them: Who do people say that I am? They answered and said: John the Baptist; and others say Elijah, and others one of the prophets. Then he asked them: And you, who do you say I am? Peter answered and said to him: You are the Christ. Then he warned them to tell no one about him.
>
> Then he began to explain to them that the son of man must suffer much and be rejected by the elders and the high priests and the scribes, and be killed, and rise up after three days. He was telling them frankly. And Peter laid his hand upon him and tried to warn him, and he turned about and looked at his disciples and reproved Peter and said: Go behind me, Satan; because you do not think the thoughts of God, but of men.
>
> (Mark 8:27–33)

Any *exousia* which is exercised in this episode is ambiguous, for the word *parrêsiạ* is found in the midst of an exchange of rebukes and counter-rebukes between Jesus and Peter. The disciples' reaction to Jesus's frank words is unusual even for Mark. Peter immediately responds negatively to the son of man saying, and this in turn leads to Jesus's harsh reply (8:33), which equates Peter with Satan and separates the thoughts of God from the thoughts of men.[5] Jesus is "rebuked" (RSV), *epitiman*, by Peter and "rebukes," *epetimêsen*, Peter in return. The same verb appears at Mark 8:30, immediately after Peter's confession: Jesus "rebukes" them to tell no one. In Mark 4:39, Jesus rebukes the sea, and elsewhere he rebukes unclean spirits (Mark 1:25, 9:25); Bartimaeus is also rebuked (by "many people") when he cries out, "Jesus, son of David, have pity on me" (10:47).

Thus the strangeness of Jesus speaking frankly is directly tied to the perplexing question (in Mark at least) of Jesus's identity and of his relation to the Christ and to the son of man. Whatever the reader makes of Jesus's *exousia* in Mark, it never provokes this sort of response from the disciples. The people are amazed at Jesus's authority and Jesus's opponents contest it, but the disciples receive it. In contrast, in Mark 8:32b Peter rejects Jesus's frank saying, perhaps because of its frankness. It is a situation of open conflict between Peter's messiah language and Jesus's son of man language. Is this the only place in Mark where the disciples, or one of them anyway, understand Jesus? Or do they understand him even here? Mark does not tell the reader what words Peter had to say when he rebuked Jesus, in contrast to the version in Matthew 16:22, but these words in Matthew also effectively "soften" the conflict.

Although *parrêsią* appears nowhere else in Mark, it is echoed in the second of the three Markan passion predictions (Mark 9:30–2):

> Going from there they proceeded through Galilee, and he did not want anyone to be aware of them; for he was teaching his disciples, and telling them: The son of man will be turned over into the hands of men, and they will kill him; and three days after being killed he will rise up. But they did not understand what he said, and they were afraid to ask him.

In this passage, the word *rhêma*,[6] "what he said," apparently refers to the passion prediction itself (9:31). Matthew's parallel (17:22–3) omits *rhêma*, but Luke 9:45 keeps it. The saying at Mark 9:30–2 also repeats Jesus's request to the disciples "not [to] have any one know it" (RSV), although here "it" apparently refers to the fact that they "passed through Galilee," or perhaps it refers to what Jesus was saying, but not to the disciples' understanding of who Jesus is.

Liddell and Scott (1940) note that *rheô*, which shares the same root with *rhêma* and *parrêsią*, also means "to flow" or "gush," as in "gush with blood."[7] Is Jesus then gushing in Mark 9:32 about the suffering of the son of man? Unlike the confrontation at Caesarea

Philippi, there is no rebuking on this occasion, but the episode does end in the disciples' failure to understand what Jesus said, *to rhêma*. In Mark, *rhêma* reverberates with *parrêsia* around the strangeness of "the son of man." However, neither *parrêsia* nor *rhêma* appears in Mark's wording of the third passion prediction (10:32–4). *Rhêma* appears only at one other point in Mark, where Peter recalls "what Jesus had told him" (14:72), that is, that Peter would betray him. And yet, it is the *son of man's* betrayal that Jesus predicts in Mark 9:31 and 10:33, just as it is the "son of man" about whom he speaks frankly in 8:32.

THE SON OF MAN

> Thus is translated into narrative the schematic opposition of silence and proclamation. We find it in the parables, in the beginning of the gospel and in its end, as well as in intermediate narratives.
>
> (Kermode 1979:140)

It is strange that Jesus speaks "frankly" at all in the gospel of Mark. It is even stranger that Jesus speaks frankly of the "son of man," *ton huion tou anthrôpou*. To what or whom does the phrase, "the son of man," refer, and how would anyone speak frankly of him? Mark represents the teaching in 8:31 in indirect quotation,[8] leaving to the reader the task of imagining the actual words of the character Jesus. If the imagined Jesus says (as a direct quote), "The son of man must suffer," or words to that effect – as he does in the parallel passage in Luke 9:22, and also in the remaining two passion predictions in Mark – then does the meaning of these words become clear? On the other hand, if the imagined Jesus says, "*I* must suffer" – which does not appear as such in any of the texts, although Matthew 16:21 presents such a statement in indirect discourse – then why does Mark say that Jesus talked about the son of man? Jesus never says, "I am the son of man," in Mark, nor exactly that in any other biblical gospel.[9]

Are we entitled to assume, as many scholars do, that the reader knows who the son of man is, and even *what* the son of man is? Is Jesus in fact the son of man, according to the story of Mark? If there is an equation, "Jesus = son of man," in the gospel of Mark, it is established not by Jesus's words but by Mark's narrative in which Jesus's predictions of suffering (for the son of man [Mark 10:33–4]) come true for Jesus himself. With this narrative self-fulfillment coincides also the self-referential theme of fulfillment of the scriptures.[10] "[T]he son of man goes his way as it has been written concerning him, but woe to that man through whom the son of man is betrayed" (Mark 14:21). Judas betrays Jesus, but *Jesus* betrays the "son of man" in his "confession" before the high priest at Mark 14:62 ("I am he [the son of God], and you will see the son of man sitting on the right of the power and coming with the clouds of the sky"). Yet Jesus "fulfills" the son of man prophecies *not* as the son of man but instead as the Christ/son of God (14:61) and the king of the Jews (15:2).

Mark alone cannot establish the equation of Jesus with the son of man. A great deal must be supplied by the reader. In the other biblical gospels, the disciples (and the reader) have much less difficulty identifying Jesus as the son of man, but in Mark the equation is at best a paradoxical one. Of course, if one reads Mark in the larger literary context of the New Testament – and nearly 2,000 years of Christian theologizing – then the paradox of Jesus's identity is resolved as a matter of faith: Jesus is both the son of man and the son of God. The serious inconsistencies between the various appearances of the phrase, "the son of man," in the gospel of Mark can be overlooked. On the other hand, if Mark could be considered solely in terms of its own narrative totality (limited and incomplete as that is) and apart from the larger biblical and theological context, then the results would be less clear. Such a naive reading of Mark is impossible in reality, but if the reader does not entertain this naive reading hypothetically, she risks missing important ideological features of the text, including the remarkable strangeness of Jesus's frank utterance of the saying about the suffering of the son of man.

Previous to Mark 8:31, the phrase "son of man" appears three times, always in direct quotation from Jesus. At Mark 2:10, "the son of man has authority to forgive sins upon earth,"[11] and at 2:28, "the son of man is lord even of the sabbath." The authority of the son of man is equal to that of God in these two sayings, although the resonance between the "son of man" who is "lord (*kurios*) even of the sabbath" (Mark 2:28) and the human "man" (*ton anthrôpon*) "for the sake of" whom the sabbath was made (2:27) may raise serious doubts about this equation of the son of man with God. However, on the third occasion, in Mark 3:28, Jesus states that "all shall be forgiven the sons of men (*tois huiois tôn anthrôpôn*) ...," using the phrase here more clearly to refer to ordinary human beings. "Son of man" and similar phrases are often used in the Septuagint in this latter way.[12]

This "sons of men" statement is sometimes not regarded by biblical scholars as a "son of man" saying. The effect of treating the verse as a "son of man" saying is to invert the role of the son of man, from divine lord to humble human being. In its parallel to this saying, the gospel of Matthew 12:31 has only *tois anthrôpois*, "men." The gospel of Luke 12:10 omits the phrase entirely, but quite similar phrases appear in Luke 16:8 and 20:34 ("the sons of this age," *hoi huioi tou aiônos toutou*) and in gospel of Thomas sayings 28[13] and 106. The "sons of men" who are forgiven in Mark 3:28 have apparently been replaced by the divine "son of man" who is spoken against in Matthew 12:32 and Luke 12:10. But in Mark, the "sons of men" are human beings.

When Jesus's family arrives on the scene shortly after Jesus's "sons of men" statement in Mark 3, the question arises of whose son or brother Jesus is (3:31–5). His answer to the crowd is, "whoever does the will of God is my brother and sister and mother." In this passage and in Mark 6:3, Jesus is identified as "the son of Mary and the brother of James and Joseph and Judas and Simon" (6:3). Perhaps both of these texts should also be read as "son of man" passages, that is, as passages in which the common humanity of "the son of man," insofar as this phrase applies to Jesus, is emphasized.

Furthermore, what is to be made of the next appearance of the words, "the son of man," at Mark 8:38: "He who is ashamed of me, ... of him will the son of man be ashamed when he comes in the glory of the father with the holy angels?" Do we have here another case of paradoxical inversion of the son of man role, in this case from the position of human lowliness to that of divine glory? If so, what does this paradox do to the significance of Jesus's "frank" saying at Mark 8:31? Is there indeed just one son of man in the gospel of Mark? What does the glorious son of man (or the ones at 13:26 or 14:62) have to do with the son who suffers and dies?[14] What is the connection of any of these sons of man with the son who "came not to be served but to serve, and to give his own life for the redemption of many" (Mark 10:45)? Are these sons of man distinct from each other, or from Jesus? But if they are distinct from Jesus, then why does Peter react as he does to Jesus's frank words in Mark 8:31?

The gospel of Mark does not answer any of these questions; it only raises them. Therefore the teaching at Mark 8:31 cannot be spoken "frankly." When the saying at 8:31 describes the son of man as suffering, being rejected, killed, and rising, it appears to contradict both the theological and the narrative significance of the first two "son of man" sayings in Mark, as well as other sayings which imply that the son of man is a divine being. Jesus's frank saying, along with other sayings about the family and the suffering of the son of man, implies that the son of man is a human being.

Jesus tells the story of the son of man just as Mark tells the story of Jesus. Mark is a gospel in which paradox and ambiguity regarding Jesus's identity appears frequently, but how could this ambiguity be presented "frankly?" Although in some cases (for example, 2:10) Jesus appears to have himself in mind when he uses this phrase, at other points the reference of the words, "the son of man," is not so clear.[15] For example, in Mark 2:28, does Jesus declare himself the lord over the sabbath, or is it the disciples eating the grain who are so identified? Are they the human sons of men (as in 3:28), or has Jesus (as divine son of man) granted them a special prerogative? How much can be presumed concerning the ability of disciples, Pharisees, or readers to identify correctly the meaning of these words, "the son of man?" In short, can these words be uttered frankly by anyone? Neither the character Jesus, nor the story of Mark in which he appears, can ever decisively resolve the relation between Jesus and the son of man. The strangeness of Jesus's frank words about the son of man arises from a failure of denotation.

DENOTATION AND CONNOTATION

> Whatever the manner in which it "caps" the denoted message, connotation does not exhaust it: there always remains "something denoted" (otherwise the discourse would not be possible) and the connotators are always in the last analysis discontinuous and scattered signs, naturalized by the denoted language which carries them.
>
> (Barthes 1967a:91)

The relationship between linguistic denotation and connotation is a theme that occupied Roland Barthes throughout his career. In his earlier, more typically structuralist writings, the issue played an important role in Barthes's understanding of language and meaning. However, even these early writings give indications of concepts which he later developed into a poststructuralist analysis of literature and culture. Connotation and denotation continued to figure as a topic of interest for Barthes in several essays that were written shortly before his death.

Barthes draws on a distinction which has been current in the philosophy of language at least since the writings of John Stuart Mill (1874).[16] Denotation is language used "normally," the "ordinary" or "proper" meanings of words in a sentence. It is what is sometimes called the "literal" meaning. Denotation is closely related to what Gottlob Frege called "reference," the ability of a word to pick out an object (whether actual or ideal) and thereby to "saturate" the function of a well-ordered sentence.[17] This in turn completes the sentence and allows it to be determined as true or false. Along similar lines, Irving Copi and Carl Cohen define denotation as the "extension" of a word – the list of objects to which the word may refer (1990:141). Denotation "translates" reality (Barthes 1988:174).

The sentence is a sign, and as such it unites a signifier (physical marks, sounds, gestures, etc.) to a signified (a mental reproduction of some object). This union is denotation. Connotation builds on denotation by adding a second level of meaning. Barthes follows here the views of Louis Hjelmslev: "*a connoted system is a system whose plane of expression is itself constituted by a signifying system*" (1967a:89–90, Barthes's emphasis). In other words, the denotative totality of signifier and signified (a "signifying system") becomes itself the signifier (the "plane of expression" or "connotator," as Barthes calls it) of some further signified (the connotation). Copi and Cohen define connotation as the "intension" of a word – a set of attributes which provides a "criterion for deciding" whether a word denotes a particular object (1990:141). However, whether connotation can be simply identified with the intension or "sense" (Frege) of a word and denotation identified with its extension or reference is a matter of some debate among philosophers of language. As Umberto Eco notes (1976:86), there is a danger of confusing semantic and logical categories.

Connotation and denotation occur only according to convention-ally-established codes. In connotation, the reference of a signifier swerves from a denotative signified to a sense "beyond" the denota-tion. If I say that the cream cheese is turning greenish-blue, the sentence denotes a change in the color of the cheese. However, that sentence also connotes that the cheese is becoming moldy. By playing on the sense of the word, connotation requires a shift in the context in which the statement is understood, with the result that the denoted meaning is obscured. Connotation is a parasite on meaning (Barthes

1967a:30): it is the "static" which "releasing the double meaning on principle, corrupts the purity of communication" (Barthes 1974:9). Denotation is *to rhêma*, the word. Connotation is *[to] pan [to] rhêma*, that is, the full or whole word, or *parrêsia*. Frankness is only possible within a connotative system.

This view of the relation between denotation and connotation is not unlike the conventional view of metaphor, to which it is closely related, as well as to the conventional understanding of fiction as secondary to, and meaningless apart from, the non-fictional. Metaphor, fiction, and connotation are all cases of what Frege called "quotation": "In direct quotation, a sentence designates another sentence, and in indirect speech a thought" (1952:65). Every narrative is a quotation, according to Frege. The story features a narrator (or implied author) who tells a narratee (or implied reader) about something. The reference of the sentences which constitute the narrative is disrupted by the separation of levels between the telling (the discourse) and that which is told (the story).[18] "The quotations from which a text is constructed are anonymous, irrecoverable, and yet *already read*: they are quotations without quotation marks" (Barthes 1979b:77).

Because of the importance of convention in these theories of connotation and of metaphor, they are fundamentally conservative. The conventions reflect and defend an accepted order of things. Any change in the conventional codes that govern the various levels of language is regarded as improper or at least irregular, as it would contribute to misunderstanding. The conventional theories of connotation and of metaphor share the idea that language has a primary level of meaning, in which it operates properly and more or less transparently. Every word in a language (at any given time) has one or more primary meanings. Everyone who knows the language has access to the primary level, the denotation or "literal" meaning, and they probably in fact learned it before learning the more subtle and fluid connotations. However, this level of denotation can be added to through accidental misuse or creative distortion to produce further levels of meaning which usually are less accessible or transparent. When a word is used metaphorically, it becomes the "vehicle" for a secondary meaning (the "tenor") which is substituted for the primary meaning. The tenor is often an imaginative extension of one of the primary meanings, and it sometimes becomes so widely accepted that it becomes in effect another primary meaning of the word. When this happens, the metaphor "dies."

Even in his early writings, Barthes was not satisfied with this view of language, and his dissatisfaction becomes apparent in his discussions of connotation and denotation.[19]

> [T]he raw material of denotation, with its dictionary and its syntax, is a system like any other; there is no reason to make this system the privileged one, to make it the locus and the norm of a primary, original meaning, the scale for all associated meanings.
>
> (Barthes 1974:7)

The privileging of denotation is ideological, according to Barthes. In a short essay, "The Advertising Message," first published in 1963 (1988), Barthes explores this idea. He imagines the case of a Martian[20] – "someone from another world" – who knows the vocabulary and syntax of "our language" quite well but is "utterly ignorant" of human culture. The Martian is "deaf" to metaphor and connotation. Yet she is able to receive "a perfectly constituted message," a denotation with no trace of connotation:

> There is indeed, here on this first level, a sufficient set of signifiers and this set refers to a body, no less sufficient, of signifieds.
>
> (1988:174)

The Martian is able to understand a sentence only in terms of the accepted denotation of its words. She is "stupid" in regard to any culturally derived information which might be inferred, no matter how easily, from the sentence. This describes the "analytical character" of denotation as distinct from connotation. The Martian is like a reader who reads the gospel of Mark in absolute isolation from the literary and theological traditions to which it has been bound. She is a reader from the outside. Such naïveté can only be approximated as an extreme, impossible limit.

Elsewhere Barthes admits that rigorous denotation is "utopian" (1983:30). However, there is a problem with the concept of denotation even at this hypothetical level. The Martian knows a human language but does not know about human culture. Could one learn a language without any understanding of the cultural matrix in which that language is bound? In other words, is denotation actually conceivable apart from connotation? And if it is not, then how can connotation be built upon denotation? Might it even be that denotation is *derived from* connotation,[21] that

112

denotation is a degenerate form of connotation? Barthes turns the traditional understanding of the denotation–connotation relationship on its head. He notes that "denotation is not the truth of discourse: ... [denotation is] a particular, specialized substance used by the other [connotative] codes to smooth their articulation" (Barthes 1974:128). Denotation is "raw" language, crude and untenable (Barthes 1977b:62–3).

Connotation defines the semiological system of myth, according to Barthes (1972:114–15).[22] It is connotation which makes possible the fictional worlds of narrative; without connotation the "readerly" text, the text of pleasure, would be impossible. Barthes contrasts the analytical character of denotation to the "total message," *pan rhêma*, of connotation, which in the case of the advertising message means always only one thing: "buy me!" The signified of every connotation, Barthes says, "is at once general, global and diffuse; it is ... a fragment of ideology" (1967a:91). The entirety of the denotative sign (signifier–signified) is itself the connotator of this ideology.

The specifics of the denotation no longer matter (every advertisement for every product connotes only this one thing), but they are nonetheless indispensable; as Barthes says, there can be no connotation without denotation. The resulting double message "disconnects" the denotative meaning and thus supports an illusion or dream (an ideology) of naturalness; this is the "innocence" of language (Barthes 1986:65–6).

> The excellence of the advertising signifier thus depends on the power ... of *linking* its reader with the greatest quantity of "world" possible: ... experience of very old images, obscure and profound sensations of the body, poetically named by generations, wisdom of the relations of man and nature, patient accession of humanity to an intelligence of things through the one incontestably human power: language.
>
> (1988:177–8, his emphasis)

Barthes concludes that the advertising message, in its use of connotation, serves as the paradigm of *all* narrative. What is true of the advertising message is true of every story, including the stories in the Bible, such as the gospels. In narrative the meaning (or in Barthes's text, *franchise*, "frankness") returns at the secondary, connotative level, after having been delivered from the primary level of denotation. The advertising message is explicit about its own doubleness: "the second signified (the [advertised] product) is

113

always exposed unprotected by a frank [*franc*] system, i.e., one which reveals its duplicity, for this *obvious* system is not a *simple* system" (1988:178, his emphases). The "natural" quality of the advertised object (or of any narrative message) arises from the symbol-system of realism which denotation produces through the flux of the sentence, but this realism is impossible apart from the artificial, ideological nature of the message. The message says one thing and tells another. It says, quite "literally," that "this is a metaphor."

What, then, does Jesus mean when he speaks frankly of the son of man? Is he saying, as readers usually assume, "This is me?" Or is his very frankness itself a sign that the son of man can never, even – or perhaps especially – in Jesus's words in Mark, be anything but a metaphor, or a fiction, that Jesus can only be the son of man in a parabolic, paradoxical story, that Jesus's own relation to the son of man is indirect and artificial – "natural" only in the sense (as Barthes makes clear) that the natural is itself always unreal, fictional, ideological?

> [H]owever discontinuous language itself may be, its structure is so fixed in the experience of each man that he recognizes it as a veritable *nature*: do we not speak of the "flux of speech"? What is more familiar, more obvious, more natural, than a sentence read?
>
> (Barthes 1986:94, his emphasis)

Jesus speaks frankly in Mark 8:32 because his saying about the son of man in Mark 8:31 comes as close as possible to a purely connotative statement. Like the advertising message, Jesus's statement cannot be taken at face value. Although no language can dispense entirely with denotation, as Barthes says, Jesus's statement comes as close to that extreme as possible. Its denotation is nonsensical, and therefore it refers to nothing. The saying's denotative content approaches zero, and it explicitly requires a connotative convention to elucidate it. This is why the absolutely naive reader (like the Martian, a limit case, but also necessarily an outsider) is unable to understand this saying; the frankness of Jesus is a symptom. Much like the modern advertising message, Mark's comment upon the saying denotes (frankly) that this is the case. Mark is frank about Jesus's frankness.

Of course, the Christian reader has no difficulty understanding Jesus's saying as rich with theological and narrative significance, just as the consumer in modern Western civilization has no difficulty understanding advertising messages. Christians are not Martians in relation to this text! Corresponding to the conventions of realism that lend to the advertising message its quality of naturalness is an elaborate set of theological conventions which enable the reader of Mark to encounter this narrative as though it were transparent. The Christian reader will unconsciously read Mark 8:32 as "naturally" and clearly identifying Jesus as both the son of man and the Christ. The believing reader is an insider, aware of the saying's connotations.

In fact, non-Christian readers of Mark will also encounter this passage as though its meaning were clear, providing they also are not Martians – in other words, providing they have been sufficiently enculturated with the generalized "Christian values" which dominate in the so-called First World and which (via mass media) are now readily accessible even to peoples and cultures in other parts of the world.[23] Although these values are increasingly secularized and the Christian element in them is questionable, the correspondence highlighted by this frankness nevertheless suggests that a strong relationship exists between Western Christian thought and the conventions of literary realism – the metalinguistic system which enables us to read a great many stories.

For Barthes's Martian reader, however, the advertising message is simple, innocent, and utterly misleading, for the denotations of advertising messages are always trivial and their connotations are of supreme importance. The Martian reader will always be mystified by the second level of meaning, the level of connotative *pan rhêma*. For the Martian who reads Mark, there is no messianic secret, no passion prophecy, no christological revelation, for these do not and cannot appear at the level of denotation. The naive reading of Mark cannot understand Jesus's frankness; like the Martian, the naive reader is an outsider, for whom the text is always parabolically obscure. Jesus's "son of man" saying in Mark 8:31 is a point of impenetrability, where the Martian, no matter how much of the language she knows, can proceed no further. In Jesus's frankness, the parabolic estrangement of the outsider, and indeed of the entire text of Mark, is confirmed.

INTERTEXTUALITY

The Word, here, is encyclopaedic, it contains simultaneously
all the acceptations from which a relational discourse might
have required it to choose. It therefore ... is reduced to a sort
of zero degree, pregnant with all past and future specifica-
tions.

(Barthes 1967b:48)

Intertextuality and connotation are closely bound together; indeed,
intertextuality is driven by connotation. "To read in any real way,
then, is to enter into connotation" (Barthes 1977b:79). Therefore,
intertextuality is not a purely individual matter, for even the most
private of readings is, like all language, ultimately a shared experience. The language of the text is always a public language. My
reading is formed in tension not only with my own reading history,
but with that of many others, even though I have no knowledge of
most of these other readers.

"Intertextuality" is the name for that which holds a textual
universe together and gives it meaning. Intertextuality refers to an
essential characteristic of every reading, namely, that there can be no
first reading, no truly naive reading, no purely denotative reading.
Every reading is always preceded by some understanding of what is
to be read. And yet, paradoxically, intertextuality also entails that the
same book can never be read twice. The second reading will
necessarily be of a "different" book – a book in a different
intertextual configuration and in a changed intertextual web. Each
reading is unique, overshadowed by a singular complex of other
readings, in which the reading reflects all the other readings, as in a
hall of mirrors. The reader is the product of her previous readings,
which she brings to every "new" reading. Yet as soon as the new
reading enters into the intertextual network, it transforms all of the
preceding readings.

Intertextuality is an uncontrollable gush or flux of meaning (from
connotation to denotation and back again), a vibration or oscillation
which can never be suppressed. Intertextuality is always at least
partly unconscious. To seek complete intertextual self-awareness (if
that were possible) would be to attempt to think the unthinkable, to
unravel meaning and separate denotation from connotation, and
ultimately, among other things, to become a naive reader, a Martian.
Insofar as the biblical texts are full of passages such as the one
considered here, the semiotician who strives to become a naive

reader moves in a direction diametrically opposed to that of traditional theological readings: she seeks a text stripped bare of all meaning, an inert, alien, inscrutable thing, a token without a type. She seeks a sort of "reading degree zero," which of course can never be found.

There are different types of intertextuality: for example, that of an author who deliberately and explicitly alludes to another work, as in James Joyce's *Ulysses* or Tom Stoppard's play, *Rosenkrantz and Guildenstern are Dead*. A second type of intertextuality is encountered whenever one text draws upon or plays with a set of codes which were originally developed in the reading of another text. In this way much contemporary science fiction and fantasy literature draws upon biblical and other ancient mythological motifs. A third type of intertextuality is formed by the reverberation between stories that have arisen from a common narrative structure or genre, although the stories may come from different periods of history or even different cultures. The familiar three-fold or four-fold plot structure of fairy tales from all over the world would be an example of this. However, the aleatory type of intertextuality described here is more remote and accidental than any of these three.

The terms "frank" and "frankness" which appear in Barthes's essay are Richard Howard's translation of the French words *franc* and *franchise*. Therefore the intertextual coincidence between Barthes's essay and the gospel of Mark lies in a merely physical resemblance, like a crude pun, between Lattimore's use of the word "frankly" for *parrêsia* in Mark 8:32 and Howard's use of "frank" and "frankness" in "The Advertising Message." This intertextual word play arises from the accidental juxtaposition of these texts in the larger intertextual web which coincides with the interests and the reading of George Aichele. The resemblance between these translated words of course cannot explain why Jesus speaks frankly in Mark's text, but it does suggest that Jesus's frankness implies a double message.

The element of chance inherent in this type of intertextuality entails a playful and perhaps even irresponsible reading. It produces a naive reading, like that of Barthes's Martian. This element of chance offends against the belief that scholarship must be systematic, rational, or even scientific. The idea that understanding arises by chance is contrary to belief in intellectual rigor and discipline. Why choose these texts, and not others also linked by some chance word play? And if this juxtaposition is unique to my reading, then why should anyone else pay attention to it? Your reading will inevitably be different. But what if *all* readings are like this in some way? If all readings, in the last analysis, are founded upon random intertextuality such as this, then a postmodern abyss of truth and meaning opens up and threatens to swallow any intelligent reading.

Fantasy writers such as Italo Calvino, Stanislaw Lem, and Umberto Eco have already imagined for their readers the possibility of a gigantic super-computer impersonally scanning every text ever written, in every language, in every translation. The computer "reads" terabytes of text in the blink of an eye, cataloging every coincidence of word or phrase. Although this cybernetic monster might generate the true name of God, and thus the end of the universe, as an Arthur C. Clarke story once suggested, it is far more probable that this computerized reading would produce a great deal of trivia, and little of interest. Some may argue that this chapter is an example of the latter.

Yet, although the focus here is on the chance and purely physical intersection of two texts, the operation of my interest is hardly by chance. Each reader brings to bear upon the text an intertextual network that both defines and reflects a field of ideologies, beliefs, and interests. The reader's consciousness is generated by this network. Within the network, not every word is of equal value. The intertextual reading context causes one word or configuration of words to stand out, to draw the reader's interest, and at the same time it obscures other possible words and configurations. No reading is ever free from the concrete particularities of such a context.

Perhaps all that the different types of intertextuality share in common is an "effect of meaning" which one text has on another, although even that effect is no doubt quite different in the different types of intertextuality. In any case the effect only arises through a reading of the texts. Texts cannot produce or affect one another without the human medium of the reader. The coincidence of words between Barthes's essay and the gospel of Mark was already there, in the sheer materiality of the texts, the ink-marks-on-paper, before my own interests drew it into the light. However, the signifying effect of these physical things could only come into play when it began to operate in my reading, or someone else's – indeed, as was noted above, it is the intertext which defines the nature of the reading. Every reading is a re-reading, just as it is a rewriting, and it is in that "re-" that the intertext appears.

In his essay, "The Task of the Translator" (1968), Walter Benjamin describes what he calls "literal translation." (Benjamin's translation theory is discussed further in chapters 3 and 6 of this book.) Benjamin is a mystic, but he is also a materialist. Translation, he says, has nothing to do with meaning. There is only the tension between two texts, which is marked only at the level of the signifier. As I have read it, Barthes's text translates Mark in this Benjaminian sense: it illuminates the text of Mark as Mark cannot illuminate itself, revealing the frankness of Jesus to be the frankness of Mark itself, and yet a frankness concealing an enigma, a revelation disguising a mystery. Can Mark be frank about the frankness of Jesus? It would take yet another frank text to assure the reader of this – and perhaps that is indeed what the gospels of Matthew and Luke attempt to do, initiating a succession of texts which culminates, but only for the moment, in my own frankness.

At a certain point in two English translations and perhaps only here, two apparently quite different originals touch one another. Richmond Lattimore translated the word *parrêsią* from the gospel of Mark as "frankly," and Richard Howard translated Barthes's word *franchise* as "frankness." This is only a physical coincidence, but it is a suggestive coincidence. It presents an intriguing answer to the question posed in part 1 of this chapter: how can Jesus (or anyone) speak frankly of the son of man? Thus this aleatory intertextual contact is not insignificant. We are here not far from Benjamin's pure or true language that appears through the translation contract between texts. The connotative play between these two texts allows each of them to illuminate the other in ways untouched by denotation. Each text interrogates and transforms the other; each one becomes an "other" for the other, complementing it even as it reveals its irreducible otherness.

Intertextuality enables reading; without intertextuality there could be no reading. However, the juxtapositions of intertextuality also refer to physical accidents of the texts which interrupt the smooth flow of reading. The coincidence of signifiers breaks through preconceptions about the gospel, and it frustrates theological expectations. Meaning becomes subject to chance, and perhaps even itself the product of chance. The prospects for textual closure become more and more remote.

Mark's text and Barthes's text touch each other, but only through the medium of the translations by Lattimore and Howard. The point of contact is a mere accident, a material resemblance. Yet this accident reveals the stuff of the text, and the necessary violence done to the text by every reading. This physical play between two English translations is *insignificant* in the Benjaminian sense: there is no transfer of meaning from one text to the other. For this contact between two texts to occur, for it to become visible, the semiotic codes must be suspended, or at least fade away temporarily, revealing only the bare stuff, the physical marks or *hulê* (sheer matter) of the text[24] that readers necessarily interpret as the signifiers.

Because these codes are the product of intertextual networks, that is, networks of meaningful reading, a paradox results: for this chance intertextuality appears at a moment of incoherence, the failure of the word "frankly" to signify. The context of Jesus's frankness collapses because of the incoherence of his saying, an incoherence that is further manifested in the exchange of rebukes between Jesus and Peter. The connotative strangeness of Jesus's saying about the son of man emerges from the denotative strangeness of the gospel of Mark's announcement that the saying was a frank one. Once again, the reader's desire for frankness has been disappointed.

> The Word is no longer guided *in advance* by the general intention of a socialized discourse; the consumer ... receives [the Word] as an absolute quantity, accompanied by all its possible associations.
>
> (Barthes 1967b:48)[25]

6

READING BEYOND MEANING

THEOLOGY OF THE TEXT

[T]here will never be ... any theology of the Text.
(Derrida 1981:258)

In the previous chapters I have explored the possibility of reading the gospel of Mark from the outside, that is, in a way which attends constantly to the obscurity of the text. These chapters have uncovered selected instances of the *resistance* of the text of Mark to meaning, and how that resistance might be overcome by the reader. In this chapter and the next one, I want to explore the theoretical questions raised by these readings somewhat further.

I agree with Jacques Derrida's claim that there can be no theology of the text. I understand the word "text" to refer to the material aspect of the signifier, the physical stuff (*hulê*) of writing. Text is therefore an instance of what Derrida calls "différance," or ineffable writing. In fact, the materiality of text cannot be comprehended by any conceptual system. There can be no theology of the text because text is the trace which escapes the closure of the self-identical "volume," the completed "work," even as it inscribes that closure. As the disruption of metaphysical identity or presence which lies at the heart of every scriptural identity, the physical material of the text is itself meaningless.

The understanding of text outlined above differs greatly from the traditional understanding of text. The metaphysical idealism inherent in the traditional understanding of textual identity, or what text is, cannot comprehend and therefore must exclude the hyletic aspect of text. The traditional understanding allows one to speak of two or more readers reading "the same text" (book, story, poem, etc.) even though not only the physical objects of the reading but the editions and perhaps even the translations involved are different.[1] This understanding of text allows readers to agree or disagree about the legitimacy of an interpretation, the authority of an edition, or the accuracy of a translation, because it assumes that the text is the same for different readers even though the text appears in quite different physical forms. The invisible, underlying stratum which allows those who hold this understanding of text to posit the identity of the various objects is the text's meaning, the spiritual essence which binds many widely varying physical copies into the unity of "the same text." Furthermore, the traditional understanding of textual identity insists that this inner meaning of the text may be read correctly. It insists on the possibility of a reading from the inside which is a reading in the "spirit" of the text.

This traditional understanding of text is therefore also profoundly logocentric (Derrida 1981). According to this understanding, text is not "really" the concrete unique ink-and-paper thing which you might hold in your hand, scan with your eyes, file on a shelf, give away, or even throw in the trash. Instead, this understanding regards text as an ideal, spiritual substance, a Platonic form or concept of which the material thing is merely a "copy." The physical object is simply the medium, the channel in and through which the spiritual reality of the text, that is, its meaning, has become incarnate. This way of thinking seems quite "natural" to readers today, and this naturalness indicates that this view is profoundly ideological. The ideological naturalness of the traditional understanding in turn indicates how deeply ingrained in contemporary readers are these beliefs regarding textual identity.

Correlated closely to this ideological understanding of textual identity is a complex economy of text. This textual economy allows texts to be owned in three distinct but complicitous ways. The conspiracy among these three types of ownership in fact forms the traditional understanding of textual identity. Meaning is at the center of this system of values; what defines each of the three types of ownership, and their relations to one another, is the *desire* for meaning. These three types of ownership together establish a law of textual identity, a system which authenticates "my property" and delimits my rights and obligations in relation to the text. The law of textual identity grounds the legitimacy of meaning in various ways, including the possibility of a proper reading (a reading from the inside), an authorized edition, or an accurate translation. This law establishes the possibility of what Roland Barthes calls the readerly text.

The system of the law of text allows the text to have three owners: the first owner, the reader, normally owns one copy of the text, a physical object, the book. The reader desires, but has no guarantee of owning, the book's meaning. The second owner, the author, is the book's historical originator and therefore according to this law does own the book's meaning – the true meaning arising in the author's intention and reflected in every copy of the book. The author secures the book's meaning. In the modern world, there is also a third owner, the copyright holder, who may also be the author or the reader (or both). This owner possesses the legal right to disseminate copies, that is, to control the event of textual incarnation.[2] Each of these owners of the text may say, "This is my book," but the term "my book" does not mean the same thing for each of them. The book that I write is not "mine" in the same way that the book that I buy is mine, even if it is the same book.

This economy of triple ownership transforms the text into what Barthes calls the "work" (1979b).[3] Similarly, some analytic philosophers reserve the word "text" for the physical object (the words on a page), and they call the ideal or spiritual substance of the text the "work." The work is a self-identical artistic entity (for example, a particular story) which may be found embodied in various texts – different copies or editions or even translations (into other languages or other media) of "the same story." Barthes identifies the work with the readerly text, which he also calls the "text of pleasure." For Barthes, the work is defined by society's recognition of an author and thus of an authority: "One must realize that today it is the work's 'quality' ... and not the actual process of reading that can establish differences between books" (1979b:79). The work is meaningful and complete; it is an object of consumption. All three of the text's owners require the work to be a union of spirit and matter, that is, that spiritual meaning be "in" the physical body of the work to give it value. This union of spirit and matter can (and must) be broken by the reader in order for understanding to occur.

For the traditional understanding of text, then, meaning is "in" the text; it is the property of the text that qualifies it as a work. This understanding of textual identity therefore requires that a distinction be made between exegesis and eisegesis: exegesis draws (or leads) meaning out of the text, and eisegesis imposes the reader's beliefs upon or reads them into the text. No confusion may be permitted between these two types of reading. It is among other things an ethical distinction: both exegesis and eisegesis claim to be proper readings from the inside, but only one of them truly is. Exegesis respects the integrity of the text and reveals that meaning which is truly within it. Eisegesis violates the text and forces another, external meaning upon it. This understanding of textual identity is profoundly metaphysical, and it regards the text as a receptacle for information. The skillful reader can extract this information more or less undamaged from the text, and without imposing too many of her own preconceptions upon the text. Furthermore, the text is in some way connected to reality – a reality outside of the text itself. Extratextual reality grounds the proper meaning of the text, which in turn is inside of the text.

Of course, the traditional understanding of textual identity recognizes that no reading is entirely free of preconceptions, no matter how objective or unbiased the reader might be. Your readings are inevitably shaped by who you are, your previous experiences, feelings, and beliefs, and your current life situations, desires, and expectations. Crossing the cognitive gap between the receiver (reader) and the sender (author) of any message is a risky and sometimes dangerous business. The traditional understanding of text assures us that there are guarantees which lessen these difficulties and overcome the dangers in the transmission of meaning. These guarantees are provided by rigorous critical techniques, often historical, but also psychological, sociological, or literary. Completely objective analysis of a text is impossible, but with proper use of technique something approaching scientific consensus can be reached. The traditional understanding affirms that within the text itself there hides an accessible meaning, which one technique or another can reliably uncover. These techniques also provide ways to bridge the referential gap between text and extratextual reality, and thus to capture meaning and thereby close the circle of understanding. In other words, the reader is able to read from the inside.

Therefore one could just as well speak of the traditional understanding of text as a "theology" of textual identity. It is this very theology of textual identity which is refused by the postmodern understanding of textual differance, the materiality of the sign. The theologically indispensable distinction between exegesis and eisegesis has been seriously eroded in recent years. First New Criticism, then structuralism, and most recently (and far more radically) various forms of poststructuralism (including the views of Derrida, Barthes, and Michel Foucault) have with increasing vigor exposed and challenged theological presuppositions on which the traditional understanding of textual identity rests. As a result of these developments, the notion that each text contains within it a single true meaning – or any meaning at all, for that matter – has been abandoned by many. The question of reference – the connection between text and reality – is now very much up for grabs.[4] The metaphysical and ethical dimensions of this theology of textual identity are increasingly difficult to deny, or to defend. Nonetheless, as the following will show, this understanding speaks to a very deep need of the reader – the desire to read from the inside. The debate regarding the nature of text is far from over.

There will never be any theology of the text, says Derrida. I agree. However, if we must do without a theology of the text, then something else will have to take its place. As the concept and the identity of "text" become increasingly problematic and paradoxical for postmodern thinkers, an understanding of reading becomes more and more desirable. One can no longer rely upon a theology of textual identity, but one can explore in its place the possibilities for an alternative theology, a postmodern theology of reading. The textual object of postmodern reading becomes uncertain, elusive, and even mysterious, but the question of what reading is can be at least partly answered. In our belief that there is a connection between text and reality, we have overlooked or minimized theologically important dimensions of reading. These include the role of the reader in the production of meaning, the influence of ideology upon reading, and the resistance to meaning inherent within the text.

THE NON-READER

> Since the design of the novel is that of an initiation rite, ... the novel (even when practiced ironically) ends by overwhelming us in spite of ourselves, authors and readers alike; in the end it calls into question everything that we have in us and everything outside of us.
>
> (Calvino 1986:195)

Reading is an endless and violent playing with text, and the reader is in a perpetual struggle with the law of text. The reader draws her life from this law even as she disturbs it; she is a vector directing the movement of the law and giving it meaning. The law establishes the book as a meaning-filled work, as the product of a worker (an author) within a system of exchange which makes it available to be owned as a piece of property. Nevertheless it is the reader who determines the value of the book, as a work, for all of its various owners. The book that is not read is garbage, that is, it is useless, worthless.

The character Irnerio, in Italo Calvino's postmodern novel, *If on a Winter's Night a Traveler*, is a "non-reader." Irnerio has taught himself how not to read. He is not illiterate, not even "functionally illiterate."[5] Irnerio refuses to read. Yet Irnerio does not refuse to look at written words. Rather, he has learned how to see strange and meaningless ink marks on pages where others see words. Irnerio is somehow beyond reading; for him the books, pages, and words are no longer transparent vehicles for immaterial ideas, but are solid, opaque objects.

> I've become so accustomed to not reading that I don't even read what appears before my eyes. It's not easy: they teach us to read as children, and for the rest of our lives we remain the slaves of all the written stuff they fling in front of us.... The secret is not refusing to look at the written words. On the contrary, you must look at them, intensely, until they disappear.
>
> (1981:49)

For the non-reader, the written words eventually "disappear" – they disintegrate into not-quite-letters, senseless shapes, blobs of darkness on the white page. This is because the non-reader looks "*at them*," at the physical marks themselves, and not at what they mean. The words disappear into sheer materiality; they become meaningless deposits of ink on paper. They are not altered physically, but they lose their signifying potential. The words cease to be filled with what the philosopher Gottlob Frege (1952) called "sense"; they become nonsensical. For the non-reader, the printed words return to what Julia Kristeva (1984) calls the semiotic *chôra*.[6] Such texts could never be more-or-less accurate copies of an ideal, transcendent original. The texts that Irnerio sees do not contain any meaning "inside" them, nor are they signifiers pointing beyond themselves.

The words also disappear for ordinary readers, but for the opposite reason, and in the opposite "direction" from the non-reader. As you learned to read, the meaning of the words gradually came to dominate the physical text itself. You learned to conceptualize past or through the concrete marks that make up words and sentences, in order to "see" meanings or ideas (signifieds) that are represented according to conventional linguistic codes. You learned to hear the language with your mind's ear. As reading became easier, the materiality of writing (as an obstruction to sense) became an almost invisible, transparent vehicle. Now that you are a competent reader, what you actually read is what the written words "say," that is, their meaning. You can only read words insofar as the stuff of writing itself has become invisible to you. What you read is the idea within the word, and you don't like it if the materiality of the word obscures the idea.

Thus the written word may disappear in either of two directions, corresponding to the two components that make up language, according to structural linguistics – the physical medium (signifier) and the intelligible content (signified). For every reader, the word is caught in a tension between these two indispensable components – a tension which cannot be maintained, but only imagined as a midpoint between two unreadable extremes. When either of the differences which make signification possible – differences between signifiers, or differences between signifieds – is foregrounded (when they become visible to the reader), the word disappears. For all those who know how to read – and this includes non-readers such as Irnerio – one component or the other must be foregrounded. Unlike Irnerio, ordinary readers choose to foreground the signified: the concepts, feelings, and other mental products derived from reading. To foreground the material signifier of the writing rather than its signified meaning, as Irnerio does, seems ludicrous and irresponsible to these ordinary readers – it goes against the grain; it is unnatural.

Non-reading refuses to read by staying close to the physical letter, the *hulê* of the written word. This would correspond to Barthes's text of "bliss," which he also calls the writerly text (1974; 1975). The writerly text resists decidable coherence; the meaning of the text of bliss cannot be controlled by any reading.

> Pleasure in pieces; language in pieces; culture in pieces. Such texts are perverse in that they are outside any imaginable finality – *even that of pleasure*.
>
> (Barthes 1975:51–2, his emphasis)

> [T]o scatter the signifieds, the catechisms ... *language upon language*, to infinity.... That difference should not be paid for by any subjection: no last word.
>
> (Barthes 1977b:50, his emphasis)

A reader can become a non-reader only by a deliberate choice; such a choice reflects upon, and rejects, the ethics, economics, and theology implied by the traditional understanding of textual identity and sketched out above. The non-reader rejects the signified, and chooses only the signifier. However, a signifier as such is more than just the material stuff that constitutes it. A signifier without a signified is impossible; as we will see in chapter 7, it is a text without ideology. Hence the non-reader is impossible. Irnerio refuses the categories of ownership, at least when it comes to books.[7] If he were not such an agreeable fellow, and actually quite moral in his own strange way, you would have to think of Irnerio as evil.

Readers can sometimes become non-readers, although only in a limited and inadvertent way. When you attempt to decipher an unusual script, or study a language with a different alphabet, or reconstruct a text that has been physically damaged, the foregrounding of the signifier is unavoidable and often unpleasant. It is then that you become a non-reader. Of course, unlike Irnerio you are still *trying* to read, to make sense of the text. Irnerio notwithstanding, no one can actually learn not to read. Thus Irnerio represents an unreachable goal; this is why his subversions of literariness do not upset us. Instead, Irnerio amuses us.

Not to read is an impossible ideal, for the unconscious habits of reading cannot be entirely unlearned. Probably only the truly illiterate person – the one who can make nothing at all out of writing – can actually see the written word as nothing but a bunch of inky squiggles. For the illiterate person, what readers perceive as a text appears to be senseless marks which cannot be significantly distinguished from other similar squiggles. What the illiterate person sees are not signifiers, for that would require that they point to signifieds. These squiggles have no signifieds. But although he has this much in common with the illiterate person, Irnerio is not illiterate.

> For Irnerio all that counts is the life lived instant by instant; art for him counts as expenditure of vital energy, not as a work that remains, not as that accumulation of life that [the reader] seeks in books. But he also recognizes, without need of reading, that energy somehow accumulated, and he feels obliged to bring it back into circulation, using [the reader's] books as the material base for works in which he can invest his own energy, at least for an instant.

> (Calvino 1981:150)

Irnerio views books merely as things. He is an artist, and literature is his medium, but not as we might expect. Books are worthy in and of themselves, but only as the meaningless stuff, *hulê*, which Irnerio glues together into larger hunks and then carves into abstract sculptures. However, non-reading is not easy, even for a master such as Irnerio. How does he decide which book is the right one for a particular sculpture? Is his decision based solely on the physical matter of the book (color or shape of cover, size or thickness of pages, binding, typeface, etc.), or is Irnerio also somehow aware of the book's signified contents? Does the text's meaning somehow affect him; are Irnerio's sculptures a kind of "reading" after all?

> I fix the books with mastic, and they stay as they were. Shut, or open, or else I give them forms, I carve them. I make holes in them.
> ... The critics say what I do is important. Now they're putting all my works in a book.... A book with photographs of all my works. When this book is printed, I'll use it for another work, lots of works.
> ... There are some books that immediately give me the idea of what I can make from them, but others don't. Sometimes I have an idea, but I can't make it until I find the right book.
>
> (Calvino 1981:149)

This non-reader is *not* the same as the naive reader described in chapter 5. The naive reader (Barthes's Martian) reads only according to the codes of denotation. The non-reader does not read at all. However, the naive reader and the non-reader have much in common. Neither is an "ordinary" reader. Both the non-reader and the naive reader stand outside of the text; for each of them there is no meaning to be found "in" the text.

Non-reading points to one of the limit-conditions that define reading: the material stuff beyond which reading cannot go. By rejecting the logocentric theology implicit in the traditional understanding of textual identity, non-reading calls this theology to our attention. The non-reader is a sort of parasite on the literate world, or indeed, on literature itself. Irnerio cannot exist unless ordinary readers exist, unless an entire immense structure of civilization exists, including authors and publishing houses and scholars and bookstores and translators, as well as economic and educational and political systems. This civilized structure allows and requires readers to be (ordinary) readers. The ramifications of this larger structure provide the world and much of the plot of Calvino's novel.

LITERAL TRANSLATION

A text lives only if it lives *on*, and it lives *on* only if it is *at once* translatable and untranslatable.... Totally translatable, it disappears as a text, as writing, as a body of language. Totally untranslatable, even within what is believed to be one language, it dies immediately.

(Derrida 1979:102, his emphases)

The reader is made possible by the misplacing of words, that is, by the removing of words from their "living," oral context by writing them. Writing invites misunderstanding (Plato 1973:96–7). Every reading is a translation, a transfer (or "metaphor") of something which allegedly lies on or in the page – Frege's "sense" – to some other place inside the reader's mind. Yet as Irnerio makes clear, when he refuses to read, that "something" is not the physical stuff of the books themselves, but something else entirely. *Hulê* cannot be translated.

For the traditional understanding of textual identity, the goal of the translator is to retrieve the authentic message of the original, source text and then to re-embody the very same message in a new, target text; this is "dynamic equivalence." Because it contains the "same" message, the target text will then be the same as the source text. As noted above, the theology of textual identity has its own doctrine of incarnation for which the spiritual "word" enters into the written "flesh" to become the literary work.[8] It is only the ideal text, the "work," which can be translated, not the concrete, material text. Compared to its meaning, the physical aspects of the translated text are unimportant, and they can be modified and rearranged and ultimately sloughed off, like a mortal human body temporarily inhabited and eventually abandoned by an eternal soul. For the traditional understanding of textual identity, translation is exegesis, saving the authentic meaning and transporting it to a new body.

Walter Benjamin's essay, "The Task of the Translator" (1968), presents an alternative view of the theological dimension of texts and the operations of language – a view that is close to Irnerio's. Benjamin's views are also discussed in chapters 3 and 5 of this book. According to Benjamin, the goal of translation is not to transfer meaning (which can somehow be detached from its linguistic embodiment) from one textual body to another, but rather to contract a kind of reciprocity between the translation and the source text, so that the reader sees through both to what Benjamin calls "pure language." This pure or "true" language is not an historical, empirical language, but rather it is language itself, that is, language without purpose, meaning, or function. Pure language is language speaking only itself, endlessly.

> A real translation is transparent; it does not cover the original, does not block its light, but allows the pure language, as though reinforced by its own medium, to shine upon the original all the more fully.
>
> (Benjamin 1968:79)

Benjamin called the attempt to realize this goal "literal translation." Literal translation seeks "a language completely devoid of any kind of meaning function, language which would be pure signifier, ... paradoxical in the extreme" (de Man 1986:96–7). The ideal of literal translation is the interlinear text, "in which literalness and freedom are united" (Benjamin 1968:82). In the space between the parallel lines of the two texts, the target text and the source text are united in a true language "without the mediation of meaning." The goal of literal translation is to establish a tension between the source and the target texts that displays the "salutary strangeness" (Steiner 1975:389) of language. The target text reflects back upon and illuminates the source text as a fragment of pure language in a way that the source text is unable to reveal by itself. In translation the original text is brought (back) to life, and the pure language imprisoned within the text is "liberated" (Benjamin 1968:71–2, 80). It is literal translation, according to Benjamin, that "saves" the text.

For Benjamin, the principal question in translation theory is: how does the translated, target text illuminate the source text? There is no question of the two texts somehow being two versions of the same thing. The value of a translation lies in its interlinear engagement with the source text, not in its infallible transmission of some meaning hidden within that text. The preferred translation will not necessarily be the most accurate one, the clearest transmission of meaning, but rather the one which stands in productive tension with the source text. Such translations are inherently and necessarily ambiguous. Literal translation emphasizes the uniqueness of the material text through the other texts with which it is juxtaposed.

Literal translation does not transfer meaning from one text to another, but it provides an intertextual site from which meanings emerge. Like a tangent to a circle, the target text harmoniously supplements and complements the source text.

Derrida argues that the interlinear space of literal translation is utopian and uninhabitable; it is sacred and untouchable space (1985:115). What readers usually want from translation is the illusion that "this is what the source text means"; readers want to be able to assume textual identity between the source and target texts. However, literal translation makes the reader aware instead of the illusion itself. Literal translation makes the reader aware of the material aspect of the text (or "pure signifier"), not the text's meaning. The reader is forced to attend to the signifier, not (as she would prefer) the signified. The reading provided by literal translation is a reading from the outside.

The text itself as a physical object, the material space of the semiotic, lacks meaning. The letters of the alphabet from which text is assembled are meaningless in themselves. The physical text is truly "literal" text, and therefore it resists interpretation. It is unreadable, non-readable, non-readerly, as Irnerio demonstrates. As George Steiner suggests (Steiner 1975:471–4; also Benjamin 1968:74–5), the purpose of language is not to reveal but to conceal, and translation tests the power of language to hide meaning.

> [T]ranslation must in large measure refrain from wanting to communicate something, from rendering the sense, and in this the original is important to it only insofar as it has already relieved the translator and his translation of the effort of assembling and expressing what is to be conveyed.
>
> (Benjamin 1968:78)

According to Benjamin, literal translation seeks to uncover the language spoken by God in creating the universe, that is, a language of naming. For literal translation, the proper name is a matter of crucial importance: the name is in a sense the point at which language is most fully realized. Proper names cannot be translated, strictly speaking, because names do not "mean" as other words do. Names stand at the very edge of language, at the boundary of signification. As Frege would say, names refer but they have no sense. In other words, names have meaning (they point to things), and yet they do not mean (they cannot be defined). Thus names are at once impossible and unnecessary to translate. The name is language beyond meaning, without meaning; it is a language "lost" by humanity (because "confused" by God) at the Tower of Babel.

The understanding of language entailed by Benjamin's theory stands at the opposite extreme from the linguistic views of Bible translators such as Eugene Nida and J.P. Louw, whose theories are dominant in the Bible translation societies today. Nida's and Louw's theories of dynamic equivalence in translation reflect the traditional understanding of textual identity. Like the non-reading of Irnerio, Benjamin's notion of literal translation would draw language back to a point of ineffability, to the edge of the human world. Literal translation empties language of significance, reducing it to a material residuum alone. Benjamin's views on translation are explicitly expressed in the discourse of theology, and they approach closely a kind of Kabbalist mysticism. In the space and the silence between the parallel lines of two texts appears pure language, the pre-Babelian language of God. Literal translation refuses to allow the separation of meaning from its physical embodiment, and as a result it devalues the entire question of meaning. The ideal of exegetical translation is rejected.

However, the absence of an extratextual realm of meaning does not liberate translation but rather constrains it, and perhaps even renders it impossible in practice. Like the non-reader, the literal translation presents an unachievable goal, but also like the non-reader, literal translation points to an important limit-condition of language and meaning.

MATERIALIST READING

[F]rom this point of view, the narrative text [of Jesus's passion in the gospels] presents itself as the "textualization" of the body of Jesus or as the text-become-body of Jesus. It is a phantasm of the text which refers no doubt to a phantasm of the body divided (articulated) into topic-regions, or places of reception of a specific category of acts.

(Marin 1980:240, n. 124)

The reader wants the text to be an authority. She desires the "work" (Barthes 1979b), a textual identity worth owning, a text to be read from the inside. The law of text ownership is equivalent to the desire for translation, and for exegesis. Barthes identified this kind of reading with the readerly text, that is, the text of pleasure, which offers the illusion of coherence and completeness. The postmodern theology of reading with which this chapter, and indeed this entire book, is concerned seeks to explore the workings of the reader's desire for the work, and especially to uncover the hyletic textual material that is ignored and excluded by this desire. In their explorations of narrative codes, strategies of authority, and the production of meaning, Barthes's writings, especially *S/Z*, present an important contribution to this theology of reading.

S/Z is an immensely complex, close reading of Honoré de Balzac's novella, *Sarrasine*. In a format which both imitates and parodies traditional biblical commentary, Barthes partitions Balzac's story into 561 more or less arbitrarily divided "lexias," which he then analyzes in terms of five "codes" which he finds operating throughout Balzac's narrative.[9] A lexia is a "phrase" (in the sense that Jean-François Lyotard [1988] has given to that term), an individual semantic unit which may range in length from part of a sentence to several sentences. The codes are the cultural and intellectual filters through which the great abstract repository of *langue* (the general repertoire of a language) becomes the limited specificity of *parole* (the concrete utterance). The field of potential signification (Kristeva's "semiotic") is formed into a narrative world (Kristeva's "symbolic") by means of these codes. The codes permit and channel the conjunction of signifier and signified; through them the signs are forged.

> Alongside each utterance, one might say that off-stage voices can be heard: they are the codes: in their interweaving, these voices (whose origin is "lost" in the vast perspective of the *already-written*) de-originate the utterance: the convergence of the voices (of the codes) becomes *writing*, a stereographic space where the five codes, the five voices, intersect . . .
>
> (Barthes 1974:20–1)

The codes provide intertextual ("already-written") structures through which *Sarrasine* creates the readerly illusion of a transparent window, a story within a story, opening on to a coherent and realistic world ("the convergence of the voices"). In the larger, "framing" story of Balzac's novella, an unnamed man attempts, and fails, to seduce a beautiful young woman by agreeing to reveal to her the identity of a mysterious old man. This revelation takes the form of another story (the inner, "framed" story) of a foolish and impetuous artist, Sarrasine, who mistakes a beautiful castrato, La

134

Zambinella, for a woman and falls in love with "her," with fatal consequences for Sarrasine. Barthes's detailed analysis of these codes, one or more of which functions in each of the lexias, reveal that they work to conceal a deep narrative incoherence, an absence or deficiency (in effect a castration). Therefore the narrative results from incoherence, as the attempt to make sense out of it; and the narrative also produces incoherence, through its own failure and incompleteness. This incoherence is the writerly in the text, which emerges eventually in even the most readerly of texts.

> This catastrophic collapse always takes the same form: that of an unrestrained metonymy. By abolishing the paradigmatic barriers, this metonymy abolishes the power of *legal substitution* on which meaning is based: it is then no longer possible regularly to contrast opposites, sexes, possessions; it is no longer possible to safeguard an order of just equivalence; in a word, it is no longer possible to *represent*, to make things *representative*, individuated, separate, assigned . . .
>
> (Barthes 1974:215–16, his emphases)

> At its discreet urging, we want to ask the classic [readerly] text: *What are you thinking about?* but the text, wilier than all those who try to escape by answering: *about nothing*, does not reply, giving meaning its last closure: suspension.
>
> (Barthes 1974:217, his emphases)

The "writerly" is Barthes's term for the resistance which the text offers to coherent meaning – not an active resistance, as though of a living presence (such as the intention of an author), but a passive, inertial resistance, a kind of friction. The writerly is lodged in the materiality of the text as writing (thus Barthes's term). The textual material disrupts the narrative codes, interrupting their operations or setting them against one another. Therefore the writerly text is most readily identified through the frustration of the reader's desire for a readerly, followable narrative. The writerly consists in those elements of the text which remain opaque to reading, refusing to be reduced to a consistent and comprehensive understanding. Such elements are present in even the most readerly and realistic narratives, such as *Sarrasine*. The writerly elements turn the reading from the inside of such stories, or of any story, into a reading from the outside.

Every instance of language is at least somewhat writerly, and there are some texts which resist any coherent reading. These latter texts are postmodern, in Jean-François Lyotard's sense of the term: "that which searches for new presentations, not in order to enjoy them but in order to impart a stronger sense of the unpresentable" (1984:81). The conflict over meaning is somehow essential to the attempt to read these writings, which are in effect all surface, a mirror surface which reflects parabolically upon itself and which never opens up to reveal unambiguously any extratextual truth. Other texts of course are highly readerly and present an illusion of clearly-identified, univocal meaningfulness. In any case, the materiality of the text appears whenever its reference is suspended or otherwise incomplete. Barthes argues that the readerly work disappears whenever the writerly text appears; the text deconstructs the work (1979b:78–9).

Through his reading of Balzac, Barthes (like Benjamin) recovers in a secular way a strand of Kabbalah, the mystical rabbinic reading of Torah[10] which attended even to physical shapes of the Hebrew letters. The Kabbalist reading has been long overlooked by the logocentric idealist tradition which has dominated Western philosophical and theological thinking, that is, the traditional theology of textual identity. Barthes's reading *praxis* yields a Benjaminian translation; the "pure language" of the Balzacian text is uncovered, and it speaks.

Fernando Belo's book, *A Materialist Reading of the Gospel of Mark* (1981), is one of the few sustained attempts apart from *S/Z* itself to apply this method and perhaps the only one to apply the method to a biblical text, although one might argue that Calvino's novel playfully hoists Barthes on his own petard. Through his reading of Barthes and of the gospel of Mark, Belo re-imports a sort of Kabbalist reading into biblical studies. Belo's "materialist reading" of Mark is not materialist merely in the sense that it is a Marxist analysis. Rather, his reading is materialist also (and perhaps more so) in that it attends to written text as a material body.

Belo follows the same method that Barthes used, adopting some of Barthes's codes and identifying others appropriate to Mark's text. Belo claims that he intends to read Mark in terms of its narrative qualities alone, and with no regard to its referential truth-value (1981:95). In order to do so, he divides the gospel of Mark into seventy-three "sequences," each made up of one or more "scenes." These sequences and even more so the scenes correspond roughly to Barthes's lexias. Here, however, Belo compromises Barthes's text-analytical method rather severely by combining it with scholarly historical–critical treatment of the gospels. Unlike Barthes's arbitrary lexias, which are "matter[s] of convenience" (1974:13), Belo's sequences consist rather of established form-critical pericopes, irreducible atoms of tradition that allegedly lie "behind" the synoptic gospels. These textual units have been uncovered by conventional biblical scholarship of the last two centuries. The bulk of Belo's book consists of detailed and often provocative reading of these sequences in terms of relevant codes.

Belo ingeniously adapts the five codes which Barthes developed for study of Balzac's nineteenth-century French Romantic novella so that they are also relevant to a first-century Hellenistic Jewish gospel. Despite this, however, Belo rarely uncovers in Mark's story the sort of remarkable narrative structures that Barthes does on nearly every page of *Sarrasine*. This is not a consequence of differences between the two object-texts. If the writerly emerges to sabotage the flow of Balzac's very readerly story, then how much more so is this the case in the gospel of Mark, which, as the preceding chapters have argued, is a very writerly text? Yet Belo's book fails to confirm that the text of Mark is indeed far more writerly than Balzac's story. Belo brings the reader inside the text, whereas Barthes shows the reader how far outside the text she always is.

In the last analysis, Belo fails to escape the grip of the traditional understanding of text. As I have argued in the preceding chapters, the long entombment of the gospel of Mark within the secure confines of the Christian canon has protected it from the sort of critical reading represented by the Barthesian approach. Nevertheless, studies of the gospels in recent years have gone far toward penetrating that security. Belo is apparently unaware of these studies. With the exception of Louis Marin's important book and the work of a few other French structuralists, Belo does not cite any of the literary and narratological studies of the gospels of the last several decades. His references to English-speaking biblical scholars are to an earlier generation. This odd mixture of traditional and radical scholarship gives Belo's readings a decidedly quirky quality.

In addition, Belo frequently accepts the judgments of traditional "bourgeois" biblical scholarship – the very judgments which he claims to be rejecting! – not only in relation to the sequences of Mark's text, but also regarding matters of dating and provenance of the gospel (1981:96–7). He furthermore, and apparently

137

unconsciously, draws upon conventional judgments in relation to many points of exegesis. Belo admits that his reading is "naive" (1981:1). This *naïveté* contributes to the insight and originality of his book. However, Belo is not at all the naive reader or "Martian" to whom Barthes refers (1988:173–8). What is most disturbing about Belo's reading of Mark at these points is its "natural" quality. Since ideology naturalizes text, which is inherently un-natural, we may wonder how free Belo's reading actually is from the effects of bourgeois ideology.

The ironic effect of Belo's reading is to "de-materialize" the Markan text in an effort to bring to it a kind of closure – a new closure, to be sure, different from that of bourgeois scholarship, but closure nonetheless. This closed text of the gospel refers to participation in an apostolic succession which continues in contemporary movements of liberation, and it turns the oppressed peoples of the world into a new Israel. To this new apostolate corresponds Belo's reading of the Markan Jesus as a Pauline Jesus (1981:206, 297), or a Jesus who abandons Judaism in order to turn to the Gentiles. One finds echoes of this understanding at several points in Belo's reading, such as his comments on Jesus's interactions with the Gerasene demoniac – pagans do not endanger Jesus (1981:130) – and on the dialogue with the Syrophoenician woman as an alteration of Jesus's strategy (1981:145).

According to Belo, Jesus is stopped by Jewish authorities before his revolutionary plans to take his *praxis* to the Gentiles can be fully realized. Belo's reading here is not foreign to the history of bourgeois biblical scholarship, despite its materialist and revolutionary orientation, and it suggests an anti-semitism which is unfortunately also not foreign to the mainstream of Gentile biblical scholarship.[11] Liberation of the oppressed is a worthy goal, but if that alone is what the gospel of Mark is "really" about, then the text has once again been closed in the name of logocentric univocity.

I share Belo's political sympathies, and I share his disgust at the theological tepidity of contemporary bourgeois churches. However, I suspect (as I think Barthes would) those points in Belo's reading where the reader's desire for a coherent, liberatory writing overwhelms the materiality of the text. Belo's reading tests my own attempt to read from the outside. At these points the reader is drawn into Belo's text, and through Belo's text into Mark's text; the reader becomes once again an insider, even though now she is a different sort of insider from the bourgeois Christian. The strengths of Belo's reading are in those places (and they are many) where his reading is itself radically shaken or disrupted by the writerly qualities of the gospel of Mark. Belo is at his best when he reads from outside, that is, when Mark's refusal of bourgeois and of Gentile readings emerges through its refusal of any totalizing reading – including Belo's own reading.

> The Gospel narrative is articulated with the indefinite play of the narratives of its readings, a play that must not be closured, even in the name of reason, even in the name of God. The debate thus opened concerns the evaluation of the power at work in the practice of the bodies which we are.
>
> (Belo 1981:294)

The gospel of Mark is not a politically neutral book. It depicts Jesus and his followers in tension with the social, intellectual, and political world of their day. However, the reader's understanding of the nature of this tension depends in Mark on the reader's understanding of Jesus's identity, and the ambiguity of Jesus's identity is a central and unresolved matter in Mark's narrative. Yet Mark is also "political" on another level: few texts do the job of confronting and rejecting the reader's desire for power and for control over the meaning of the text as well as Mark does. It has been my concern in the previous chapters to explore ways that the text of Mark resists reading. My objections to Belo's book do not center upon his political reading of Mark, but upon his apparent desire to have his reading be the only reading, the correct reading. This creates a conflict which may be inherent in any reading, but which is suppressed all too often.

Belo's ability to call Mark's textual resistance to our attention emphasizes the degree to which many readers have failed to see that resistance. It is this ideological dimension of Mark – its resistance to the reader's understanding – which is uncovered by a materialist reading. Yet precisely this resistance of the text can never be read but can be encountered by the reader only in what Barthes calls the unreadability, or writerliness, of text. Belo's reading reveals the alienness of Mark's story, and this revelation results from close attention to the materiality of text.

Belo's book carries profound implications for those who engage in theological enquiry beyond the confines of traditional religious institutions.[12] His book concludes with a long "Essay in Materialist Ecclesiology" in which he sketches an "ecclesial" understanding of the "collective Son of man" as a material presence in the world – as a body composed of hands, feet, and eyes. This body, which is inherently political, is in Mark's view (as interpreted by Belo) Jesus's body. It is not a body to be abandoned in an ascension to some spiritual realm, but rather it is Mark's textual body itself enmeshed in the ideologies of its readers, in this physical world, the only place where the kingdom of God might be.

> The *continuity* [between Jesus and the son of man in Mark] thus refers us to the *figure of the collective Son of man* at the level of the erased text; this figure ... functions in the register of a continuity that is indicated by the ascensional schema in which *the starting point is earth*.
>
> Let us demythologize this figure. ... What will be left of the figure of the collective Son of man will be the communist program of his practice, [and] his subversiveness.
>
> (Belo 1981:287, his emphases)

For Belo, this means re-opening the question of bodily resurrection, for he insists that salvation in the gospel of Mark is always salvation of the body. The "body of Christ" is no easy theological metaphor here. Belo argues that the messianic narrative of Mark lies in fundamental opposition to the bourgeois theological discourse of institutional Christianity. It is this traditional discourse which keeps the church from being able to read Mark in politically liberative fashion.

By playing the culturally determined pressures toward signification (the codes) over against the writerly resistance offered by the materiality of the text, Belo's materialist reading of the gospel of Mark treads a fine line. At every step his reading threatens to obliterate the very thing which makes it possible. On the one hand, the reader wants to read from the inside. This desire is inherent in the intertextual context of every reading. The reader's desire to produce a coherent reading is very powerful, and perhaps irresistible. On the other hand, Mark's writerly resistance to any reading places the reader on the outside. It is the materiality of Mark's text that refuses the hegemony of bourgeois theology and opens a space for Belo's alternative reading.

READING FROM THE OUTSIDE

> If one grasps that every signifying practice is a field of
> transpositions of various signifying systems (an inter-textual-
> ity), one then understands that the "place" of enunciation and
> its denoted "object" are never single, complete, and identical to
> themselves, but always plural, shattered, capable of being
> tabulated.
>
> (Kristeva 1984:60)

Benjamin's notion of literal translation, Calvino's non-reader,
and Belo's materialist reading offer approaches to a postmodern
theology of reading which stress the physical, concrete aspects of
texts.[13] In contrast, the traditional understanding of text and its
associated theology of textual identity views text as an incarnate yet
ultimately spiritual word. For this traditional understanding, the
postmodern position sketched in this chapter has always been
marginal, often heretical, and generally disregarded. The possibility
and the implications of a reading from the outside have been ignored
by traditional theories of textual identity, as well as by much of the
Jewish and nearly all of the Christian theological tradition.

The postmodern theology of reading sketched out here reads the
text from the outside. This reading uncovers the carnality of the
word in the materiality of text, apart from any possible signification.
This theology of reading is concerned with what Gilles Deleuze and
Félix Guattari call the "flow" of language, apart from or even
logically prior to the point at which the linguistic flow "breaks" into
meaningful text, although that priority can never finally or actually
be realized. Deleuze and Guattari explicitly identify this flow with
hulê (1983:36), sheer physical stuff, and they contrast it to the
"machine" which breaks or interrupts the flow. I take this machine
to be the intertext, or ideology, which enables readers to read the text
from the inside.[14]

What this postmodern theology of reading desires, therefore, is
the "new word," the word which is as yet or once again meaningless
– not really a word, but only potentially one. It seeks this word in
nonsense, incoherence, and gibberish. (This is not glossolalia, for
which "speaking in tongues" is already Spirit-filled.) Like literal
translation, reading from the outside is both materialistic and
mystical. It therefore attends closely to those points where language
resists rational or empirical analysis, where the rules of meaning are
broken. These points of resistance involve questions of fictionality,

141

connotation, and metaphor, among others.

The postmodern theology of reading rejects the theology of textual identity, and in so doing it makes problematic the very meaning of "theology." Nevertheless, the word "theology" cannot be discarded, for it points to the ongoing, inevitable, and inescapable slide of language and thought toward metaphysical (logocentric) closure. We cannot escape from the conceptual need for coherence, completeness, and identity.[15] The desire to read from the inside brings with it the inevitable return of the traditional understanding of text. All language and thought, even the most atheistic, the most secular, and the most scientific, is caught in the gravitational field of this great black hole which is indicated in various ways by words such as "presence," "sense," and "reference." Only poetry in its most radical, linguistically incoherent forms comes close to escaping from the vortex of the desire for meaning. With such poetry, language is at its most concrete; it is hyletic. This is the maximum degree of the writerly.

The postmodern theology of reading is intensely interested in books, writings, scripture.

> [T]o describe systems of meaning by postulating a final signified is to side against the very nature of meaning.... Scripture is a privileged domain for this problem, because, on the one hand, theologically, it is certain that a final signified is postulated: the metaphysical definition or the semantic definition of theology is to postulate the Last Signified; and because, on the other hand, the very notion of Scripture, the fact that the Bible is called Scripture, Writing, would orient us toward a more ambiguous comprehension of the problems, as if effectively, and theologically too, the base, the *princeps*, were still a Writing, and always a Writing.
>
> (Barthes 1988:242)

In Barthes's terms, the theology of textual identity, or reading from the inside, seeks the "Last Signified." The postmodern theology of reading, or reading from the outside, rejects the Bible as authority, just as Belo rejects the appropriation of biblical truth by bourgeois theology, and just as Irnerio rejects the demand of every writing, the demand to be read. This postmodern theology reads the Bible against the grain of established theological truth. By claiming ownership of the Bible, the church claims to read it from the inside. Reading from the outside liberates the Bible from the church's hermeneutic control, or as Barthes might say, reading from the outside reads the Bible as "Writing." It rejects the necessity of canon. For reading from the outside, the Bible becomes just another text, or rather, many texts. For this postmodern theology of reading, the Bible is many bibles, an expanding and contracting and multiple text, a shimmering of texts which cannot be contained in any one book.

For the postmodern theology of reading, exegesis *is* eisegesis.[16] The term "exegesis" is an ideological subterfuge used to conceal a preference for one type of eisegesis over others, to make one way of reading into the text appear to be the natural and normal reading out of what the text had to say within it. The works of Calvino, Benjamin, and Barthes, among others, have made it clear that there is no such thing as an objective meaning hidden within any text. The notion of a scientific critical exegesis is as dangerous in its own way as the proclamation of the "true meaning of the Bible" (as inspired by God) on the part of fundamentalist religion, to which the traditional theology of textual identity is functionally equivalent.

There are no limits to eisegesis; the possibilities for misreading any text are endless. As a spiritual translation from the materiality of the text, every reading is a misreading, turning the text into what it is not. Still, just because there are no correct interpretations, it does not follow from this that there are no *incorrect* interpretations. An incorrect reading of the gospel of Mark would be analogous to a reading of *Sarrasine* which held that La Zambinella was not a castrated man after all, but really a woman.[17] The reader who reads *Sarrasine* and understands La Zambinella to be a woman, or a gay man, does not read "the same story" as another reader who understands the conventional denotation of "castrato." An alternative set of codes which permit the understanding of "castrato" as, for example, "a type of woman" is not inconceivable, but such a reading would substantially transform the readerly narrative structures of *Sarrasine*. It would require a rewriting of the English language. Each reading is a rendering of the hyletic text (the material aspect of the signifier) which justifies itself in terms of a set of conventional, culturally derived codes. If there are "wrong" readings, for example, that La Zambinella is a woman, it is because in this specific, concrete context, the codes that readers have accepted won't permit such a reading. For contemporary readers, at this time, "castrato" and "woman" cannot be equivalent.

What this postmodern theology of reading seeks is to understand the tensions between the resistance inherent in the physical aspects of a text and the ideological pressures brought to bear upon the text by its readers.[18] Reading is a juggling of codes, trying to get all the meanings to work out right. The reader's desire for meaning inevitably disincarnates, and therefore mutilates, the text. The material text – physical marks on the page – is torn out of one context and transported (translated) into a different one. The material text remains "the same" physically, but as a result of the changed context, the meaning has changed. It is a misunderstanding – but then, in this sense, all readings are inevitably misreadings.

Therefore I, too, have misread Calvino, Benjamin, and Belo. Like Irnerio, I reshape Belo's work to fit my own desire – I read into it. As a middle-class North American white man, and thus an oppressor in fact if not in intention, I am perpetually in danger of reclaiming Belo's radically neo-Marxist reading of Mark for the sort of bourgeois theology over against which he sets his own reading. That is a risk which I must take, or else not read at all (that is, not translate) and remain silent. But this non-reading would be quite unlike that of Irnerio, whose non-reading culminates in the work of art.

I read Belo's book within the context of an attempt to work out a new way to think about reading and texts, including my own role in relation to the texts. I seek a materialist reading of Belo's materialist reading. I do not read Belo in the context in which he reads the gospel of Mark, and yet Belo's reading is not entirely unlike Irnerio's non-reading, either. One misreading leads to another. In addition, Belo permits a reading from within another context, the context of "the other." Every (re)reading changes the context and opens a way for the other. Therefore, my reading is also not entirely foreign to Belo's, even as it cannot be identical to his. My reading stands over against his book, touching it (I hope) as a tangent to a circle, that is, a literal translation.

Every text is a specific, material product of concrete acts of production. For the traditional theology of textual identity, the materiality of language is only the temporary and ultimately transparent medium for the spiritual contents of meaning. In contrast, for the alternative, postmodern theology of reading, the marks on the surface of a page are not merely the vehicle or channel of a fundamentally independent meaning. The written text does not pass meaning on from an earlier, extratextual realm (such as the mind of an author) so that it may eventually be translated back to a different, but also extratextual, location (the mind of a reader).

Instead, these written marks are opaque, inert, and resistant to the desire for meaning. The differences through which they signify are themselves without meaning. The material body of a text conceals even as (and more than) it reveals. Different texts are not copies of some ideal original, and they cannot be collapsed into some universal, spiritual identity.

This postmodern theology of reading seeks to become aware of tensions between the reader's desire for meaning and the text's resistance to meaning. This theology therefore also offers a way of non-reading, in much the same way that Irnerio's book-sculptures offer a way of reading. Reading from the outside presents a different reading, an alternative reading, from the main streams of the Jewish and Christian traditions. It is a reading of the hyletic otherness of text which may well appear to traditional readers as a mutilation of the text. It looks so intensely at the text that the words disappear, not into ideas as they do for reading from the inside, but into meaningless marks. The postmodern theology of reading can never be more than a prolegomenon, a not-quite-theology, a *via negativa* which can only announce what it is not.

> [O]ne should read in desirous anticipation of what a text will be; one should read texts of the past in a nihilistic perspective, almost as if they were in a state of becoming.
>
> (Barthes 1985:112)[19]

7

TEXT, INTERTEXT, IDEOLOGY

TEXT VS. IDEOLOGY

To act as though an innocent discourse could be held against ideology is tantamount to continuing to believe that language can be nothing but the neutral instrument of a triumphant content. In fact, today there is no language site outside bourgeois ideology: our language comes from it, returns to it, remains closed up in it.

(Barthes 1976:10)

A bumper sticker in support of the National Rifle Association's stand against gun control laws used to be common in the American Midwest. It said:

Guns don't kill.
People kill.

I don't understand the appeal of this slogan, because it seems to me that the problem is that people do indeed kill other people, and they frequently do so with guns, and thus the propositions on the bumper sticker are irrelevant to the implicit conclusion. But then, an appeal to logic is generally not a function of bumper stickers.

It is a matter of considerable controversy today whether or not, or in what sense, texts may be said to "have" ideologies. More particularly, do the biblical texts possess a single ideology, or several ideologies? If so, what is the ideology of the Bible? Arguments about whether or how texts might possess ideologies bring the NRA bumper sticker to my mind. I imagine biblical scholars (or other literary scholars) driving down the road, with similar signs on the rear bumpers of their cars:

146

Texts don't kill.
People kill.

And indeed, people do kill other people with texts, and this is why ideological criticism is critical to textual analysis. Ideologies are handles by which readers clutch texts, so that we may use them as bludgeons or knives or machine-guns, to claim our own piece of the world, or to eliminate our enemies. The texts that we read, and the biblical texts especially, are soaked in human blood.

When one addresses the question of the relation of text to ideology, it is easy to become abstract and theoretical, far removed from the concrete world in which specific people suffer and die for their beliefs, or as a result of the beliefs of others. Yet even this bloodless, metaphysical enquiry must encounter the world of suffering and death. The disagreements about the relation between text and ideology may appear to be merely semantic ones, but they arise because actual people use words such as "text" and "ideology" in remarkably different ways from one another, and because these words are actually quite important to us. How readers think about texts and ideologies is a symptom of how we think and act in other respects. Our use of these two terms is itself ideological, and it illuminates the ideologies which inform the various ways of understanding texts and the histories of their readings.

Some people think that texts are univocal, that is, that each text is a clear and largely unambiguous expression of a single ideology. This claim belongs most obviously to religious fundamentalism. However, it also belongs to any reading which identifies a single true meaning for a text and equates that meaning with its author's intention[1] or the text's effect on some privileged reader, either historical or ideal. This view is also held by some ideological critics, who view each text as always already possessing an ideology, and for whom reading presents the invitation to either accept or reject that ideology.[2] The only question is whether the reader has understood the text correctly or not.

I reject the claim of textual univocity. I think that if the distinction between text and ideology is erased, so that text and ideology are identified with one another, then textual critics and scholars are out of business, and more importantly, readers are let off the hook. If each text contains an ideology and directs its own reading, then the reader becomes a passive observer (in some ways like the couch potato in front of a TV) who either "gets the message" or does not, but who bears no responsibility for the meaning which her reading uncovers. Such a reader would have no control over the text's meaning; instead, the text would control the reader's understanding of it. As a result, any two competent readers would have no dispute over the text's meaning. This, however, is contrary to our experience of texts, both as individual readers and as participants in conversation with other readers, conversations which continue for as long as the text is read.

I believe that no text is bound to one and only one ideology. On the face of it, this belief of mine seems foolish. It is hard to imagine Adolf Hitler's *Mein Kampf* appealing to anyone but a Nazi, or *The Communist Manifesto* supporting the interests of anyone but a Marxist. Perhaps these are extreme cases. Or perhaps the ideology which informs my own readings keeps me from imagining these texts in other contexts. It does appear, however, that some texts are in fact more "available" to multiple readings – that is, more polysemic – than are others; for example, it would not be hard to argue that lyric poems are usually more polysemic than fix-it-yourself manuals. But I would also want to argue that even the least poetic of texts is somewhat polysemic. Even the clearest fix-it-yourself manual will be subject to various readings.

The diversity of readings that many biblical texts have received allows me to question whether any reading of the Bible can be the correct one. If biblical texts were univocal, such cases could not arise. Competent readers often arrive at opposed readings of the same biblical texts. Some may question whether or how the text involved in this case is truly "the same text" for these two very different readers. Or a single competent reader may be unable to decide which of two or more contradictory readings of the same text is to be preferred. In this second case, it is precisely the "sameness" of the text that presents the problem. Of course, one might also question the competence of these readers. However, to deny the competence of those who read differently, or those who cannot clarify obscure texts, is one way to contest the reading of the text. The question of who is a competent reader, or what the criteria for competence are, itself reflects beliefs about what a text is and what reading accomplishes. These beliefs in turn reflect fundamental metaphysical and epistemological positions.

If I hold that texts are receptive to multiple and even contradictory readings, then I must distinguish between text and ideology. I define "text" as the material aspect or *hulê* (Husserl 1962) of the signifier.[3] A text may consist of ink marks on a page, the vibration of a string, or electronic pulses in a wire. It may be the vapor trail of a 747, the smell of sour milk, or the color of the sky. These different types of text may require different ways of reading; my focus in this book is on "books," human writings. Not everyone would agree with this definition of text, but my definition does allow me to say that, at least in some cases, two readers have disagreed about the meaning of the *same* text, and to specify in what way the text is the "same."

It follows from this definition that no interpretation can completely digest any text. No meaning can entirely absorb the text. No understanding can wholly comprehend a text. After the reading has combed, stroked, diced, beaten, and strained the written signs – after every possible reading has done this – there remains a residue which resists signification.[4] That residue is the materiality of the signifiers themselves – for example, the ink and paper forming letters on a page – which I call "text." This materiality is the sheer physical stuff, or *hulê*, of the signifier.[5] This hyletic aspect of the sign can never be directly perceived as such, but only inferred; therefore the text is *not* what is in the reader's mind. The reader reads the text as always already meaningful, filtered through what is often a thick layer of codes, that is, culturally determined preunderstandings. This meaningful layer, which is often called "text," actually hides the text from the reader.

Nevertheless pristine text, prior to *any* reading, must be postulated as other than the codes and preunderstandings supplied by readers; otherwise reading becomes entirely solipsistic. The claim that "the text is ideological" would then be no different from statements that "the text is textual" or "the ideology is ideological." "Text" serves here as something like what Immanuel Kant called a "regulative principle" (1929:211), a phrase which he applied to the "analogies of experience."[6] The distinction between text and ideology is a necessary one, even if it cannot be practically realized. It is the unreachable goal of reading from outside to uncover the concrete, hyletic text, the text itself. We approximate to an encounter with this pure text when we see a book in an unknown language, or an unknown alphabet;[7] if there were non-readers such as Italo Calvino's fictional character Irnerio,[8] they would see the hyletic text itself.

I define "ideology" as an intertextual weaving of texts. Ideology is not the texts themselves but the way in which an indefinite set of texts is juxtaposed and held together in the practice of some reader. This also is a rather limited definition, and there is much more to ideology than this. But if we are going to talk about texts, this approach makes more sense to me than to define ideologies in terms of "ideas" or something of that sort. In relation to texts, *ideology is intertext*.

Intertext is not something that readers create, but rather something that *creates readers*. Each human being can be understood as the juxtaposition of all the texts that she has heard, read, written, told, or enacted, a perpetually incomplete totalizing that constantly grows and diminishes as she adds new texts to her reading repertoire and forgets old ones. The individual reader stands at the junctures of an indefinite web or network of texts; the individual *is* that web or network. "This 'I' which approaches the text is already itself a plurality of other texts, of codes which are infinite or, more precisely, lost (whose origin is lost)" (Barthes 1974:10). The reader is an ideological intertext. "[T]he work of ideology is also to construct coherent subjects" (Judith Newton and Deborah Rosenfelt, quoted by Tina Pippin in Jobling and Pippin 1992:204).

Nonetheless, the individual human being can also be regarded as a hyletic, material body, that is, as a text (Calvino 1981:155–6). The human body certainly has the potential to signify many things. Conversely, many of the later writings of Roland Barthes (especially 1975, 1977b) play with the metaphor of the written text as a body. The text is a body which feels pleasure or bliss, a body which "rustles." I argue in chapter 3 that the gospel of Mark "rustles" in the story of the raising of Jairus's daughter. From this postmodern point of view, everything is either a text or an intertext, a "flow" or a "break" (Deleuze and Guattari 1983:36).

There can be no intertext without or apart from texts. The intertext is nothing but texts, and yet the intertext is not itself a text. Ideology is the intertextual "glue" that both joins texts to one another and configures the way that they are joined. Furthermore, as Barthes noted, ideology naturalizes the text; its function is to make the text, that very un-natural thing, appear familiar and normal. "[I]deology [is] the conceptual glue of culture, that which makes culture seem natural" (Alice Jardine, quoted by Pippin in Jobling and Pippin 1992:204). Ideology does this by providing a set of conventional codes or filters through which the text may be read. These codes allow the reader to recognize the text as a "work" (Barthes 1979b), to identify it, and to make sense out of it. Ideology creates an illusion of reality; it makes the meaning of the text seem obvious.

Ideology is therefore not something extra added to texts but rather the way in which a set of texts is assembled, a picture puzzle that turns out different for each reader. Yet ideologies are *not* themselves individualized; rather, they are embodied in the discourse of groups, what Barthes called the "sociolect." Ideologies are not merely theoretical constructs. Although ideologies have abstract structures, they are concretely enacted upon and through human communities. Ideologies are in fact powerful forces within the human world, for they invariably privilege some groups of human beings and deprivilege others. Ideologies are what make thought and action possible, and they also make some thoughts and actions *impossible*. Ideologies are therefore always contested, and they are therefore always violent.

The reader is relatively free to choose the texts that she reads and even to change her readings of individual texts. However, the reader has much less control over her ideology, and she can change it only at the cost of considerable discomfort and disruption in her life. Intertextuality and thus ideology can be either conscious or unconscious; most often it is completely unconscious, but never is it completely conscious. What ideological criticism is always trying to do is to bring portions of the intertextual network to greater self-awareness, and therefore to make the reader conscious of how un-natural all of this textual naturalness is. In effect, ideological criticism attempts to read the intertext. This is what this book has attempted in part to do, in relation to the gospel of Mark. However, the reader can never free herself from the reading filters provided by intertextuality; like all readers, she is trapped in the fundamental, hermeneutical circularity of all criticism.

IDEOLOGY AND MEANING

The innumerable writings that dominate our lives are made intelligible by a preordained agreement as to their referential authority; this agreement, however, is merely contractual, never constitutive.

(de Man 1979:204)

The Cartesian separation between material texts and mental ideologies might be taken to imply that texts could "have" ideologies just

151

as bodies "have" minds.[9] Yet this mind–body metaphor is deceptive, for it implies that texts are living organisms, that is, that texts have spiritual ideologies "in" them as human bodies have rational souls. The hyletic text is nothing more than insignificant blobs of ink on paper; the text is completely passive, inert. It is the reader who actively "brings" ideology to the text, thereby resurrecting the dead written words. The reader intertextually enacts an ideology *through* the text and upon the extratextual world. From this point of view there is no significant distinction between a reading and the practices generated in relation to that reading; reading is "always already" profoundly hermeneutical, never objective or disinterested. The reader always reads from one socio–historical, intertextual position or another, and thus every reading affects the reader's thinking and behavior. Hence my imagined bumper sticker slogan.

However, an ideology is a Transcendental Signified (Derrida).[10] The coherence of an intertextual network of signifiers (texts) is the meaning (the ultimate signified) that governs the meaning of each text in the network. For example, in order to make any sense out of the text of the gospel of Mark, the reader must insert it into an intertextual network, "locating" its genre and defining its reference, its coherence, and its value as a book. Understanding of the text happens only within an intertextual and therefore ideological context. This intertextual network determines in this way the meaning of every text that the reader reads and weaves these meanings together into a sense of "how things are" or "reality." As Barthes put it, ideology is the signified of connotation (1967a:92–3). I have thus begged my own question in the foregoing, because there can be no signified without a signifier – no ideology without a text – and vice versa. It is not quite correct to say that readers bring ideologies to texts, because texts don't even *exist* as signifiers until they are read, and the ideological network cannot exist apart from the texts. Every signifying text is always already read; there is never an act of reading which does not involve location of the textual site (as more or less natural and obvious) within an intertextual context. Texts and ideologies belong together; no production or consumption of text is ever free from ideology.

Although the signifier–signified binarism of classical structuralism has been deeply undermined by poststructuralist analysis, this point still remains an important one. What poststructuralism challenges is the ideality and self-identical totality of the sign as signifier–signified. It does not contest the signifying relation itself, but rather it claims that the signifying relation is always incomplete. Poststructuralism points to the densely concrete and specific contexts in which texts are read, to intertextual particularities of reading, and to the contingent, and in principle incomplete, nature of every reading.

The question, Do texts have ideologies? becomes then the question, What is text without intertext? Can there be a reading which is not intertextual? Text without ideology is hypothetical and unreal – not something that readers ever encounter. However, there are texts, as I have defined the word, for which there is no intertextual context. These are the texts which are not read. The number of texts which will never again be read must be huge. Texts which have been forgotten, lost, or destroyed, never to be recovered – so obscured by time that no one attempts to recover them – these texts have no intertext. They are cultural garbage. Ideology makes the text memorable; the text that is remembered is the text that "possesses" an ideology. Other texts that because of the language used, or physical features of the writing, remain indecipherable to the reader's eyes or impenetrable to understanding – these are also texts without intertext. They are nonsense. Ideology makes the text meaningful; the text that makes sense is the text that "possesses" an ideology.

The texts that the reader throws away or forgets – that become garbage – are those texts that are unsuited to the reader's ideological needs. These texts may be "unredeemable," but they are more often simply irrelevant and unimportant to the reader. These texts could be deciphered, because the necessary codes are available. However, no one is interested in deciphering them. On the other hand, the texts which continue to resist the reader's understanding may be important to her at first, but there are no available codes through which these texts may be read. If the reader does not succeed in making sense out of them, in finding or creating such codes, then she throws these texts away, too.

Such texts approach (in different ways) a "zero degree" of ideology.[11] They are meaningless. However, these meaningless texts do not dwell in some idealistic limbo in which texts do not have ideologies; these texts are concrete, physical things. The alienation of these texts from the reader, and vice versa, places the texts in tension with their context in such a way that ideological criticism of them is tenuous and uncertain, and perhaps impossible. But then, ideological criticism of such texts is never done; no one criticizes texts that no one reads. Only to the extent that the reader can (and does) fit these texts into larger, intertextual networks can the texts be reclaimed from the garbage heaps of culture.

These meaningless texts present a limit of textuality, an almost-no-context, yet the fact that this situation does exist for innumerable texts is also important. Texts can change or lose ideologies. In other words, texts can move within the intertextual network; their juxtapositions with other texts can change. Texts can also drift away from the network and be forgotten. We are returned to the distinction between text and ideology, in a way that questions the nature of the connection between them. The intertextual codes are not themselves in the texts, for no text is self-explanatory. Nor is the text a surplus or repository of many (perhaps infinite) meanings, as some[12] have suggested.

Instead, the materiality of every text continually resists meaning, and thus it evades ideology. The text itself – the *hulê*, the material space of the semiotic (Kristeva 1984:32–4) – is deficient in meaning. The text *resists* the reader's coherent reading; the text grates against meaning and therefore the reader must force ideological codes upon it. All texts are devoid of meaning, but some are easier to read into, partly because of the specific context of reading (which changes) and partly because of the physical characteristics of the text itself. Different texts offer different degrees of evasion or resistance: Kafka's novels are more resistant to meaning than are Dickens's novels, and the gospel of Mark is more resistant than is the gospel of Luke.[13] Conversely, different ideologies tolerate the resistance of texts to different degrees; some ideologies are more "flexible" than others.

Hyletic text *lacks* meaning; it presents an absence of meaning which the reader continually desires to fill up. It is readers who *demand* meaning. The reader's ideology satisfies this desire for meaning. Therefore all reading is intertextual; reading is an endless juxtaposition and interchange of texts, that is, a kind of translation.[14] The reader is made possible by the mis-placing of the word which is writing; the reader is a translator who re-places the word, moving the meaning to a foreign body in a new place, a new time. All readers are translators, those who take immaterial meanings from their proper places (the meaningful words that make up the story) and move them someplace else. Ideological criticism must attend closely to the specific, concrete contexts, that is, the "places" where the intertextual play of reading occurs.

THE PRACTICAL CONTEXT

Ideological criticism is today precisely condemned to operations of theft: the signified, exemption of which is the
materialist task par excellence, is more easily "lifted" in the
illusion of meaning than in its destruction.

(Barthes 1977a:208, his emphasis)

The text is ontologically distinct from its intertextual reading
context. The intertext can change while the text, as defined above,
remains the same. However, the immediate context in which a text
is read is always epistemologically prior to the text. Every text
"possesses" an ideology because every text is always read in a unique
context; the notion that a text might be read without any context,
that is, the idea of an ideologically neutral reading, is hypothetical
and belongs to logocentric idealism. Reading always entails a specific
context. No reader actually encounters a text except in the context
of a concrete situation, itself composed of innumerable texts. This
context necessarily limits the range of ideologies to which the text is
"available."

To state this theoretical point in a more practical way, each text
– except for those "garbage" texts which are not read at all – will
always be owned by some group(s) and denied to others. It is a
function of ideology to identify "proper" owners of the text and to
serve as a protective fence around the textual property, in order to
prevent its theft by others. Ideology makes this fence seem quite
natural and normal – that the text *is supposed to* mean just what its
owners say that it does. It is ideology, therefore, that divides insiders
from outsiders (Mark 4:11–12, 25).[15] Identification of ownership
excludes others from ownership; ideology monopolizes the text.
Thus it is not true that any text is available to any ideology. Texts
"possess" ideologies for precisely this reason, and if they didn't have
ideologies, they would be worthless – that is, garbage.

Ideology transforms the text into the "work" (Barthes 1979b).
The relation between text and work is discussed further in chapter
6. The work is a law: an authority, something worth keeping. The
work is the product of a worker (an author) within a system of
exchange (or translation) which makes it available as a piece of
property. "Three things are postulated here: a *determination* of the
work by the outside world (by race, then by history), a *consecution*
of works among themselves, and an *allocation* of the work to its
author" (Barthes 1979b:78). Ownership provides power to affiliate

the text with other texts, through dissemination of text, authorization of translation, or promulgation of "correct" interpretation. The owner controls the intertext and thus the reading of the text. Identification of ownership is an important function of ideology – perhaps the most important one.

Thus it would be better to say that ideologies possess texts, rather than that texts possess ideologies. The question of the ideology of the Bible then becomes the question of who owns the Bible. Ownership of biblical texts may be defined in terms of scholarly expertise, in which case the scholarly Society of Biblical Literature may own the Bible. Or else it may be defined in terms of copyright law, in which case the National Council of Churches has a claim to ownership, for it holds the copyright to the RSV. Or ownership may be defined in terms of divine inspiration, or uninterrupted tradition (continuity with ancient owners), or in some other fashion congenial to the various religious groups that claim to own the Bible.

It is no coincidence that modern awareness of and interest in ideology arises alongside of legal recognition of copyright and an ethics which condemns plagiarism. Copyright laws and plagiarism rules can be defined as codes which determine meaning, insofar as they guarantee the contents of the text to be the "original" or "authentic" work. These laws and rules make explicit the fence that keeps the non-owner from the text. The conjunction of codes of copyright, plagiarism, and so forth with print culture is also not coincidental, and the arrival of electronic culture already demands a thorough revision, and perhaps abandonment, of current notions of intellectual property. These are all ideological matters: ideology not only provides the means of appropriating the text but also defines what counts as appropriation.

However, no written text can entirely guarantee its proper context – its authoritative intertext. The ideological struggle of conflicting readings is an unavoidable product of the technology of writing. This is the point of Socrates's famous Myth of Theuth in the *Phaedrus* (section 275), and also of the Seventh Letter of Plato (1973). Questions of the relation between writing and language, and between writing and ideology, have long been central concerns of the Western philosophical tradition.[16] All writing is copied and therefore false; in other words, writing is inherently plagiaristic. Reading is never final or finished. Reading plays endlessly and violently with the work, and with the law of the work. Readers either accept the owners' reading, or they reject it. In any reading context, counter-readings will be possible.

The counter-reader is a thief, one who steals the text from its proper owner. The counter-reader abuses the codes and mis-reads the text, because only the proper owner may determine correct usage. A counter-reading, or "reading against the grain," involves a violent transfer or inversion of context, liberating the text from one owner–reader's ideology and claiming it for another ideology. The counter-reader offers an abnormal or "bad" translation of the text, in which the old words acquire new meanings, different meanings from those that the owner would give it. We return once more to the separation of text from ideology. If counter-readings are always possible and even perhaps desirable, and if all ownership of texts is ideological and thus subject to contest, then no text finally belongs to anyone or any context. It is impossible to think or talk about conflicting readings without supposing some genuine distinction between text and ideology, but it is also impossible to *read* a text in a non-ideological manner. In order to assert that texts have ideologies and that texts are never free from some ideological context or other, we must also assume that texts and ideologies are not the same thing.

Every reading is ideological, including the readings of the gospel of Mark and other texts in this book, and including your reading of this book. Fredric Jameson refers to this as "rewriting the text" (in Jobling and Pippin 1992:229–30). Because every writing is already a reading, rewriting requires a new reading, that is, a counter-reading. The violence of rewriting the text reflects the violence with which the current owners have appropriated the text and the degree to which they have secured its reading.

Some counter-readings will be possible and other counter-readings will be impossible within the same reading context. Thus it may be that no single reading of the biblical exodus and conquest stories can be shared by Native American and African-American readers, for Black readers may want to identify with the Israelites, but Indians may choose to side with the Canaanites. Precisely what (in the context) makes the text valuable to one group will make it hateful to another. This limitation is built into the distinction between text and ideology offered above, because the relation between text and context is always the product of intertextuality. Context is always finite, always particular, always concrete; context is itself always a multiplicity of texts.[17]

Counter-readings are acts of stealing the text. They are also revolutionary acts of liberation. For example, Tina Pippin (1992b) re-reads the Jezebel stories in the book of Kings in order to take them from white, male owners and offer them to others, such as poor and Black women, who have been excluded from ownership. What allows Pippin to read the Jezebel stories as she does, when other competent readers reject her views? How far can she press her alternate readings? To whom (if anyone) is Pippin accountable for her readings, and why? To what extent (if any) can appeal to "the text" be used, either by her or by her opponents?

Likewise, when Pippin reads the Apocalypse of John as an unredeemably misogynist text (1992a), and when other scholars, even other feminist scholars, disagree with her reading, who speaks for the proper owners of the text? The disagreement is a dispute over property rights. However, if the text is recognized as unredeemable by a potential counter-reader, does this reader in effect acknowledge the legal rights of current owners? When Pippin says that the Apocalypse is unredeemable for women, is she saying that this text *cannot* be stolen? Even though she disagrees with the ideology of the text's current owners, is she saying that they are none the less the only rightful owners?

Different ideologies of reading are implied by the tension between these metaphors of "redemption" and "theft" of the text. The metaphor of redemption respects the laws of ownership and thus the law of the work. Redemption implies a legal and relatively non-violent system of exchange; it also suggests a return of things to their proper standing or "place." The metaphor of theft does not respect the law. Theft stands outside of the law and is inherently violent; it rejects all claims to propriety. Things which are not redeemable might still be stealable, and vice versa. When Pippin says that the Apocalypse cannot be redeemed, is she implying that it *must* be stolen?

> It is theft that prevents the gift and the countergift from entering into an exchangist relation. Desire knows nothing of exchange, *it knows only theft and gift* ... the essential process is not exchanging, but inscribing or marking.
>
> (Deleuze and Guattari 1983:186, their emphasis)

Much of the revolutionary quality of counter-reading is that it threatens to break open the Bible itself. "Holy Scripture" is profoundly ideological. The biblical canon is the ultimate form of ownership, an immensely powerful intertext, and an authoritative context for specific biblical texts. Canonizing also freezes the historical formation of the texts. At what point in its history does "the text" actually appear as a complete thing? This question is particularly pertinent to the gospel of Mark (see chapter 2). When is the text of Mark "finished?" The text is finished when it enters the canon.

The biblical canon provides an authoritative intertextual context for each of the biblical writings. Text is the material aspect of the signifier; however, the physical form in which many biblical texts appear has a great deal to do with this authoritative context, and thus with ideology. Expensive paper with gilt edging and fancy binding, the presence and extent of an apparatus, whether scholarly or pious – all of these express a great deal about the text's importance, its *value* to its *owners*. However, more significant than any of these features is the collection of many disparate texts under one cover and one title, which suggests a coherent and complete whole.

The historical conjunction of the desire for canon and the technology of writing ("Scripture") is not a coincidence; the decision to disseminate the message leads to the need to authenticate it. As time passes, institutions change, and in the modern world of print culture, publication and copyright effectively freeze the text. And now, in the brave new world of electronic texts, even this techno-logical and legal canonization threatens to come undone. Perhaps it will be this transformation of the medium more than any theological revolution which liberates the biblical books from their canonical captivity.

Even within the traditional canon, however, every reader favors some writings more than others (the canon within, or beyond, the canon), using the favored texts as an intertextual lens through which the others may be read – for example, reading the gospel of Mark in the light of the gospels of Matthew and Luke.[18] In that sense, at least, every reader is a counter-reader, for canon implies a notion of wholeness or completeness. To break up the canonical text is to reject any canonical reading. Nevertheless, the privileging of some texts rather than others is one of the major benefits of establishing a canonical multi-text such as the Bible in the first place, because this privileging has "rescued" the more writerly texts in the Bible, such as Mark, for the faith of believing readers.

However, as long as communities of readers continue to recog-nize the biblical canon as authoritative, readings of the Bible such as

Tina Pippin's will be (correctly) understood to be dangerous and revolutionary. Insofar as Pippin's readings of the Apocalypse challenge – and in fact reject – the canon, they break the intertextual context; insofar as she does not go on at this point and re-canonize the biblical texts, the Apocalypse is nullified or, as Barthes says, "dispersed." Pippin steals John's Apocalypse from its owners but does not claim ownership for herself or any others! Through which set of codes may this text then be read? The text's value as a possession is voided, or at least rendered uncertain, and the Holy Word is transformed into cultural garbage. Ideological criticism of the Bible here serves an anti-sacramental function.

Often hand-in-hand with religious institutions, scholars have attempted to make biblical texts readable and believable – to turn them into what Barthes called "texts of pleasure." In doing this, contemporary scholars continue in modern, scientific ways an old tradition of reading the Bible, a tradition which was already authorized by and institutionalized in believing communities very early on. It seems quite unlikely that any of the biblical writings, either Jewish or Christian, could have been accepted as canonical unless an ideology allowing their proper interpretation were already in place.

The reading of any text – even the most ancient ones – is always a contemporary reading. The context of every text is always *here* and *now*. This is not to say that readers today cannot have some sense of the ways that ancient readers understood the text, but it is to say that our awareness of such ancient readings is itself always conditioned by our present contexts and commitments, that is, by our ideologies. This is true also of our understanding of historical conditions under which the text was written. The privileging of an ancient reading as the text's proper meaning is therefore nothing more than the privileging of the *contemporary* intertext through which the ancient reading is understood. Ancient readings always stand at an inherent disadvantage to the contemporary readings through which they are necessarily filtered.[19] Ancient reading will always be alien to present understanding, and reading will therefore always be anachronistic.

Historical scholarship of the Bible has tried to overcome the foreignness of the texts, to translate or bridge the gap of millennia separating the reader from the people who produced the texts originally. It has sought to remove alienness from the texts – to explain the texts, to make sense out of them. It has done so by locating the "authentic" meaning of biblical texts in the texts' historical origins, understood as the intentions of their authors or the understandings of the communities to which they were initially addressed. More recently, the attempt to reconstruct inherent literary or narrative structures of the texts, as reflected in the understanding of an ideal or qualified reader, has added to this repertoire of scholarly techniques.

The concept of anachronism as a fault of scholarship is essential to the ideology of historical objectivity that has belonged for two hundred years now to owners of the Bible. For this scholarly tradition, anachronism destroys the delicate historical bridge which connects the contemporary reader to the past. Anachronism threatens the scientific historical enterprise, and the theological one as well, with a breakdown of scholarly discipline. The ideal of an ideologically neutral reading is essential to modernist literary, historical, and scientific hermeneutics, and it is itself an ideological subterfuge of great sophistication. The model of objective, scientific scholarship which forbids anachronism and other historical errors itself belongs, together with individualism, nationalism, capitalism, colonialism, and patriarchy, to what Barthes called "bourgeois ideology."

Stealing the text is inherently anachronistic, for the very concept of anachronicity is ideological, that is, a means by which one set of owners (scholars) protect their claim upon the text. Counter-readings of biblical texts tend to pull those texts out of the context defined by this ideology, and so it is no surprise that the charge of anachronistic "reading out of context" is a common one leveled against counter-readers such as Pippin. Counter-reading replaces one intertext, one set of codes, with another. The counter-reader is perceived as abusing and mis-reading the text, although what her reading makes clear is that *every* reading mis-reads the text.[20] Every counter-reading is therefore a form of ideological criticism.

The critique of ideology requires also a critique of the critic. To the extent that ideological criticism continues to maintain a façade of scholarly objectivity, its potential for revolutionary change will be crippled. If the ideological critic is a counter-reader, the charge of anachronism will pose no problem, as the counter-reader is already outside of the law of the owner and gives it no heed. She is condemned in advance to reading out of context. However, not all ideological criticism is necessarily counter-reading. Intertextual awareness does not require that the reader desire a change of the text's owners. Indeed, some ideological critics might wish only to restore a privileged set of codes and to protect the text for currently legitimated owners. If these proper owners are identified as original owners, then criteria of anachronicity become once again relevant.

THE IDEOLOGY OF LANGUAGE

The social intervention of a text (not necessarily achieved at the time the text appears) is measured not by the popularity of its audience or by the fidelity of the socioeconomic reflection it contains or projects to a few eager sociologists, but rather by the violence that enables it to *exceed* the laws that a society, an ideology, a philosophy establish for themselves in order to agree among themselves in a fine surge of historical intelligibility.

(Barthes 1976:10)

It is a commonplace to state that all language is social. Language is always shared; there are no private languages. Yet this statement can be understood in two radically different ways.

One theory states that the purpose of language is to share information, to convey ideas from one party to another. Language is trustworthy and neutral, like a static-free telephone connection – a transparent channel for ideas. Language is disinterested. Access to language is open to anyone with sufficient mental capacity. If language "belongs" to anyone, then it belongs to the gods, who benevolently share it with humanity. Language unites us. According to this theory, texts do not have ideologies because texts are instances of this common good, language. Or, if texts are ideological, it is because they reflect an ideology which is objectively there, in some extratextual referent – it is "real" or "true" in some sense. The counter-reader is always wrong, foolish, or evil. Although it is rarely made explicit, this theory is dominant in the modernist historical scholarship described above.

An alternative theory of language states that the purpose of language is to control and even to conceal information, to protect the secrets of one group from the "others," the enemy, anyone who is not one of "us" – the outsiders. I share language only with those who are like me in some way or another. Language is coded; it is a game played according to obscure rules, an opaque wall dividing those who know how from those who don't (Isaiah 6:9, Mark 4:11–12). Language is a curse and an obstacle to all who live in the world after

Babel.[21] Language divides humanity, separating civilized people from the barbarians.

According to this second theory, whoever controls language controls wealth and power, and there are many contestants for the prize. Because there is no disinterested language, and insofar as texts are the products of language, generated through language and traversed by language, texts are always interested. Texts are the playing fields of ideology. They always belong to someone. The counter-reader disrupts the play and betrays the secret, and sometimes she even changes the rules of the game. Thus the counter-reader is a poet, a cheat, a saboteur.

I think that the relation between texts and ideologies is more complex and muddy than the first theory of language can allow. No one speaks quite the same language as anyone else, and yet nothing is less private than language. Texts are not vehicles of a separable meaning, and yet texts have no meaning "in" them. There is no one correct reading of a text. Language conceals at least as much as it reveals, and probably more. Even the most fluent masters of any language cannot unlock all of its secrets. All language – and narrative most of all – is riddled with indeterminacies which cannot be controlled or overcome by any reader, including the author, as the preceding chapters have argued.

This tendency of language to be contested by ideology is intensified in the case of writing, which frees text from the immediate, determining context of the spoken word. Writing detaches the signifier from the signified and makes apparent the need for an interpretive bridge to re-connect them. The relation between written text and its message is always doubtful, for the physical stuff (*hulê*) of the inscribed letters has no inherent meaning. The creation of alphabets and transcription of oral traditions make possible and necessary the distinction between linguistic medium and significant content. Either content or medium may change, independently of the other: an old text may acquire a new meaning in a new situation, or (in a "dynamic translation") the meaning may pass from one language to another, or from writing to film, etc. This is what Socrates feared (Plato 1973), and what the gospel of Mark well illustrates: writing opens up a plurality of possible meanings, none of which can be authoritative. This polysemy turns understanding into misunderstanding, and therefore writing is both powerful and dangerous. It is magical. The deceptions inherent in all language are made evident in writing. As Jacques Derrida and others have more recently claimed, writing is prior to speech, if not chronologically, then at least ontologically.[22]

How then do *I* read? How have I been reading in the foregoing chapters? Can I read on behalf of anyone but the contemporary legal owners of the biblical texts? How could I read on behalf of anyone but myself? Even to raise the question in this way is false, however, for it implies that "I" am somehow separate from my reading – that this reader, "I," is not intertextual but rather extratextual.

> Do I then exist *before* my language? Who might this *I* be, owner of precisely that which causes me to exist? How can I live my language as a simple attribute of my person?
>
> (Barthes 1987a:52, his emphasis)

In his 1971 essay, "Writers, Intellectuals, Teachers," Barthes sketched out two types of ideological criticism (1977a:206–8; see also 1987a:72). The first criticism is anarchic and seeks "an asemic word"; it "anticipates a new, unprecedented state in which the efflorescence of the signifier would not be at the cost of any idealist counterpart, of any closure of the person" (1977a:208). The second criticism speaks from within a concrete moment of historical crisis: "the liquidation of the old criticism can only be carried forward *in* meaning (in the volume of meanings) and not outside it." Barthes holds that the second criticism, which I take to be a criticism from the standpoint of the oppressed, those who do not own the text, is the "more historically correct." I think that he is right: this is the genuine counter-reading, a reading from the outside. The counter-reading will always be that of those who are oppressed and marginalized, and the dominant reading, the reading of the owners, will inevitably be oppressive. The truly liberative reading will always be provisional, always shifting, on the run, and utopian: "the wretched of the earth" will *never* own a text.

However, only Barthes's first type of criticism is an option for me. By every definition that I know, I belong to the category of "oppressor": white, Anglo, male, Gentile, straight, middle-class, middle-aged, Middle American. If I turn away from the interests of my class, my gender, my race, then what are my options? I can't steal something that I already own. Any counter-reading which I might attempt would be rightfully suspect. I try to read in sympathy with "the other," whoever she may be, but I cannot read *as* the other. This is one reason why the question of text and ideology is so very uncomfortable to people like me – that is, to oppressors.

How then can I claim also to read from the outside? My reading is hardly non-ideological. I will not appeal to some utopian universalism of the spirit, which itself would be just another disguised form of logocentric idealism. There can only be particularities of the flesh, concrete contexts in which actual human beings read actual texts. I want to turn the power of texts, including biblical texts, *against* my own ideology. This can only lead, for my reading of the text of the gospel of Mark, to a rewriting which destroys the owners' readings. Insofar as I read from the outside, it must be an impossible, utopian outside, not the very real outside of the oppressed counter-reader. Thus I find myself necessarily in the company of Irnerio, the impossible non-reader of chapter 6, and the impossibly naive Martian reader of chapter 5. The resurrection of the word does not entail for me a re-creation or renewal of meaning. This is diametrically opposed to the desire to redeem biblical texts for women or other oppressed readers. Here again is the tension between "redemption" and "theft." I can neither steal the text nor do I wish to redeem it. What then shall I do? My desire is nothing less than self-destructive, and my reading will end only in my own obliteration.[23]

POSTSCRIPT:
"GET RID OF IT"

THE TEXT AS BODY

But why do you write? – **A**: I am not one of those who think with an inky pen in their hand, much less one of those who in front of an open inkwell abandon themselves to their passions while they sit in a chair and stare at the paper. I am annoyed by and ashamed of my writing; writing is for me a pressing and embarrassing need, and to speak of it even in a parable disgusts me.

B: But why, then, do you write? – **A**: Well, my friend, to be quite frank (*im Vertrauen gesagt*): so far, I have not discovered any other way of getting rid (*loszuwerden*) of my thoughts. – **B**: And why do you want to get rid (*loswerden*) of them? – **A**: Why I want to? Do I want to? I must. – **B**: Enough! Enough!

(Nietzsche 1974:146)

The existence of the reader–consumer of the text demands a counterpart, namely, the writer–producer. Every writer is first and foremost a reader. For the traditional understanding of text, the text is a logocentric construction which bridges the gap between reader and writer, a "work" that connects these two activities even as it holds them apart and reinforces their distinct identities. As we saw in chapter 6, hermeneutics, the traditional theology of textual identity which Derrida rejects, treats the text as a vehicle which transports a message from the writer–sender to the reader–receiver. For this theology of the text, the text is a metaphor, a fleshly body inhabited by and carrying (*meta pherein*) a living spirit; this message–spirit "in" the text transforms it into "the work." Friedrich Nietzsche's aphorism #93 from *The Gay Science*, quoted above, both plays with and finally demolishes this transportation metaphor: for speaker "A," the text is excrement or vomit, a foreign, improper body, something the writer "must" expel from her own, proper body. Or, if one prefers to think of the work as a child, as some do, then it is a child whose delivery comes not as a blessing, but as relief and liberation after many hours of unavoidable and painful, perhaps even life-threatening, labor.

Nietzsche's character "A" speaks frankly, although whether she speaks for the actual author of the aphorism, the historical Nietzsche, may be another matter. Character "A"'s frank word, like Jesus's *logon* at Mark 8:31–2a ("the son of man must suffer much and be rejected by the elders and the high priests and the scribes, and be killed, and rise up after three days. He was telling them frankly"[1]), is an index of the *lack* of meaning in this text. Does Nietzsche as the genuine author attempt to pull back a veil here and reveal his true intent – the real reason why the real man writes? Could such a revelation of meaning and identity ever be achieved without ambiguity? Suppose that character "A" were to say, frankly and without any possibility of irony, "This is truly why I write: I must get rid of my thoughts." Could not the reader (since character "B" has by now abandoned the dialogue) even then continue to ask "A" what she means by the words that follow? "Why must you 'get rid of' your thoughts? How does writing get rid of them? What about your thoughts is so objectionable?" Then suppose further that character "A" were to answer that question, again quite frankly. This would in turn lead to further questions from the reader, thereby opening up an endless chain of such questions. This endless string of questions would not be deterred or deflected by any definitive answer, for there could be no truly definitive answer to such questions.

What connection could be established between any physical text and the intentions of its writer? "[L]iterature is like schizophrenia: a process and not a goal, a production and not an expression" (Deleuze and Guattari 1983:133). According to Nietzsche, the act of textual "production" is not an "expression" (of its writer's intent) but rather an expulsion, an excretion. Insofar as the writer (whether author or translator) creates the text, she does so as a reader, that is, intertextually. Writing is the way the reader *eliminates* what she has read.

If the attempt to understand the act of production requires postulation of abstract entities such as "history" or "work" –

whether the labor be that of a proletarian class or that of a mother – then that attempt too is in danger of returning to the logocentrism of the traditional theology of the text. Nietzsche's scatological rewriting of the Romantic childbirth metaphor of literary–artistic creation refers implicitly to the material text, the physical object which appears as an overlooked by-product, as an afterbirth ("a pressing and embarrassing need"), of the "expression" of "ideas." The material text, Husserl's *hulê*, is this signifier which does not signify (Deleuze and Guattari 1983:243–4). As a result, attention to the physical aspect of the text does not foster communication but rather blocks it, even though communication is impossible without the textual *hulê*. That meaningful communication is impossible without this meaningless material is a paradox implicit in every text but made especially evident in postmodern texts.

The fundamental metaphysical questions regarding the integrity and identity of the work of literature must therefore be explored in relation to the hyletic body of the text. This concrete materiality of writing is the "real" or "true" text[2] which gives the work its existence. However, for all practical purposes, this physical body of the text does not exist. The materiality of the text is itself always *invisible*, except to non-readers such as Italo Calvino's character Irnerio, and unspeakable, except when the text speaks only itself or, as Roland Barthes says, when language "rustles." The *hulê* of the text is language itself speaking, and it is language speaking itself.

To make the same point in theological terms, textual *hulê* is the voice of God, as opposed to the word of God. This materiality of the text has no value as an authority/truth/source of knowledge; in fact, the material text has no value at all.[3] How could it? Textual *hulê* can never actually be experienced. Even for theoretical purposes, *hulê* can only be imagined as a hypothetical limit. Nevertheless, the sheer materiality of the text must be postulated as "real," somehow over against the reader, if we are to understand the relationship between text and ideology. Otherwise the text becomes whatever the reader desires it to be, and if that were the case then readers would never throw away, lose, or burn books, and readers would never read books, either, for that matter.

In this postmodern world, we can no longer believe that language identifies or reflects an extralinguistic reality. Following Barthes, we think of language as a play of codes, an exercise of power – not the ancient *poiêsis*, but instead the ability to manipulate countless bits and pieces of information. These are of course simply different ways to think about the same thing, but the difference in perspective is crucial. Postmodern creative power is the ability to reshuffle and replay the information bits endlessly. Who puts these potentially-signifying fragments together; who "means?" Who produces the meaningful text? Reading rewrites the text. The one who produces the text is always the reader, the human being living in relation to other human beings. However, as we saw in chapter 7, the living human consciousness is also put together, an assembled subject, an ideological and intertextual weaving of texts. What we call "reality" is the intertextual product of countless textual fragments, that is, the dialectic of the readings of many such readers. Concrete, hyletic texts drift among the many fragments of "reality," where they are caught up in numerous and contradictory readings.

For the reading from outside, the text is an inert, resistant body, opaque to all connotation. For this reading an intertextual web is not available. It is *only in this sense* that concrete texts do not have ideologies; only under these circumstances can texts be meaningless. As for the physical textual object itself being ideological, one might just as well, following Nietzsche's aphorism, say that excrement is ideological, for within the human (intertextual) context, excrement *is* ideological, which is precisely my point about the distinction and the relation between text and ideology.

At a crucial point in Franz Kafka's story, "The Metamorphosis," the father and sister of Gregor Samsa, the salesman who has become a gigantic insect, together realize that they must eliminate him from their lives. These characters assume the role of the text's implied reader, reading the text of their son and brother's body. Their situation parallels that of the actual reader, for whom the impediment of the material text must be removed before she can get on with the story.

> "I won't utter my brother's name in the presence of this creature [the sister says], and so all I say is, we must try to get rid (*loszuwerden*) of it. We've tried to look after it and to put up with it as far as is humanly possible ..."
>
> "We must try to get rid (*loszuwerden*) of it," his sister now said explicitly to her father ..., "it will be the death of both of you, I can see that coming. When one has to work as hard as we do, all of us, one can't stand this continual torment at home on top of it. At least I can't stand it any longer."
>
> (Kafka 1948:124)

Later Gregor's sister says to her father, "You must just try to get rid (*loszuwerden*) of the idea that this is Gregor. The fact that we've believed it for so long is the root of all our trouble" (Kafta 1948:125). Getting rid of the "creature" (*Tier*, but also *Untier*) allows the father and sister to retain the memory of the human son and brother that the repulsive insect once was, before it utterly destroys their lives. Removal of the proper name, Gregor, from the referent signals that its transformation into an unspeakable monster is now complete. Gregor's body has ceased to signify, in any ordinary sense of the word. It has become pure language, the material text.

The act of reading is the ideological production or construction of the reader through an always violent confrontation with the text's hyletic disruptions of identity. This ideological confrontation between the reader and the text both destroys identity and establishes it; reading establishes as violent both the identity of the reader and that of the text. What is the connection between the physical text and the intertextual context, or ideology, provided for it by the reader? The reader is constructed by the intertext, upon and around the text, like a pearl around a grain of sand. Like the writer, the reader finally "gets rid of" the hyletic remains (corpse, excrement, rubbish) of the text, which she sweeps out of sight and obliterates with her interpretations. If writing is the elimination, or expulsion, of the text, then reading must be so, too.

THE BODY AS TEXT

> The charwoman stood grinning in the doorway as if she had good news to impart to the family but meant not to say a word unless properly questioned.... "Oh," said the charwoman, giggling so amiably that she could not at once continue, "just this, you don't need to bother about how to get rid (*weggeschafft werden*) of the thing (*Zeug*) next door. It's been seen to already."
>
> (Kafka 1948:131)

Near the end of Kafka's story, "The Metamorphosis," the charwoman assures the Samsa family that Gregor's corpse has been disposed of. Everything is once again in its proper place (*Es ist schon in Ordnung*). She alone has read from the inside the inscrutable parable of metamorphosis. The charwoman alone recognized that Gregor could still understand their words, that is, that he was still in some sense human, despite his monstrous physical transformation. It is she who straightens up the story.

Kafka's story reverberates in curious ways with the story of the anointing of Jesus in Mark 14:3–9:

> And when he was in Bethany in the house of Simon the leper, and at dinner, a woman came with an alabaster vessel full of ointment of nard, pure and precious; and she broke open the jar and poured the ointment over his head. But there were some who grumbled among themselves: Why was there this waste of ointment? The ointment could have been sold for upwards of three hundred denarii and the money given to the poor. And they scolded her. But Jesus said: Let her be. Why are you hard on her? She has done a good thing for me. For always you have the poor with you, and you can do them good whenever you will, but you do not always have me. She did what she could, she took the opportunity to anoint my body in advance for my burial. Truly I tell you, wherever the gospel is preached through all the world, what she did will also be spoken of, in memory of her.

Those who are present at the anointing of Jesus in Simon's house are indignant and reproachful at the nameless woman's waste of great wealth, the expensive ointment that she pours over Jesus's body. To this disturbing juxtaposition of great wealth and Jesus's reference to the poor ("always ... with you") is added the conjunction of the gospel and memory; as "what she did will also be spoken of" whenever the text of Mark is read, Mark's story is talking about itself again. Like Kafka's charwoman, the woman in Bethany obliterates the body. Despite the disciples' indignation, she has done them a service, performing a menial task ("she did what she could") so that they may get on about their insiders' business of preaching the gospel, as they do in the two added endings of Mark.[4] Whether the woman with the ointment is also a disciple is not stated, but she too is an insider, for Jesus approves of her extravagant action.

Matthew 26:6–13 follows Mark's version of the anointing of Jesus closely, abridging the story slightly. In Luke 7:36–50 and John 12:1–8, the woman "anointed" (*êleiphen*: Luke; *êleipsen*: John) Jesus's feet, rather than "poured" (*katecheen*) the ointment over his head, as happens in both Mark and Matthew. This seems to reduce the extravagance of the gesture. In Luke's quite different version, all reference to the poor and to the waste of money have been removed.

In addition, Luke has substantially altered the theme of the story, so that the story concerns the forgiveness of sins. John 12:4–6 also redirects the focus of the story by impugning Judas's motives for concern over the great expense of money and thereby explicitly conjoining Jesus's anointment and Judas's betrayal.

All of the synoptic gospels omit John's conjunction of anointment and betrayal, but Mark and Matthew do immediately follow the anointing story with the story of Judas going to the high priests and arranging to betray Jesus. In Matthew 26:14, Judas's betrayal is logically connected to the anointing of Jesus as the effect to its cause, by the conjunction *tote*, "and at that time." Mark 14:10 connects the anointment scene with Judas's betrayal by the conjunction *kai*, "and." The effect of this is that the significance of the connection between the scenes is left uncertain.

Nevertheless, even as the text of Mark anoints Jesus, it also betrays him. The woman's costly nard is an allegory of hermeneutical richness, covering the mere flesh of the signifier, Jesus's body, and preparing it/him for burial, just as the intertextual context prepares the naked text-body for the reading of faith. This reading of faith is the reading from the inside of Eucharistic consumption, of "body" and "blood," which follow immediately upon the episode of Judas arranging to betray Jesus, in the story of the last supper and the upper room (Mark 14:17–26). Thus Mark's story presents the sequence anointment ⇒ arrangement of betrayal ⇒ last supper.

Jesus's body has indeed disappeared by the end of Mark, more concretely than in the other biblical gospels, where Jesus seems to hang around interminably. John in particular stresses the continuing presence of Jesus's body. Yet although Jesus's body has completely disappeared by Mark 16:8, swallowed up in the silence of the terrified women, the body of Mark's text lingers on. Indeed, the body of the text is manifest in the women's silence, for they have now become outsiders: "to those who are outside all comes through parables, so that they may have sight but not see, and hear but not understand, lest they be converted and forgiven." If the women say "nothing to anyone," it is because there is nothing to be said, nothing that *can be said*. They are choking on the unspeakable hyletic body of the text.

The empty tomb with which Mark closes signifies the breaking of the mythic spell, the great disenchantment. The text itself is revealed as an "empty tomb." The empty tomb is a point of fantastic escape or liberation, that is, liberation from referential meaning. Through it, the gospel of Mark admits the inescapable fictionality of its language. The silence of the women's fear in Mark 16 reflects this moment of revelation – a revelation that the true story cannot be told.[5] The text of Mark admits its own failure as a narrative to present the reader with a coherent story. At the same time Mark speaks the unspeakability of the transcendent, the impossibility of a Transcendental Signified.

Unlike Gregor's body, however, the body of the text cannot be easily swept away. For Mark, no closure of the text is possible without suffering (Donahue in Kelber 1976:78). Along with the frightened women on Easter morning, the reader has yet to encounter the resurrected Jesus. An extratextual encounter with a signified savior might provide a definitive answer to the text's riddle, but Mark's text alone cannot supply that. As in saying 2 of the gospel of Thomas ("Let him who seeks continue seeking until he finds. When he finds, he will become troubled. When he becomes troubled, he will be astonished, and he will rule over the All" [Cameron 1982:25]), the speechless flight of the women from the tomb at the end of Mark's story itself lies at a point of being troubled and astonished.

Indeed, another text will be required to close Mark's text, or maybe it will take several other texts. Eventually a potentially endless string of commentaries and other intertextual readings of the gospel of Mark, including of course this book, will respond to Mark's own textual inadequacies. The general strategy of these books is to complete the uncompleted, to identify that which lacks identity, and thus to bring the reader's difficulties with Mark to an end. Even this book, which explicitly tries *not* to do that, may through its own illusions of completeness produce that effect anyway.

Within the New Testament, both the gospel of Matthew and the gospel of Luke attempt, in differing ways, to speak of the Transcendental Signified, disguising the failure which Mark admits (as does the gospel of Thomas). By giving us tales of encounters with the risen Jesus, Matthew and Luke allow the reassuring resurrection to sweep away the troublesome Crucifixion, both justifying and interpreting it. For these gospels and for the gospel of John, the resurrection accomplishes something. The incoherent non-disjunction of crucifixion and resurrection in Mark is transformed into systematic succession – that is, what was disordered and incomplete in Mark becomes well-ordered in the other gospels (Marin 1980:29).

Matthew and Luke unite death and resurrection in a continuous narrative, thereby overcoming any loss along the way and making sense of the whole story. Thus they allow the reader to see the "real" meaning of both crucifixion and resurrection: the triumph of the Christ. In each of these two gospels, the reappearance of the body of the Lord coincides with the disappearance of the body of the text; Mark's ambiguities have indeed been swept away. Mark's reader must either embrace a risen one who has not appeared or else get rid of the entire story as rubbish (*Zeug*). In either case, the reader's "astonishment" at the end of Mark, and likewise her astonishment at the entire gospel, has itself come to an end.

NOTES

INTRODUCTION

1   "The exterior or the other of the text is thus contained for us in the very
constitution of the text as a text which is only accomplished as meaning
by a constant displacement outside of itself, than by a gesture of
transcendence" (Marin 1980:216, n. 3). "The Other is neither an object
in the field of my perception, nor a subject who perceives me: the Other
is first of all a structure of the perceptual field without which this field,
in its totality, could not function as it does.... When I in my turn and
for myself grasp the reality of what the Other was expressing, I do
nothing except explicate the Other, develop and realize the corresponding possible world.... In short, the Other as structure is *the expression
of a possible world*, it is the expressed grasped as not yet existing outside
of that which expresses it" (Deleuze 1989:123).

2   Irnerio is discussed further in chapter 6.

3   Or increasingly, of magnetic or optical recording/playback devices,
computer media, processors, etc. In the electronic world, the question
of "what is text?" becomes even more complex, as "direct" reading by
humans of text (magnetic or laser alterations of tape, disk, etc.) is not
presently possible without machinery. Yet even "electronic text" has a
material, recorded aspect. Electronic text changes the *hulê*; it does not
dispense with it.

4   See Aichele 1991b.

5   Every translation "renders" a text in three senses of that word: it
presents the text, it interprets the text, and it clarifies (as one clarifies
fat, by boiling it) the text. A word-by-word or literal translation such
as Lattimore's tends to display the ambiguities of the text rather than
to explain or elucidate them.

6   For an example of differences between "literal" and "dynamic equivalent" translations, see Aichele 1992c. Other examples appear in the
following chapters.

1 JESUS FRAMED

1 The transliteration/translation combinations in Mark, and especially "talitha cum," are discussed further in chapter 3.

2 Taylor 1953:553 suggests a liturgical significance.

3 These repetitions range from small phrases (such as the words of the voice from heaven or the cloud, Mark 1:11, 9:7) to sizeable episodes (such as the feeding miracles in Mark 6 and 8). See Neirynck 1972.

4 For example, Nineham 1963:413, 416–17. Conversely, Taylor (1953) insists on the general historical plausibility of the scenes discussed in this chapter. For an alternative view, see Kermode 1979:110ff.

5 See Marin 1980:98–9. This theme appears in much popular contemporary literature, for example, Jorge Luis Borges's "Three Versions of Judas" and Nikos Kazantzakis's *The Last Temptation of Christ*.

6 All stories are to some extent self-referential (Aichele 1985, chapter 3; see also chapter 3 in this book). However, when self-referentiality becomes crucial to a story, this creates a loop or short-circuit of meaning. An analogy would be:

> The following sentence is true.
> The preceding sentence is true.

Both of these sentences are true, but they are about nothing beyond themselves. If Mark's story "fulfills scripture" by regarding itself as scripture, then this is true of Mark as well. Such self-referentiality is a striking characteristic of some postmodern stories, such as Italo Calvino's *If On a Winter's Night a Traveler* (see chapter 6).

7 On Mark's treatment of Judas and Peter, see Fowler 1991:247; Marin 1980:120ff., 155ff.; and Kermode 1979:62. "We are thinking in effect of considering two coupled functions named 'Peter' and 'Judas' which, between them, constitute a complete performative in [J.L.] Austin's sense: the production of an enunciation and the execution of an action" (Marin 1980:232, n. 78).

8 Not by name, but as "one of you" (Mark 14:18), "one of the twelve, the one who dips into the dish with me" (14:20); thus the phrases apply equally well to Peter or to any of the disciples. Matthew 26:25 makes the reference to Judas explicit.

9 Mark's enigmatic references to the young man are central to the debate about the "secret gospel of Mark." See Crossan (1985), chapters 6–7. Compare also the references to the "other disciple" in John 18:15–16.

10 I assume that Mark ends at 16:8; Peter does appear again in the shorter added ending to Mark, and presumably as one of the eleven (16:14) in the longer added ending.

11 Compare Marin 1980:222, n. 28.

12 The phrase "son of man" in Mark is discussed further in chapter 5.

13 Burnett's (1992a) discussion of the narrative function of Jesus's proper name in Matthew is pertinent here.

14 Recent studies using literary-critical methodologies, as well as some more traditional approaches to Mark such as Kelber 1976, have rejected Kähler's judgment.

15 See Aichele (1992b).

16 The beginning and the multiple endings of Mark are discussed further in chapter 2.

17 For example, Donahue in Kelber 1976:62: "... Mark has constructed the trial narrative in such a way that it embodies major theological concerns of his Gospel. The trial itself is considered an entree to Mark's theology." However, Donahue also recognizes that "belief for Mark is rooted in irony and paradox" (in Kelber 1976:78).

18 See Burnett (1992b, especially 156–8), and the works which he cites.

19 The general relation between texts and ideologies, and the possibility that a counter-reading might "steal" a text, are discussed in chapter 7.

2 DESIRE FOR AN END

1 Aristotle's theory of poetics is closely connected not only with his metaphysics (via the concept of mimesis) and his logic, but also with his views on ethics (via the concept of character), politics, and rhetoric. These connections cannot be pursued here.

2 See also Barthes 1985:17.

3 The striking similarity between this line of argumentation and that of the classical cosmological proof (derived from Aristotle) of the existence of God cannot be pursued here.

4 The "serial," whether television, novel, or comic-book, produces a distinct phenomenon from the sequel or prequel, for many serials are constructed as though they were episodes in stories which are in principle endless (and which have no fundamental narrative unity to them, according to Aristotle). Nonetheless, it may be impossible in practice to distinguish between a serial and a series of sequels; compare, for example, the original *Star Trek* TV show with the *Star Trek* movies.

5 Many manuscripts add "the Son of God" at the end of verse 1 (compare RSV).

6 See for example Italo Calvino's *If On a Winter's Night a Traveler*, which is discussed further in chapter 6. This second-person novel features the attempt by "you" to read Italo Calvino's novel, *If On a Winter's Night a Traveler*. Many postmodern narratives feature self-referential characteristics such as this. Perhaps the best-known example is Flann O'Brien's *At Swim-Two-Birds*.

7 Aichele (forthcoming).

8 This ending is "uncontested" in that all of the endings of Mark include it, although not all include it as or at the end. It is also the ending in fact of the gospel of Mark in codices Vaticanus (B) and Sinaiticus (ℵ) from the fourth century. These two manuscripts are widely regarded by scholars as containing the oldest complete texts of the gospels. The evidence in Patristic sources for the supplementary endings is older than these manuscripts by a century or more. Nonetheless, Nineham argues that the version of Mark known to the authors of Matthew and Luke ended at 16:8 (1963:439).

9   See Boring 1991:50, Nineham 1963:440, Taylor 1953:609. "Mark begins *in medias res* and ends without closing" (Boring 1985:147, n.14); contrast Magness 1986:90, 119.

10 For example, Rhoads and Michie 1982:35ff., especially 39; Fowler 1991:61.

11 For example, Taylor 1953:609–10.

12 Few if any scholars regard either of the added endings as original. For further discussion of textual evidence for Mark's endings, see Aland and Aland 1987:287–8.

13 This ending appears in several manuscripts from the fifth century and following (including codices L, ψ, 099, 0112). In most of these manuscripts, this text is followed in turn by the longer added ending discussed below, but in one case (the Old Latin codex k) the shorter added ending alone closes the text of Mark.

14 See Taylor 1953:614.

15 See Mark 1:14, 38, 39. The healed leper "proclaims" also (1:45), as does the demoniac (5:20). The verb may be used self-referentially in 13:10 and 14:9. In the longer added ending, note also 16:15, 20 (used of the disciples).

16 This includes codices A, C, D, W, and θ. Although Irenaeus, and possibly Tatian and Justin, knew of the existence of the longer ending in the second century, Eusebius and Jerome in the fourth century claimed that the best manuscripts did not have the longer added ending.

17 These include Jerusalem, Phillips, Scholar's Version (longer added ending in square brackets), and RSV (longer added ending in italics and a smaller typeface). NEB prints both added endings (the shorter first). TEV and Lattimore place both added endings in square brackets (in reverse order in Lattimore).

18 With the possible exception of John 7:53–8:11.

19 Presumably it is Judas who is now absent from the group – none of the eleven are mentioned by name.

20 Lattimore: "the agony"; RSV: "the birthpangs."

21 See note 26.

22 See Nineham 1963:453, and Taylor 1953:612, 615.

23 The relation between ideology and theology is pursued further in the Introduction and in chapter 7.

24 See Barthes 1974, 1975, 1977b. Also Kristeva 1984:*passim*. "There is no limit to what can be said in the text.... The text's so-called *composition*, however, assigns a 'boundary to the infinite,' and thereby fulfills the text's first criterion: to avoid becoming a free-flow 'escape' of the signifier, this discourse must provide itself with guardrails" (209).

25 Crossan (1985) and others have argued persuasively that the Transfiguration and the Walking on the Sea (Mark 6:45–51) were originally resurrection stories which Mark has transplanted back into pre-death settings. Nonetheless, the fact that this transplanting has already been written into Mark seriously undermines the significance of these stories as resurrection appearances. See, for example, Kelber 1976:150ff.

26 Compare Kelber in Kelber 1976:175: "The young man [in Mark 14:51]

mimics Jesus' escape from death and almost comically exposes the failure of the plot to kill Jesus. He plays the role of transition from the Gospel's disintegrating process toward reintegration." Kelber's reading requires the reader to fill in many gaps surrounding the only two uses of *neaniskos*, "young man" (14:51, 16:5) in Mark.

3 TALITHA CUM

1 The same is also true of Mark 14:36, where Jesus prays, "Abba, Father." It may be that "Abba" had theological significance to early Christians.

2 Witnesses for *talitha koum* include the two oldest complete manuscripts of Mark, the fourth-century codices B (Vaticanus) and ℵ (Sinaiticus). On the use of Aramaic in relation to the gospels and Acts, see Black (1967; especially 277–80). Black makes a strong case that codex D is closer to Aramaic than either B or ℵ; whether this means that D is closer to the "original" words of Jesus is not my interest here. Black's (and others') views concerning an Aramaic original "behind" the gospels has been strongly contested by Guenther (1992) and others.

3 See Taylor 1953:296.

4 See, for example, Nineham 1963:162, 204. Taylor rejects this view.

5 Given the mystery that surrounds the "secret gospel of Mark," there is a possibility that some version of Mark was indeed kept for esoteric use only. However, that would not be the (canonical) version of Mark considered here, which has presumably been cleansed of dangerous material. For discussion, see Crossan 1985, chapters 6–7. The letter concerning the "secret gospel of Mark" appears in Cameron 1982.

6 Additional miracle stories appear in the next several chapters of the gospel, and they include the story of which Mark 7:34 ("ephphatha") is a part. Also included of course is Mark 7:11, the saying about Corban, although that is not part of a miracle story.

7 The parallel stories in Matthew 8:18, 23–34, 9:18–26, and Luke 8:22–55 reflect some of these fantastical qualities, but others have been removed; see Aichele 1991a.

8 See Hedrick 1993:9.

9 The word *parakousas* can also mean "overheard."

10 This seeming haste may be simply an effect of Mark's parataxic narrative style. In any case, it contributes to the overall effect of the story.

11 A noteworthy exception is Taylor (1953:295), who at least keeps his options open. Hedrick (1993:9–13) considers both options before deciding that the girl is dead.

12 Compare Mark 9:27, 16:6. Note also the conjunction of *katheudê* and *egeirêtai* with *parestêken* and *paradoi* in a very different setting in Mark 4:26–9. Here too an allegorical reference to death and resurrection is possible.

13 The reference, hermeneutic, and proairetic codes are three of the five reading codes described and used by Barthes throughout his reading of

Sarrasine (1974). See especially 17–21. Further discussion of these codes appears in chapter 6 of this book. Further discussion of connotation and denotation appears in chapter 5.

14 Literal translation will also be discussed in chapters 5 and 6.

15 The question of self-referentiality is also pursued in chapter 1, in relation to Mark's reference to itself as "scripture."

16 See Aichele, 1991b.

17 For example, Mark 1:1, 8:35, 10:29, 13:10, 14:9, 16:15; see also Mark 13:14, 16:8.

18 This question addressed by this chapter appeared on and was discussed by the IOUDAIOS discussion group on the Internet (IOUDAIOS-L@lehigh.edu) from January 6–14, 1993. I am grateful to the participants in that discussion, including Bruce Whittmarsh (who asked the initial question), Stan Kulikowski, Alan Humm, Larry Hurtado, Jim Strange, Don Westblade, Herb Basser, Rochelle Altman, and Ira Robinson.

4 THE TEXT READS ITSELF

1 Section 275. In the Seventh Letter attributed to Plato, the possibility of writing the truth is questioned, paradoxically, in a written document (section 341 = Plato 1973:136); see also Derrida's remarkable essay on the *Phaedrus* passage, "Plato's Pharmacy" (1981).

2 The following diagram is borrowed and adapted from Barthes (1967a:89–90).

3 The non-reader is discussed further in chapter 6. The naive reader is discussed further in chapter 5. Literal translation is discussed further in chapters 3 and 6.

4 See Kermode 1979:27–8, who also compares this text to Mark 4:11ff. Kafka's story has also been published separately from *The Trial* under the title "Before the Law" (*Vor dem Gesetz*) (1958).

5 In striking contrast is the doorkeeper parable of Mark 13:34–6.

6 This is the Revised Standard Version. Lattimore curiously has "the secrets of the Kingdom of God."

7 Compare "he said to them" in Mark 4:21 and 24, but note also Mark 4:11.

8 See Fowler 1991:101–2. Although not parallel to Mark 4:24–5, saying 70 of the gospel of Thomas echoes a similar address to the reader:

> Jesus said, "That which you have will save you if you bring it forth from yourselves. That which you do not have within you will kill you if you do not have it within you."

Many of the sayings in the gospel of Thomas reflect this reference to their own reading (see especially sayings 1 and 2).

9 Compare Lattimore's translations of the identical wording at Mark 10:38, 13:33, and 13:35 (see also 10:42). RSV translates Mark 4:13 as "Do you not understand ...?" NEB, TEV, and the Jerusalem Bible adopt similar strategies.

10 See Nineham 1963:140; Fowler 1991:184.
11 See Kermode 1979:33.
12 Mark 1:1, 14, 15, 8:35, 10:29, 13:10, and 14:9 (and 16:15). Whether the words "the gospel" are self-referential in Mark is a matter of some disagreement. Nevertheless, whatever Mark says about "the gospel" applies also to the story of Mark itself.
13 For example, Taylor 1953:258.
14 See Crossan 1980; Tolbert 1989.
15 See Moore 1992, chapters 1–3.
16 The ideological and theological dimensions of reading are discussed further in chapters 6 and 7.
17 See Hartman and Budick (1986), especially the essays by Fishbane, Kugel, Stern, Dan, Kermode, and Solotorevsky.
18 See Fishbane in Hartman and Budick (1986).
19 Faur (1986) describes the multiple and even mutually contradictory quality of midrashim, as well as the distinction between oral and written Torah.
20 Could this meta-canonical function, rather than the canonical status which the New Testament eventually acquired, have prompted the astonishing adoption by early Christians of the codex form of manuscript, at a time when Jews and nearly all others in the Mediterranean world were still using the scroll? See Roberts and Skeat 1983, who hint at something like this (57–9, especially 59, n. 3) but do not pursue it.
21 This has become apparent in biblical scholarship as the great manuscript discoveries at Qumran and Nag Hammadi, among other things, have led to wider awareness of the fluidity of "canon" in early Judaism and Christianity.

5 JESUS'S FRANKNESS

1 John 7:4, 13, 26, 10:24, 11:14, 54, 16:25, 29, 18:20.
2 Mark 4:11–12 is discussed at greater length in the Introduction and chapter 4 of this book.
3 See also *Apocryphon of James* 8:1–9, 11:15.
4 Acts 2:29, 4:13, 4:29, 4:31, 9:27, 9:28, 13:46, 14:3, 18:26, 19:8, 26:26, 28:31 (the final sentence in Acts). See Mealand 1990:596–7.
5 Fowler (1991) claims that there is no "uptake" by characters in Mark on Jesus's "son of man" statements. This exchange may be an exception, although no other character uses the phrase. The Cynics were also subject to rebuke (Vaage 1992:33); however, the Cynics' words and behavior are characterized by a sense of humor which seems absent from the episode at Caesarea Philippi.
6 Schlier derives *parrêsia* from *pan* + *rhê-*, the root from which *rhêma* is also derived, in Kittel V 1967:871, n. 1 (citing Plato, *Gorgias*, 461e). *Rhê-/rheô* apparently serves as root for a number of Greek words, including *rhêsis*, *rhêma*, *rhêtos*, and *rhêtra*, which have overlapping meanings. Of these words, only *rhêma* occurs in the New Testament.

NOTES

See also Liddell and Scott (1940), who derive *parrêsia* from *pas* + *rhêsis*, and Debrunner *et al.*, in Kittel IV 1967:75, n.19. Note the phrases *meta pasês parrêsias* in Acts 28:31 and *en pasê parrêsia* in Philippians 1:20 (compare 2 Corinthians 3:12, 7:4).

7

> "In *Cratylus* ... Plato characterizes the position of Heraclitus with *rhoê* (*rheô*) as 'flowing,' and hence as 'flux.' *Rheô*, then becomes a metaphor for change, particularly the flux that renders absolute knowledge impossible... as far as knowledge (or *understanding*) is concerned, any form of *rheô* got buried and became the suppressed, negative term in the philosophical traditions.... if by Mark's time *rhêma* connoted the impossibility of certainty in knowledge, then how could the disciples understand even when Jesus spoke to them 'frankly' (entombed *rheô*, or flux, in the bold speech of *parrêsia*)? What is encrypted in Mark 8:32 in *parrêsia* (namely *rheô* as 'flux') seems to 'rear its connotative head' in *rhêma* in 9:32!... That is, the very word *parrêsia* carries within it the *impossibility* of understanding (in *rheô*), which then the entire narrative of Mark 'works out' in its presentation of an enigmatic Jesus."
> (Fred Burnett, private correspondence, December, 1992)

8 According to Lattimore's translation, and the RSV. Lattimore's translation reproduces some of the ambiguity of the Greek text (which has no punctuation) by replacing quotation marks with less decisive punctuation.

9 Perhaps the nearest to an explicit identification of Jesus as the son of man in Mark is found at 14:41–2: "behold, the son of man is betrayed ... see, my betrayer is near." However, see John 6:53–6, 8:28, and 9:35–7. Also compare Matthew 16:13, 15, to Mark 8:27, 29, and see also Luke 22:47–8. These latter tendencies reflect what I have elsewhere called the de-fantasizing of Mark by other canonical gospels.

10 The self-referentiality in Mark of "the fulfillment of the scriptures" is discussed further in chapter 1.

11 Here we find a "son of man" saying conjoined with the word *exousia*. Fowler argues that this "son of man" saying should be read as the narrator's commentary, not Jesus's words (1991:114, 116n.); Fowler also treats Mark 2:28 as such a commentary (1991:103–7).

12 Both with and without definite articles. For example, LXX Psalm 11:2, 9, 30:20, 32:13, 44:3, 52:3, 57:2, 88:48, 106:8, 15, 21, 31, 113:24, and 144:12. Perhaps the best-known examples are in Ezekiel (2:1, 3, 6, 8, 3:1, etc.). Ecclesiastes uses "sons of man," *hoi huioi tou anthrôpou*, at 1:13, 2:3, 3:10, and 9:12. Contrast Genesis 6:2, "the daughters of men," *tas thugateras tôn anthrôpôn*.

13 Oxyrhynchus Papyrus 1 (= Thomas 28) has *tois huiois tōn an(thrôp)ôn*, "the sons of men."

14 The suffering son of man appears also at Mark 9:9, 12, 31, 10:33, 14:21 (perhaps), and 41. See also Mark 12:6.

15 See Vermes and Black in Black 1967:310ff. In Mark 9:11–13, a parallel

is established between the son of man and Elijah. If Elijah = John the Baptist, then the son of man = Jesus – this is a common reading of this saying. But what if these verses are read as Elijah = son of man? Note the similarities between 9:12b and 9:13, bracketed by "it is written about (*gegraptai ep[i]*) [the son of man, Elijah]." Could Jesus be proclaiming here that John the Baptist is the son of man? A clear distinction between John and the son of man is suggested by Matthew 11:19 (par. Luke 7:34), to which Mark has no parallel.

16 Connotation and denotation are discussed further in chapters 2, 3, and 4.

17 See Frege's essay, "On Sense and Meaning" (1952); also Aichele 1985. Compare Eco: "a denotation is a cultural unit or semantic property of a given sememe which is at the same time a culturally recognized property of its possible referents." (1976:86).

18 This understanding is most fully developed in Chatman (1978).

19 In *Criticism and Truth*, originally written in 1965–6, Barthes used "primary language" and "literal reading" instead of "denotation," and "second language" instead of "connotation" (1987a:69). He expressed dissatisfaction with the implications of this terminology.

20 Or, he says, an "Iroquois." Barthes apparently thinks of Martians and Iroquois as being equally foreign to "our language." Elsewhere he speaks of the "mythology" which associates Mars with impartial judgment. "Mars [is] merely an imagined Earth, endowed with perfect wings, as in all dreams of idealization" (1979a:28).

21 Copi and Cohen (1990:142) argue that extension (denotation) is determined by intension (connotation), not vice versa.

22 However, in this passage, Barthes also equates myth with metalanguage, not connotation. Compare the diagram in 1972:115 to those in 1967a:90. His further discussion of myth in *Mythologies* (1972:114–17) concerns connotation.

23 There are no more Iroquois, at least in this sense!

24 See Husserl 1962:226ff.; also Kristeva 1984:31ff., Deleuze and Guattari 1983:36.

25 I am indebted to Professor Richard Hutcheson (SUNY/Potsdam) for invaluable assistance in the preparation of this chapter. An earlier version of the chapter appeared in the 1992 Society of Biblical Literature (SBL) *Seminar Papers* (Atlanta: Scholars Press).

6 READING BEYOND MEANING

1 This of course also applies to different media. For example, is the RSV of the gospel of Mark the same text in an expensive leather-bound edition, a cheap paperback edition, a digitized electronic version, and a recorded "talking book" version?

2 The advent of electronic culture, with readily available technologies of textual reproduction, transmission, and transformation, seriously threatens the stability of this triple economy. Hence electronic culture is in some ways more receptive than its predecessors to postmodern ideas.

3 Foucault notes some logical difficulties in the concept of "the work" (1979:143–4).
4 See Aichele 1985, especially chapters 3 and 4.
5 Nor is Irnerio a product of either oral or electronic culture. Irnerio belongs entirely to print culture.
6

> ...the *chôra*, as rupture and articulations (rhythm), precedes evidence, verisimilitude, spatiality, and temporality.... all discourse ... moves with and against the *chôra* in the sense that it simultaneously depends upon and refuses it.
>
> (Kristeva 1984:26)

> ...Previous to the ego thinking within a proposition, no Meaning exists, but there *do* exist articulations heterogeneous to signification and to the sign: the semiotic *chôra*.
>
> (Kristeva 1984:36, her emphasis)

See also Kristeva 1984:239, n. 12.
7

> ... we do not form oppositions of *named*, fractionized values; we skirt, we avoid, we dodge such values: *we take tangents*; strictly speaking, this is not a change of course; the fear is that we fall into opposition, aggression, i.e., into meaning.
>
> (Barthes 1977b:140)

8 Compare Marin 1975:56.
9 The *hermeneutic* code both provides and delays the answers to questions; the *semic* code concerns nuances and implications ("flickers of meaning") of the utterance; the *symbolic* code specifies multiple levels of meaning; the *proairetic* code lays out an empirical sequence of actions; the *reference* code addresses the cultural repository, the authorities of knowledge (Barthes 1974:17–21).
10 See Scholem 1987, and Faur 1986.
11 See also Belo 1981:262ff., 281–4.
12 See Aichele 1992a.
13 Calvino, Benjamin, and Belo provide examples of what I have elsewhere called "concrete theology": "In order to exceed the limits, theology must uncover the not-itself which lies unnamed at its center, its hidden eccentricity and non-identity: it must become concrete" (Aichele 1985:138–9).
14 The relation between intertext and ideology is pursued further in chapter 7.
15 See Aichele 1985: *passim*.
16 A better term than either of these for what happens in interpretation may be one recently proposed by Gary Phillips, "intergesis," which suggests a reading between the texts, or intertextual reading (1992).
17 When I teach *S/Z*, I have the students read *Sarrasine* first. Several usually come up with such readings.
18 For a variety of explorations of this issue, see Culley and Robinson (1993).
19 An earlier version of this chapter appeared in the electronic journal *Postmodern Culture*, May, 1993 (Oxford University Press).

7 TEXT, INTERTEXT, IDEOLOGY

1   In contrast, I understand an author to be a special sort of reader, but
    nothing more. "There can be no writing without reading" (de Man
    1979:202). All reading is rewriting, and all writing is reading. The
    ideology of a text's producers is no more inherent in the text than is the
    ideology of its consumers.

2   Fowl (1995) identifies and quotes several of these critics.

3   See Aichele 1985, especially chapter 1.

4
> The text's principal characteristic and the one that distinguishes
> it from other signifying practices, is precisely that it introduces,
> through binding and through vital and symbolic differentiation,
> heterogeneous rupture and rejection: jouissance and death. ...
> [H]eterogeneity is that part of the objective, material outer world
> which could not be grasped by the various symbolizing struc-
> tures the subject already has at his disposal.
>
> (Kristeva 1984:180)

5   See Husserl 1962:226ff.; also Kristeva 1984:31ff., Deleuze and Guattari
    1983:36.

6   See Jameson 1972:109; Barthes 1987b:71–2.

7   Compare Jameson 1991:249. Ideology is operative in the historical
    production of the text (in the linguistic conventions of the author, the
    first audience, etc.), but this ideology is no more "in" the text than is
    the ideology of the contemporary reader, as these instances indicate.

8   Irnerio is discussed further in chapter 6.

9   See Jameson 1972:104–5. This idea of course is a variation on the
    widespread modernist theme of form vs. content or container vs.
    contained.

10 Barthes calls this "the Last Signified" (1988:242).

11 See Jameson 1972:158.

12 Paul Ricoeur is perhaps the best-known advocate of this view.

13 Compare Penchansky's distinction between the "juicy stories" of
    Judges and the "Deuteronomic Template" (in Jobling and Pippin
    1992:35–41). See also Barthes 1975:36.

14 See Schaberg in Jobling and Pippin 1992:222.

15 See Schaberg in Jobling and Pippin 1992:224.

16 See Ong 1967; Derrida 1973, 1976, 1981.

17 This is how I understand Barthes's claim that "[e]very text [is] ... itself
    the intertext of another text [and] belongs to the intertextual"
    (1979b:77).

18 The relation between canonicity and reading is pursued further in
    chapter 4.

19 When Fowl (1995) compares the Abraham stories in Genesis to the
    readings of these texts by Philo, Paul, and Justin Martyr, he notes the
    ideological codes through which Philo, Paul, and Justin rewrite
    Genesis, but he does not note the codes through which he then reads
    the four texts. To do so would open up an infinite intertextual
    regression.

20 Compare Steiner's discussion of translation as "mistaking" (1975: 379–80); see also Derrida 1979:171.
21 See Steiner (1975:473) and of course Wittgenstein (1953). See also Jameson's comments on "discursive struggles" (in Jobling and Pippin 1992:232).
22 See note 18. See also Deleuze and Guattari 1983:184ff. and especially 202–3.
23 I am indebted to Stephen Fowl's 1992 paper for the SBL Ideological Criticism Group, "Texts Don't Have Ideologies," which provided the impetus for this chapter (Fowl 1995).

POSTCRIPT

1 The significance of "frankness" in relation to Mark 8:31–2a is discussed further in chapter 5.
2 Once again, this applies not only to printed writing, strictly speaking, but to all "text" as defined in chapter 7. Even electronic texts cannot exist without a material aspect, such as the magnetic alterations of a disk or the illuminated pixels of a display screen. The fact that the reader can physically rewrite the electronic text much more easily than she can rewrite a printed text does not alter this fundamental materiality in any way. Of course different physical media *do* influence the production of the text in different ways, many of which have ideological implications (for example, gender in language, the economics of publishing, or the accessibility of relevant technology).
3 Even for the book collector, the ancient bundles of ink and paper are of no value except that they stand in some relationship to the work, for example, of Chaucer or Dante or Goethe.
4 The endings of Mark are discussed further in chapter 2.
5 Something quite similar appears in the disciple Thomas's refusal to speak in saying 13 of the gospel of Thomas:

> Jesus said to His disciples, "Compare me to someone and tell Me whom I am like." Simon Peter said to Him, "You are like a righteous angel." Matthew said to Him, "You are like a wise philosopher." Thomas said to Him, "Master, my mouth is wholly incapable of saying whom You are like." Jesus said, "I am not your master. Because you have drunk, you have become intoxicated from the bubbling spring which I have measured out." And He took him and withdrew and told him three things. When Thomas returned to his companions, they asked him, "What did Jesus say to you?" Thomas said to them, "If I tell you one of the things which he told me, you will pick up stones and throw them at me; a fire will come out of the stones and burn you up"
>
> (Cameron 1982:26–7).

BIBLIOGRAPHY

Aichele, George (1985) *The Limits of Story*, Chico, CA: Scholars Press.
——(1991a) "Biblical Miracle Narratives as Fantasy," *Anglican Theological Review* 73/1:51–8.
——(1991b) "Translation, Narrative, and Theology," *Explorations* 9/4:61–80.
——(1992a) "Post-Ecclesiastical Theology," *Explorations* 10/3: 5–14.
——(1992b) "Two Fantasies on the Death of Jesus," *Neotestamentica* 26/2:485–98.
——(1992c) "Two Theories of Translation, With Examples From the Gospel of Mark," *Journal for the Study of the New Testament* 47:95–116.
——(forthcoming) "Fantasy and the Gospels: Theological and Ideological Implications," *Journal for the Fantastic in the Arts*.
Aland, Kurt and Aland, Barbara (1987) *The Text of the New Testament*, trans. Erroll F. Rhodes, Grand Rapids, MI: Eerdmanns and Leiden: Brill.
Aristotle (1967) *Poetics*, trans. Gerald Else, Ann Arbor, MI: University of Michigan Press.
Auerbach, Erich (1957) *Mimesis, the Representation of Reality in Western Literature*, trans. Willard Trask, Garden City, NY: Doubleday and Co.
Balzac, Honoré de (1974) *Sarrasine*, trans. Richard Miller. In R. Barthes, *S/Z*, New York: Hill and Wang.
Barthes, Roland (1967a) *Elements of Semiology*, trans. Annette Lavers and Colin Smith, New York: Hill and Wang.
——(1967b) *Writing Degree Zero*, trans. Annette Lavers and Colin Smith, New York: Hill and Wang.
——(1972) *Mythologies*, trans. Annette Lavers, New York: Hill and Wang.
——(1974) *S/Z*, trans. Richard Miller, New York: Hill and Wang.
——(1975) *The Pleasure of the Text*, trans. Richard Miller, New York: Hill and Wang.

——(1976) *Sade, Fourier, Loyola*, trans. Richard Miller, New York: Hill and Wang.

——(1977a) *Image, Music, Text*, trans. Stephen Heath, New York: Hill and Wang.

——(1977b) *Roland Barthes*, trans. Richard Howard, New York: Hill and Wang.

——(1978) *A Lover's Discourse*, trans. Richard Howard, New York: Farrar, Straus and Giroux.

——(1979a) *The Eiffel Tower and Other Mythologies*, trans. Richard Howard, New York: Hill and Wang.

——(1979b) "From Work to Text," trans. Josué V. Harari, in *Textual Strategies*, Ithaca, NY: Cornell University Press.

——(1983) *The Fashion System*, trans. Matthew Ward and Richard Howard, Berkeley and Los Angeles: University of California Press.

——(1985) *The Grain of the Voice: Interviews 1962–1980*, trans. Linda Coverdale, Berkeley and Los Angeles: University of California Press.

——(1986) *The Rustle of Language*, trans. Richard Howard, Berkeley and Los Angeles: University of California Press.

——(1987a) *Criticism and Truth*, trans. Katrine Pilcher Keuneman, Minneapolis: University of Minnesota Press.

——(1987b) *Writer Sollers*, trans. Philip Thody, Minneapolis: University of Minnesota Press.

——(1988) *The Semiotic Challenge*, trans. Richard Howard, New York: Hill and Wang. (French original: *L'aventure sémiologique*, Paris: Editions du Seuil, 1985.)

Belo, Fernando (1981) *A Materialist Reading of the Gospel of Mark*, trans. Matthew J. O'Connell, Maryknoll, NY: Orbis Books.

Benjamin, Walter (1968) *Illuminations*, trans. Harry Zohn, New York: Schocken Books.

Berg, Temma F. (1989) "Reading In/To Mark," in *Semeia* 48:187–206.

Black, Matthew (1967) *An Aramaic Approach to the Gospels and Acts*, 3rd edn, Oxford: Oxford University Press.

Borges, José Luís (1962) *Ficciones*, trans. Anthony Kerrigan (ed.) New York: Grove Press Inc.

Boring, M. Eugene (1985) "The Christology of Mark: Hermeneutical Issues for Systematic Theology," in *Semeia* 30:125–53.

——(1991) "Mark 1:1–15 and the Beginning of the Gospel," in *Semeia* 52:43–81.

Burnett, Fred (1992a) "The Undecidability of the Proper Name 'Jesus' in Matthew," in *Semeia* 54:123–45.

——(1992b) "Exposing the Anti-Jewish Ideology of Matthew's Implied Author: the Characterization of God as Father," in *Semeia* 59:155–91.

Calvino, Italo (1981) *If On a Winter's Night a Traveler*, trans. William Weaver, New York: Harcourt Brace Jovanovich, Inc.

——(1986) *The Uses of Literature*, trans. Patrick Creagh, New York: Harcourt Brace Jovanovich, Inc.

Cameron, Ron (ed.) (1982) *The Other Gospels*, Philadelphia: The Westminster Press.

Chatman, Seymour (1978) *Story and Discourse*, Ithaca, NY: Cornell University Press.

Carroll, Lewis (Charles Dodgson) (n.d.) *Through the Looking Glass*, New York: Grosset & Dunlap.

Copi, Irving and Cohen, Carl (1990) *Introduction to Logic*, eighth edn, New York: Macmillan Publishing Co.

Crossan, John Dominic (1980) *Cliffs of Fall*, New York: The Seabury Press.

——(1985) *Four Other Gospels*, Minneapolis: Winston Press.

Culley, Robert C. and Robinson, Robert B. (eds) (1993) in *Semeia* 62, Atlanta: SBL/Scholars Press.

Deleuze, Gilles (1989) "Michel Tournier and the World Without Others," in Mike Gane (ed.) *Ideological Representation and Power in Social Relations: Literary and Social Theory*, London and New York: Routledge.

——and Guattari, Felix (1983) *Anti-Oedipus*, trans. Robert Hurley, Mark Seem, and Helen R. Lane, Minneapolis: University of Minnesota Press.

de Man, Paul (1979) *Allegories of Reading*, New Haven: Yale University Press.

——(1983) *Blindness and Insight*, Minneapolis: University of Minnesota Press.

——(1986) *The Resistance to Theory*, Minneapolis: University of Minnesota Press.

Derrida, Jacques (1973) *Speech and Phenomena*, trans. David B. Allison, Evanston, IL: Northwestern University Press.

——(1976) *Of Grammatology*, trans. Gayatri Chakravorty Spivak, Baltimore: The Johns Hopkins University Press.

——(1979) "Living On: Borderlines," trans. James Hulbert, in *Deconstruction and Criticism*, New York: Seabury Press.

——(1981) *Dissemination*, trans. Barbara Johnson, Chicago: University of Chicago Press.

——(1985) *The Ear of the Other*, trans. Peggy Kamuf and Avital Ronell, New York: Schocken Books.

Dewey, Kim E. (1980) "Paroimiai in the Gospel of John," in *Semeia* 17:81–99.

Eco, Umberto (1976) *A Theory of Semiotics*, Bloomington: Indiana University Press.

Faur, José (1986) *Golden Doves with Silver Dots*, Bloomington: Indiana University Press.

Foucault, Michel (1979) "What Is an Author?" trans. Josué V. Harari (ed.) in *Textual Strategies*, Ithaca, NY: Cornell University Press.

Fowl, Stephen (1995) "Texts Don't Have Ideologies," in *Biblical Interpretation* 3/1:15–34. (Originally presented to SBL Ideological Criticism Section, 1992.)

Fowler, Robert (1991) *Let the Reader Understand*, Philadelphia: Fortress Press.

Frege, Gottlob (1952) *Translations from the Philosophical Writings of Gottlob Frege*, Peter Geach and Max Black (eds) Oxford: Basil Blackwell.

Guenther, Heinz O. (1992) "The Sayings Gospel Q and the Quest for Aramaic Sources: Rethinking Christian Origins," in *Semeia* 55:41–76.

Hartman, Geoffrey H. and Budick, Sanford (eds) (1986) *Midrash and Literature*, New Haven: Yale University Press.

Hedrick, Charles W. (1993) "Through the Looking Glass: Was She Dead or Only Asleep? Narrative Criticism and Jairus's Daughter," presented to Westar Institute, Spring 1993.

Hennecke, Edgar and Schneemelcher, Wilhelm (eds) (1963) *New Testament Apocrypha*, vol. I., trans. R. McL. Wilson, Philadelphia: The Westminster Press.

Husserl, Edmund (1962) *Ideas*, trans. W.R. Boyce Gibson, New York: Macmillan Publishing Co.

Jameson, Fredric (1972) *The Prison-House of Language*, Princeton: Princeton University Press.

——(1975) "The Ideology of the Text," in *Salmagundi* 31–2:204–46.

——(1991) *Postmodernism, or the Cultural Logic of Late Capitalism*, Durham, NC: Duke University Press.

Jerusalem Bible, trans., (1966) *The Jerusalem Bible*, The New Testament, Garden City, NY: Doubleday & Co.

Jobling, David and Pippin, Tina (eds) (1992) in *Semeia* 59, Atlanta: Scholars Press/SBL.

Joyce, James (1986) *Ulysses*, New York: Random House.

Kafka, Franz (1948) *The Penal Colony*, trans. Willa and Edwin Muir, New York: Schocken Books. (German original of "The Metamorphosis": "Die Verwandlung," Berlin: Schocken Verlag, 1935.)

——(1958) *Parables and Paradoxes*, various trans., New York: Schocken Books.

——(1964) *The Trial*, trans. Willa and Edwin Muir, revised and additional trans. E.M. Butler, New York: Alfred A. Knopf, Inc.

Kähler, Martin (1964) *The So-called Historical Jesus and the Historic, Biblical Christ*, trans. C.E. Braaten (ed.) Philadelphia: Fortress Press.

Kant, Immanuel (1929) *Critique of Pure Reason*, trans. Norman Kemp Smith, London: Macmillan & Co. Ltd.; reprinted New York: St. Martin's Press.

Kazantzakis, Nikos (1960) *The Last Temptation of Christ*, trans. P.A. Bien, New York: Simon and Schuster.

Kelber, Werner (ed.) (1976) *The Passion in Mark*, Philadelphia: Fortress Press.

——(1983) *The Oral and the Written Gospel*, Philadelphia: Fortress Press.

——(1990) "In the Beginning Were the Words," *Journal of the American Academy of Religion* 58/1:69–98.

Kermode, Frank (1967) *The Sense of an Ending*, Oxford: Oxford University Press.

——(1978) "Sensing Endings," in *Nineteenth-Century Fiction* 33:144–58.

——(1979) *The Genesis of Secrecy*, Cambridge, MA: Harvard University Press.

Kittel, Gerhard (ed.) (1967) *Theological Dictionary of the New Testament*, vols. IV & V, trans. Geoffrey Bromiley (ed.) Grand Rapids, MI: Eerdmans.

Kristeva, Julia (1984) *Revolution in Poetic Language*, trans. Margaret Waller, New York: Columbia University Press.

Lattimore, Richmond, trans., (1979) *The Four Gospels and the Revelation*, New York: Dorset Press.

Liddell, Henry George and Scott, Robert (eds) (1940) *A Greek–English Lexicon*, new edn, revised by Henry Stuart Jones and Roderick McKenzie, London and Oxford: Clarendon Press.

Lyotard, Jean-François (1984) *The Postmodern Condition: A Report on Knowledge*, trans. Geoff Bennington and Brian Massumi, Minneapolis: University of Minnesota Press.

——(1988) *The Differend*, trans. Georges Van Den Abbeele, Minneapolis: University of Minnesota Press.

Magness, J. Lee (1986) *Sense and Absense*, Atlanta: Scholars Press.

Marin, Louis (1975) *Critique du Discours*, Paris: Editions de Minuit.

——(1980) *The Semiotics of the Passion Narrative: Topics and Figures*, trans. Alfred M. Johnson, Jr, Pittsburgh Theological Monograph Series 25, Pittsburgh: The Pickwick Press.

Mealand, David L. (1990) "The Close of Acts and Its Hellenistic Greek Vocabulary," in *New Testament Studies* 36:583–97.

Mill, John Stuart (1874) *A System of Logic*, eighth edn, New York: Harper & Brothers.

Moore, Stephen D. (1992) *Mark and Luke in Poststructuralist Perspectives: Jesus Begins to Write*, New Haven, CT: Yale University Press.

NEB, trans., (1971) *The New English Bible*, New York: Oxford University Press.

Neirynck, Frans (1972) *Duality in Mark: Contributions to the Study of the Markan Redaction*, Bibliotheca Ephemeridum Theologicarium Lovandiensium 31, Leuven: Leuven University Press.

Nestle, Eberhard *et al.* (eds) (1979) *Novum Testamentum Graece*, 26th edn, in *Greek–English New Testament*, Stuttgart: Deutsche Bibelgesellschaft.

Nietzsche, Friedrich (1974) *The Gay Science*, trans. Walter Kaufmann, New York: Random House. (German original: *Die Fröhliche Wissenschaft*, Stuttgart: Alfred Kröner Verlag, 1956.)

Nineham, D.E. (1963) *Saint Mark*, Harmondsworth, Middlesex: Penguin Books.

O'Brien, Flann (1966) *At Swim-Two-Birds*, London: Penguin.

Ong, Walter, S.J. (1967) *The Presence of the Word*, New Haven, CT: Yale University Press.

Phillips, Gary A. (1992) "'What is Written? How are You Reading?' Gospel, Intertextuality and Doing Lukewise: A Writerly Reading of Lk 10:25–37 (and 38–42)," Society of Biblical Literature *Seminar Papers*, Atlanta: Scholars Press, 1992.

Phillips, J.B., trans., (1957) *The Gospels in Modern English*, London: Geoffrey Bles.

Pippin, Tina (1992a) *Death and Desire: the Rhetoric of Gender in the Apocalypse of John*, Louisville, KY: Westminster and John Knox.

——(1992b) "Jezebel Re-Vamped," presented to SBL Semiotics and Exegesis Section.

Plato (1973) *Phaedrus*, trans. Walter Hamilton, Harmondsworth Middlesex: Penguin Books.

Rhoads, Donald and Michie, Donald (1982) *Mark as Story*, Philadelphia: Fortress Press.

Ricoeur, Paul (1967) *The Symbolism of Evil*, trans. Emerson Buchanan, New York: Harper and Row.

Roberts, Colin H. and Skeat, T.C. (1983) *The Birth of the Codex*, British Academy, London: Oxford University Press.

RSV, trans., (1971) *Holy Bible*, Revised Standard Version, 2nd edn, Division of Christian Education of the National Council of Churches of Christ in the United States of America, New York: Thomas Nelson.

Sandmel, Samuel (1978) *Anti-Semitism in the New Testament?*, Philadelphia: Fortress Press.

Scholars Version, trans., (1990) *New Gospel Parallels*, vols 1, 2, *Mark*, ed. Robert W. Funk, Sonoma, CA: Polebridge Press.

Scholem, Gershom (1987) *Kabbalah*, New York: Dorset Press (1st edn, Jerusalem, 1974).

Serres, Michel (1982) *The Parasite*, trans. Lawrence R. Schehr, Baltimore, MD: The Johns Hopkins University Press.

Steiner, George (1975) *After Babel*, New York: Oxford University Press.

Stoppard, Tom (1967) *Rosencrantz and Guildenstern Are Dead*, New York: Grove Weidenfeld.

Taylor, Vincent (1953) *The Gospel According to Saint Mark*, London: Macmillan & Co., Ltd.

TEV, trans., (1966) *Good News for Modern Man*, Today's English Version, New York: American Bible Society.

Todorov, Tzvetan (1973) *The Fantastic*, trans. Richard Howard, Cleveland, OH: Case Western Reserve University Press.

——(1977) *The Poetics of Prose*, trans. Richard Howard, Ithaca, NY: Cornell University Press.

Tolbert, Mary Ann (1989) *Sowing the Gospel: Mark's World in Literary–Historical Perspective*, Minneapolis: Fortress Press.

Vaage, Leif E. (1992) "Like Dogs Barking: Cynic Parresia and Shameless Asceticism," in *Semeia* 57:25–39.

Wittgenstein, Ludwig (1953) *Philosophical Investigations*, trans. G.E.M. Anscombe, New York: The Macmillan Co.

INDEX OF NAMES
AND TERMS

193

INDEX OF BIBLICAL
AND RELATED TEXTS